Perfect Days in...

ROME

Travel with
Insider
Tips

GW00418731

Contents

 TOP 10 4

That Rome Feeling 6

For chapters: see inside front cover

TOP 10

Not to be missed!

Our top hits – from the absolute No. 1 to No. 10 – help you plan your tour of the most important sights.

⭐1 CAPITOLINO ► 50

The elegant Piazza del Campidoglio – laid out by Michelangelo, with the Palazzo Senatorio, Rome's city hall, and the Capitoline Museums – was the city's hub in ancient times.

⭐2 FORO ROMANO ► 52

Atmospheric ruins of world history where you can walk in the footsteps of powerful men such as Julius Caesar, Mark Antony and Cicero, and philosophise about the transient nature of things.

⭐3 COLOSSEO ► 60

The largest arena of antiquity where the emperor had fearless gladiators fight wild beasts – *panem et circenses* or 'bread and circus' – in the classic Roman mega-spectacle.

⭐4 CAMPO DE' FIORI ► 86

Popular vegetable market where Roman women shop in the morning and at night the city's youth meet up around the statue of the heretical monk Giordano Bruno.

⭐5 PIAZZA NAVONA ► 88

The most beautiful and interesting Baroque square in Rome (left) is a papal creation that is today an open-air stage for street performers, artists and throngs of sightseers.

⭐6 PANTHEON ► 92

This ancient temple has remained almost unchanged for 2,000 years. First a pagan altar, then a church, and later the final resting place of Italian kings – a tourist highlight.

⭐7 FONTANA DI TREVI ► 124

Baroque fountain ensemble where Marcello Mastroianni played the Latin lover in Fellini's famous film *La Dolce Vita*. Throw a coin into the fountain to return to the city.

⭐8 BASILICA DI SAN PIETRO ► 154

St Peter's Basilica is the heartbeat of Christendom – with Michelangelo's imposing dome, the inviting Piazza San Pietro and the Baroque genius of Bernini.

⭐9 MUSEI VATICANI ► 162

The largest museum in the world with 1,400 rooms – you will need to be prepared to set aside some time just to admire Michelangelo's frescoes in the Sistine Chapel.

⭐10 MUSEO E GALLERIA BORGHESE ► 126

1,000 works of art by Raphael, Caravaggio, Canova and Bernini are housed in the former summer palace in Villa Borghese Park.

THAT
ROME

Find out what Rome is all about and savour its unique flair (almost) like a native Roman.

THE STAIRS TO END ALL STAIRS

Nobody can resist them! In Italian, the **Spanish Steps** (➤ 136) with their sensual Baroque curves are known quite unspectacularly as the Scalinata di Trinità dei Monti – Stairs of the Trinity of the Mountains – but they are Rome's greatest magnet for tourists. From the top, you will have a magnificent view over the ochre-coloured palazzi as far as the dome of St Peter's and, below, of the Piazza di Spagna bursting with life – go there, sit down and take in everything going on around you.

ESTATE ROMANA – ROMAN SUMMER

The Romans used to pull down their shutters in August and head off to the seaside. Today, the financial crisis has meant that many of them stay at home. However, the resourceful Romans have now rediscovered cultural pleasures in the **Estate Romana** (➤ 44) summer festival (www.communeroma.it).

There are concerts, readings and an open-air cinema. The performances in the Baths of Caracalla are among the highlights. For years, it was closed because of the danger that sections would collapse. The stage was then simply moved out of the risk zone – and the fabulous view of the imperial baths remained.

ICE CREAM IN STYLE

There are no ice lollies in Rome, here ice cream is eaten in style! *Gelato* is celebrated properly: in an ice cream parlour and scooped, in the traditional way. The *limone* flavour still has the tang of lemon, you can taste the almond liqueur in *amaretto* and *bacio* is as sensual as a chocolate kiss. *Cono o coppa*, in a cone or cup, is the eternal question. Visit the famous, more than 100-year-old, **Giolitti** ice cream parlour (✚ 202 B1; Via Ufficio del Vicario 40; daily 7am–2am) behind the parliament, where Rome's smart set likes to meet for their *gelato* treat.

NIGHTLIFE ON A HILL OF SHARDS

Dancing on the rubbish heap of history? Not a problem in Rome! In ancient times, the merchants in the indoor markets sold their oil,

FEELING

The Testaccio district buzzes with night-time action

That Rome Feeling

olives, wine and grain in beautiful amphorae and simply threw the shards *(testa)* away. Today, the hippest discotheques, such as the gay bar L'Alibi, and expensive trattorias like Checchino dal 1887 (Via Monte Testaccio 30, www. checchino-dal-1887.com, Tue–Sat) are located on the ecological rubble mound, the **Testaccio** (➤ 118).

PICNIC IN THE PARK

If it is so hot that the lipstick in your handbag starts to melt, and your head and feet are worn out from your marathon through Rome's museums, you can recover in the magnificent park of the **Villa Borghese** (➤ 126). And the best way to do it is with a picnic basket from GiNa (➤ 143) complete with salmon sandwiches, wine, olives, cheese and even a tablecloth.

MULTICULTURAL MARKET: PORTA PORTESE

You will find everything here – possibly even the Gucci wallet that was stolen from you yesterday

Idyll in the gardens of the Villa Borghese

(empty, of course). In addition, shoes, belts, clocks, clothes and cheap kitsch. The great bargain hunt between Viale Trastevere and Porta Portese begins early (✚ 207 D3; Sun 7am–2pm). Another flea market, the **Mercatino Flaminio**, Piazza della Marina (✚ 202 A4; Sun 10am–7pm), is a more elegant alternative.

THE ANCIENT LIE DETECTOR

The ancient "Mouth of Truth" on **Piazza Bocca della Verità** (➤ 184) was made famous by the film *Roman Holiday* when Audrey Hepburn and Gregory Peck flirted in front of the man-sized marble sculpture of a face. Today, many young couples still make a pilgrimage to the ancient lie detector that supposedly bites those who do not tell the truth. Try it out!

ICE-COLD FOUNTAIN WATER

Do as the Romans do! Drink delicious spring water straight out of a *fontanella*, one of the city's many drinking **fountains**. The trick: close the spout with your finger so that the water jets up through the smaller opening, higher on the spout, and straight towards your mouth.

The Magazine

THE
ETERNAL CITY

The first glimpse of Rome is bewildering – massive ruins, crumbling walls, stately palazzi, towers and domes are all jumbled together. Buildings of every epoch jostle side by side. The 3,000-odd years of the city's history lie all around.

The city on the seven hills may seem eternal, but its history can be easily divided into four periods: nearly 1,200 years of history includes the ancient era of the first Etruscan settlements on the Palatine Hill to the great days of the Republic and its decline in the late Imperial period. After the devastation of the Barbarian invasions in the early Middle Ages the papacy emerged as the centre of power. The heydays of the princes of the church were, however, the Renaissance and Baroque, where they took Rome to new heights. 1871 Piedmontese troops conquered the Papal States and Rome became the capital of a united Italy, with the Vatican as an independent enclave.

Classical Rome

According to legend the city on the Palatine Hill was founded on 21 April 753BC by the twins Romulus and Remus, who were said to have been suckled by a she-wolf. Romulus, who slew his brother in battle, named the city after himself. What is certain is that there was an early Stone Age settlement on the Palatine in the ninth-century BC. Later came the Etruscans, who drained the the marshy ground where the Forum is today. When the last Etruscan king was deposed in 510BC, the Roman Republic that was established would last for five centuries. After the three Punic Wars (264–146BC) against Carthage in North Africa, Rome ascended to a world power dominating the entire Mediterranean.

In 44BC the appointment of the successful commander, Gaius Julius Caesar, as dictator for life saw the emergence of single rulers. Following Caesar's assassination in 44BC, Mark Antony formed an alliance with Caesar's nephew Octavian, who then became the first emperor Augustus (▶ 12). Rome was now the undisputed ruler of the Mediterranean but was beset by internal conflicts. After years of terror under Nero, who used the Christians as a scapegoat for Rome's devastating fire in AD64, Emperor Vespasian took control, restored law and order set about creating magnificent buildings such as the Colosseum (▶ 60).

The death of the philosopher emperor Marcus Aurelius in AD180 saw the final decline the Empire. Constantine (303–367) and his successors abandoned the once proud Rome and made Constantinople (Byzantium) the capital. In the power vacuum of the 5th and 6th century, Germanic tribes sacked Rome several times and in 476 Germanic mercenaries under Odoacer deposed the last Roman emperor, Romulus Augustulus.

Medieval Rome

By the middle of the 6th century Rome had deteriorated to a provincial city in the Byzantine Empire, and the metropolis had shrunk to 50,000 inhabitants. In this dark hour the power of the Bishops of Rome was strengthened but even powerful popes, such as Leo the Great (440–461)

Even more impressive by night; the ruins of the Colosseo, the largest surviving monument of Roman antiquity

The Magazine

Reclining statue, one of two representing the Nile and the Tiber, at the Palazzo Nuovo

and Gregory the Great (590–604), were unable to defend Rome, forcing the papacy to seek Christian patrons in the north against the Lombards. This culminated in the Frankish king Charlemagne being crowned Emperor of the Holy Roman Empire by Pope Leo III on Christmas day in the year 800. Rome's situation improved but the centuries-old power dispute between emperor and papacy, both secular and ecclesiastical power was inevitable and culminated in 1084 with the pillage of Rome. The papacy had taken a major knock, exacerbated 300 years later, when the French declared their

THE FIRST EMPEROR

In 31BC, Octavian, nephew of Julius Caesar, defeated his rival Mark Anthony, lover of the Egyptian queen Cleopatra, at the Battle of Actium. He was proclaimed Emperor, taking the name Augustus, "favoured by the gods", and brought peace to the Roman world. The beautiful Ara Pacis Augustae (► 108), decorated with family portraits, was erected as a reminder of this, and statues of him sprang up all over the Empire. A mixture of modesty and arrogance, he lived in a simple house on the Palatine, while making the city splendid, saying, "I found Rome built of brick, I leave it clothed in marble."

THE PRISONER OF THE VATICAN
In 1870, Pius IX retreated to the Vatican, leaving Rome to become Italy's capital. Here he, and three succeeding popes, remained, refusing to recognize the Italian state. The situation was resolved in 1929 when Pius XI and Benito Mussolini signed the Lateran Treaty recognizing Rome as the capital of Italy and making the Vatican City an independent sovereign state and the world's smallest "country".

own candidate pope, and the papacy moved to Avignon in France for 69 years. Stability was only gained in 1417, when Pope Martin V declared that the papacy would henceforth control the city council. Rome and its papal ruler were restored, paving the way for the great days of papal power.

Papal Rome
Under Nicholas V (1447–55), the first Renaissance pope – and founder of the Vatican Library (▶ 171) – and his successors Rome was steered to new heights. Artists such as Bramante, Michelangelo, Raphael, Bernini and Borromini created their works by papal order. As powerful politicians the princes of the church conquered large parts of central Italy – to the chagrin of the major powers of Spain and France – and in 1527 the French sacked the city.

As part of the Counter-Reformation, at the beginning of the 16th century, the popes of Rome expanded even greater splendour on Rome. By the 18th century the hedonistic, party-loving Rome was drawing travellers from cooler northern climes. Johann Wolfgang Goethe lived – and loved – here in 1786, under the pseudonym Filippo Möller

> "... party-loving Rome was an essential stop on the Grand Tour"

(▶ 111) while in 1820 the poets John Keats and Percy Shelley lived in a villa at the base of the Spanish Steps.

In 1798, Napoleon invaded, and made Rome a Republic, which was only returned to Pope Pius VII in 1814. The spirit of nationalism was born, culminating in the 1860 establishment of the Kingdom of Italy. Rome held out as an independent papal state until 1870 when it became part of a united Italy. Pius IX fled to the Vatican, declaring himself a prisoner.

Modern Rome
In 1871 the city became Italy's new capital and underwent a modernisation programme, with districts radiating out from the centre. Mussolini also left his mark with the development of the EUR (Esposizione Universale di Roma) district between Rome and Ostia, built for the cancelled World Exhibition of 1942. In the 50s, the influx of hundreds of thousands of poor southern Italians necessitated the rapid construction of featureless suburbs. The beautiful *centro storico*, however, has remained largely spared (thus far!) by such architectural sins.

ART IN ROME

3,000 Years of Creativity

In Rome, man-made beauty is everywhere. Like some magnet composed of stone and paint, Rome's art has been pulling in crowds from around the world for centuries, making the city an essential destination for culture. Architecture, sculpture or painting, art is all around you, an integral part of the physical city that covers 3,000 years of artistic and historic development and represents astounding creativity.

It can be overwhelming; Rome has no "one-stop" museum covering a comprehensive survey of its art. Instead, art is scattered all over the city, much of it still in the buildings and settings for which it was created. It's this that adds an extra dimension to what's on offer, and there's a sense of serendipity to tracking down art in Rome. Of course, you don't want to miss must-sees such as Vatican City (▶ 149), Palazzo Altemps (▶ 97) and the Borghese galleries (▶ 126), but there are many hidden treasures off the beaten track where you may find yourself alone with a great statue or picture.

Detail of a battle on the Colonna Traiana in Trajan's Forum

The Classical Ideal

The Romans inherited their concept of the beauty of the human form from the Greeks, and museums still display supreme examples of this ideal, often in the form of Roman copies of long-lost Greek originals. Head for Palazzo Altemps (▶ 97) and the Vatican's Pio-Clementino (▶ 162) to see some of the best, or take in the Etruscan art at the Villa Giulia (▶ 141).

> "there's a sense of serendipity to tracking down art in Rome"

For home-produced classical art, there's the choice of architecture, sculpture and painting: Roman buildings surviving virtually intact, such as the Pantheon (▶ 92) and Colosseo (▶ 60), monumental forms that marry architecture to sculpture such as the triumphal arch of Septimius Severus (▶ 53) or the Colonna Traiana (▶ 73).

For Roman sculpture, take in works such as the *Dying Gaul* in the Capitoline Museums (▶ 73) or the iconic *Laocoön* in the Vatican Museum (▶ 162), one of the world's most dynamic pieces of sculpture; while painting is represented by the beautiful and decorative wall frescoes in the Palazzo Massimo alle Terme (▶ 132).

The Dark Ages and Beyond

Christian art made its appearance in Rome in the fourth century, when the Emperor Constantine decriminalized the new religion. Though few paintings remain, Rome boasts a clutch of early churches, many decorated with mosaics in the Byzantine style with figures of saints that are often also

Looking up at Michaelanglo's magnificent dome of the Basilica di San Pietro

The Magazine

full of charming detail of everyday life, such as those in San Clemente (► 67) and Santa Prassede (► 138). Later medieval art includes Arnolfo di Cambio's ciborium, a stone altar canopy in Santa Cecilia in Trastevere (► 111) and the city's only Gothic church, Santa Maria sopra Minerva (► 96).

Choir stall in Basilica di San Clemente

Renaissance to Neoclassicism

By the 15th century the Renaissance, that great rebirth of artistic and intellectual expression, was well underway, and the following 400 years were the zenith of artistic productivity. With the popes and the great Roman aristocratic families as patrons, just about any noteworthy artist worked in Rome.

The result was an astounding variety of art. Head for the Musei Vaticani (Vatican Museums, ► 162) to see work by early Renaissance artists such as Fra Angelico, Botticelli, Perugino and Pinturicchio, then take in Basilica di San Pietro itself (► 154), a triumph of the High Renaissance, whose design was influenced by superstars such as Michelangelo. His most monumental work, in the form of the astonishing frescoes he painted in the Cappella Sistina (Sistine Chapel, ► 166) is also in the Vatican, where it contrasts with Raphael's gentle and luminous frescoes. There's contrast too, in the shape of Caravaggio's (► 26) dramatic output, scattered in churches and galleries throughout the city.

Drama and energy are the keynotes of Bernini's sculptural work, which you can see in the Borghese (► 126) as well as magnificent churches such as Santa Maria della Vittoria. Baroque architecture combined with a touch of rococo in the 18th century, producing ensembles such

HOW TO PAINT THE SISTINE CEILING

Open-mouthed in the Cappella Sistina (► 166), forget the art for a moment and think about the sheer practicalities of painting a ceiling on this sort of scale. Virtually every day for four years, Michelangelo climbed the 18m (60ft) high scaffolding and stood all day, painting with his arm and hand above his head with paint and plaster dripping in his eyes.

As fresco involves applying pigment to an incised outline on wet plaster, he had first to plaster the area, then get the paint on at a speed that enabled him to cover the prepared surface in the course of a single day. He wrote plaintively to his brother: "I wish simply to eat a hot meal in peace."

as the Fontana di Trevi (▶ 124) and the Spanish Steps (▶ 136), until neoclassicism brought a more restrained note, personified by the slick marble perfection of Canova's sculpture.

Into the Modern Age

From the 19th century, it is planning and architecture that have taken centre stage, with great piazzas laid out and boulevards carved through medieval areas. Mussolini was a prime mover here, creating the Via della Conciliazione as an approach to the Basilica di San Pietro and the Via dei Fori Imperiali, as well as entire new districts and buildings such as Termini station, with its undulating canopy, which was finished in the 1950s.

This trend has continued into the 21st century with the construction of some truly innovative complexes, such as Richard Meier's Ara Pacis building (▶ 108), Renzo Piano's Auditorium Parco della Musica, Zaha Hadid's MAXXI, the *National Museum of the 21st Century Arts,* and the transformation of the Scuderie Quirinale into one of Rome's most exciting and modern exhibition spaces.

A Touch of Recycling

If you're wondering why quite so many classical buildings in Rome are so comprehensively ruined, you've only got to look about you. For centuries after the fall of Rome, palaces, temples and public buildings provided a handy source of ready-dressed building material, which medieval and Renaissance builders cheerfully plundered. Stone, columns and pillars from the Colosseum, Forum and countless other ancient structures were re-used in new buildings – just go to 12th-century Santa Maria in Trastevere (▶ 102) and take in the 22 granite columns that line its nave – all purloined from the third-century Baths of Caracalla (▶ 80).

The cultural centre Auditorium Parco della Musica on the Olympic site

Buon APPETITO

As everywhere, Roman eating habits are changing. The cliché of pasta served up in family-run trattorias now vies with new-style restaurants, which have kept the best of traditional Roman cuisine but added a 21st-century twist.

The changes have definitely been for the better. Twenty years ago, the options were limited – glitzy expense-account slanted restaurants, humble trattorias or a rough-and-ready pizza dive, and that was about it. Nowadays, you can eat in wine bars, salad bars, gastropubs and decent ethnic restaurants, in surroundings where traditional fusty decor has given way to light and air and stone, steel and glass.

Rome does still offer simple family-run restaurants, where tables spill onto secluded piazzas and the menu features all the classic Roman specialities. Even here, though, times are changing, with the rise of the *nuova trattoria*, eating houses retaining the traditional, unfussy dishes and ingredients but served with a new oomph. This is mainly due to young creative chefs in the kitchen, and greatly improved wine lists. Such places pride themselves on the supreme freshness of their ingredients and their provenance, with menus and attentive waiters

> "unfussy ingredients and dishes but served with a new oomph"

The Magazine

proudly detailing the sources of the meat, fish and vegetables. This is a direct result of the Slow Food movement, which originated in Italy and has spread worldwide, and emphasizes the importance of local producers and organic produce.

On the Menu

As with almost any Italian city or region, Rome has a plethora of culinary specialities unique to the city. Among these are the widely available *saltimbocca alla Romana* (ham-wrapped veal flavoured with sage) and *bucatini all'Amatriciana* (pasta with a fiery chilli-hot tomato and pancetta (Italian bacon) sauce).

Other culinary influences include those introduced over the centuries by the city's Jewish population – restaurants in the old Ghetto and elsewhere serve wonderful and otherwise little-known dishes

Above: Market at the Campo de' Fiori; left: Freshly made pizza is one of the culinary delights of Rome

PIZZA, PIZZA, PIZZA

Pizza is taken pretty seriously in Rome and the city's *pizzaioli* have always taken pride in their thin, flat and crisp *pizza romana*, cooked in five minutes in a blisteringly hot wood-fired oven. *Pizzerie* are normally open during the evening and very few places serve pizza at lunchtime – if they do, they could be aiming squarely for the tourist market. Come dinnertime, make sure you head for one that specifies it's got a *forno a legna* (wood-fired brick oven); *pizze* aren't the same from an electric number. Toppings are pretty limited and the staples you can expect to find include *margherita* (tomato and mozzarella), *napoli* (tomatoes, anchovy and mozzarella), *funghi* (mushroom) and *quattro formaggi* (four cheeses). Variations on the theme include *calzone* (pizza dough sealed around a filling) and *pizza bianca ripiena* (a thick pizza split and filled with ham, cheese and vegetables).

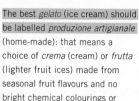

GELATO AL LIMON Insider Tip

The best *gelato* (ice cream) should be labelled *produzione artigianale* (home-made): that means a choice of *crema* (cream) or *frutta* (lighter fruit ices) made from seasonal fruit flavours and no bright chemical colourings or artificial flavourings.

You can have a *cono* (cone) or *coppa* (tub), and expect to choose at least two flavours, even for the smallest size. You'll be asked if you want *panna* (whipped cream), which will be dolloped on top.

Il Gelato di San Crispino (left and ► 144), I Tre Scalini (► 114), Giolitti (► 6), and Ciuri Ciuri (► 78) are among the best of Rome's *gelaterie*.

such as deep-fried artichokes *(carciofi alla giudia)*, pasta and chickpea broth, and *minestra d'arzilla* (ray fish soup). Traditional trattorias will often feature an antipasto buffet, a wonderful selection of seasonal vegetable dishes, all prepared *alla Romana*. This range of starters is great for vegetarians, who otherwise, like everywhere else in Italy, are pretty badly served, more because of a lack of comprehension than anything else. If you don't eat meat, don't despair; there's plenty of other dished to try.

Waste Not, Want Not Cuisine

Some of Rome's most typical specialities however, might not be high on your list of "must tries". Traditional cooking is based on the *quinto quarto* – the so-called "fifth quarter" – or what is left of an animal when everything that would normally be considered edible has been stripped from the carcass. This penchant for the obscure originally had little to do with taste, and everything to do with poverty, long the culinary mother of invention.

In practice this meant – and still means – menus filled with items that might startle even the most adventurous diner. The most traditional Roman specialities include tripe *(trippa)*, oxtail braised in celery broth *(coda alla vaccinara)*, strips of cartilage *(nervetti)*, brain *(cervello)* – delicious with peas – the pancreas and thyroid glands *(animelle)*, and *pajata*: baby veal's intestines with the mother's milk still inside (cooked in lard for added effect). And how about *lingua* (tongue), *guanciale* (pig's cheek) and *insalata di zampa* (hoof jelly salad)? Restaurants in the Testaccio district, once the slaughterhouse area, specialize in dishes featuring offal.

A State Within a State

Step into the Piazza di San Pietro and you leave Italy. This is the Vatican State, a tiny enclave in the heart of Rome, from where the Pope rules the world's billion-plus Catholics, and whose clout equals that of any of the world's heads of state.

Background to the Church

The first head of the Christian church was St Peter the Apostle, traditionally thought to have been executed for his faith in the circus built across the Tiber, on the spot now occupied by the Vatican, by the Emperor Caligula. Successive popes, following Peter's footsteps, based themselves in Rome, conquering land all over central Italy. These territories, known as the Papal States, meant the popes combined their roles as religious leaders with that of temporal monarchs, and all that entails.

For over a thousand years all went well, but in 1870 Italy was united, the papacy lost its lands and the pope retreated into self-imposed imprisonment inside the Vatican. Here, successive pontiffs railed against the Italian state, declaring it illegal and its elections meaningless. The situation was finally resolved in 1929, when Mussolini signed a treaty of reconciliation, establishing the Vatican as an independent state, but one whose power henceforth would be purely spiritual. In return for this, the Vatican got a huge cash payment, tax-free status and a role as a moral influence in Italian legislation. This state of affairs continues today, with modern popes focusing on the spiritual affairs of their worldwide flock.

Left: Ceiling of the Sala delle Muse in the Musei Vaticani; centre: View of the basilica from the Priory of the Knights of Malta; right: Swiss Guard on duty in Vatican City

The Magazine

Who and What's Inside the Vatican

Vatican City (► 149) covers an area of less than half a square kilometre, most of which is occupied by the Basilica di San Pietro (► 154) and palace buildings. These house the museums (► 162), and are also home to the Curia, the papal civil service who are responsible for the day-to-day running of the church. They're aided by the papal ambassadors, the nuncios, who represent the Vatican all over the world; in return, many major powers have their own ambassador at the Holy See. The Pope is guarded by his own Swiss Guard (see panel above) and his representative retains observer status at the UN.

The 900 residents – including 25 nuns – shop in the Vatican super-market, buy their medicine in the Vatican pharmacy, and use the Vatican post office and bank, which issue their own stamps and currency. There's a heliport, a publishing house, responsible for the daily newspaper, the *Osservatore Romano*, and a radio and TV station.

Giuseppe Momo's spectacular spiral staircase (1932) in the Musei Vaticani

Greek and Roman busts and statuary in Museo Chiaramonti in the Musei Vaticani

A Treasure House of Art

Most visitors come to the Vatican to see the art, a heritage which encompasses the very fabric of the Vatican buildings as well as the huge collection of painting, sculpture, manuscripts, reliefs, tapestries and books that's housed within the Vatican and Basilica di San Pietro. The basilica (► 154) is home to some great art, including Michelangelo's Pietà (► 157).

But the wow factor reaches its zenith in the Musei Vaticani (► 162), which house some of the world's greatest works of art.

A Spiritual Powerhouse

For many visitors to the Vatican, however, the art is utterly peripheral. For 2,000 years, pilgrims have journeyed to Rome, to pray at the tomb of St Peter, Christ's first appointed head of the church, and catch a glimpse of his successor, the Pope. In early April 2005 millions of the faithful bid farewell to the popular Polish Pope John Paul II in St Peter's Square. Shortly thereafter, on 19 April 2005, they witnessed the election of Cardinal Joseph Ratzinger as Pope Benedict XVI. After his resignation on 28 February 2013 Pope Francis followed him on to St Peter's throne.

SEEING THE POPE

When Pope Francis is in Rome he holds a general audience in St Peter's Square Wednesdays at 10:30 and on Sundays at noon he delivers the Angelus prayer from the Vatican window. Tickets are free, but you will need to apply well in advance to the Prefettura della Casa Pontifica, 00120 Vatican City (or download the application form www.papalaudience.org/tickets) then collect your ticket when you arrive in Rome. There's more information on the Vatican website (www.vatican.va).

Life Inside Rome in the 21st Century

The nearly 3,000-year-old city is considered the queen of all world cities, one where imposing Baroque palaces sit side by side with magnificent churches and the venerable ruins of the Roman Empire. But the Eternal City also has modern problems: noise, traffic pollution and prohibitive rentals in the inner city.

Left: Enjoying a drink in a Roman bar; right: Busy shopping street in the city centre

Urban challenges

In the 50s the poet and film director Pier Paolo Pasolini documented the waves of poor migrants that arrived in the Eternal City from the Mezzogiorno region in the south. The city offered plenty of work opportunities but lacked affordable housing for the hundreds of thousands of newcomers. The solution was the *borgate*, sprawling suburbs of hastily constructed high-rise developments that now surround the attractive old *centro storico*. In his films *Roma* and *La Dolce Vita* the great film director Federico Fellini immortalized the absurd contrast between these suburban wastelands and the urbane and fashionable Via Veneto.

Romans also have to deal with congestion, strikes and a public transport system that is *a singhiozzi* (stuttering). The underground Metro system only has two lines, a network that is shorter than the early Christian catacombs. The construction period for a third Metro line has already taken longer than that of the Colosseum, which was built in just eight years. Buses run intermitedly and certainly not on schedule. As a result, most of Rome's nearly three million residents have cars and run the exhausting daily traffic guantlet. The roads are also full of speeding Vespas and scooters that flit between the traffic. Rome is particulary challenging and dangerous for pedestrians and cyclists.

The Holy Year and Rome's salvation

For a long time Rome was considered a *città pigra* by the rest of Italy, a 'lazy town' with an administration that turned a blind eye to construction scandals, corruption and mismanagement. However, that changed for the better under the leadership of two successive mayors, Francesco Rutelli and Walter Veltroni, energetic Green and Social Democrat representatives. The Holy Year of 2000 even saw a small miracle in the coming together of two organizational geniuses, Pope John Paul II and Mayor Francesco Rutelli, who undertook to revitalize the city. Crumbling facades were restored, churches

Left: The Metro; right: Piazza Rotonda, perfect for a *passeggiata* – evening stroll

were re-roofed, roads repaired and the best museums – such as the Galleria Borghese (which had been closed for renovation for decades) – were reopened. Rutelli's successor, Walter Veltroni, undertook a cautious modernization of Rome, establishing modern architecture, such as the Auditorium-Parco della Musica, the MAXXI Museum by Zaha Hadid and Richard Meier's modern glass structure housing the ancient Ara Pacis. Rome has also joined the electronic age: *ragazzi* sit in public parks with their laptops and surf the internet; Romans enjoy their *caffè* – keeping one eye on the pretty tourist and the other on the iPhone – the electronic *dolce vita*.

> "a 'lazy town' with an administration that turned a blind eye to construction scandals"

CARAVAGGIO
ART'S BAD BOY

Fashions in art come and go; the big boys, the Michelangelos, Leonardos, Raphaels and Berninis, are a constant, but every age rediscovers the genius of some less stellar figure, and Caravaggio is the new darling of the 21st century.

The Man and the Myth

Born in Milan *c.* 1571, Michelangelo Merisi moved to the town of Caravaggio (after which he is known) with his family in 1576. Aged 21, and already quarrelsome and aggressive, he travelled to Rome, arriving with no money and nowhere to live. He found work as a hack artist, producing secular, often

almost homoerotic, pictures that attracted the attention of Cardinal del Conte, who soon commissioned Caravaggio to decorate the Contarelli chapel in the church of San Luigi dei Francesi (► 107).

It was his big break. Caravaggio's marvellous paintings of St Matthew, with their intense naturalism and supreme handling of light and shade, caused a sensation, and a string of prestigious commissions followed.

St Matthew and the Angel (1602) in the San Luigi dei Francesi church

Madonna di Loreto (*c.*1605) in the
Cavalletti Chapel, church of Sant'Agostino

Genius and enfant terrible

However, his artistic development
went hand in hand with a reputation
for bad behaviour, heavy drinking,
arrogance and brawling. In 1606 he
killed a young man in a street fight
and was forced to flee for Naples.
The rest of his short life is the story
of incredible artistic production, flight and violence. After a few months in
Naples, he fled to Malta, then Sicily, each time leaving a string of offences
behind him and the law hot on his heels. In 1609 he returned to Naples,
hoping to receive a papal pardon that would enable him to return to Rome.

In the meantime, he was injured in yet another street brawl and left
Naples not long after to head north, carrying with him his three last pictures. His ship sailed without him after a stop on the malaria-ridden coast
of Tuscany, where Caravaggio caught a fever and died, alone, at Porto
Ercole on 18 July 1610. His body was never found.

Caravaggio: the First Baroque Artist

Caravaggio's work stands out for several reasons: the extreme realism of
his paintings – he used the poor as his models and painted from life; his
handling of light; and the dramatic intensity of his work. Many of his
contemporaries branded his work as vulgar, lacking any sense of the ideal
or sacred, and the drama too high. The irony is, that it's precisely these
traits that make him a painter for modern times. Contemporary audiences
love the *chiaroscuro*, the shafts of light, the dirty, scruffy models and the
edgy undertones of his work. He was among the first truly baroque artists,
but it took 20th-century critics to rediscover his genius.

ACQUA VITAE

Rise early, before the traffic builds up, to hear one of Rome's most quintessential sounds – the gentle splash and gurgle of water. No other city has more fountains than Rome.

Every piazza has its own, ranging from the monumental to the homely, and modern Romans have inherited the classical delight in living in a city where the sight and sound of falling water forms the backdrop to life. Classical Romans took access to clean running water for granted, and it's estimated that Imperial Rome provided around 250 gallons of water per capita per day to every citizen. A network of aqueducts brought water from the Sabine Hills to the city – you can still see the arches around the city outskirts.

Incredibly, much of Rome's water still comes from these ancient sources, notably the Acqua Vergine, the Acqua Paola and the Acqua Felice. The supply failed during the chaos of the post-Roman era, but by the 15th to 16th centuries the Popes restored the supply and built new fountains. The nobility vied with the Popes to make them works of art; tritons, nymphs, dolphins, gods and goddesses abound, along with quirkier embellishments that range from recycled Egyptian obelisks and Roman sarcophagi to stone tortoises, books and wine barrels.

THE TOP TEN
In addition those on the Piazza San Pietro (ill. ➤ 153) and Piazza Farnese (➤ 105)

Fontana di Trevi (➤ 124)

Fontana del Tritone, Piazza Barberini: dolphins supporting a Triton (1643, left)

Fontana delle Tartarughe, Piazza Mattei: Bernini's turtle fountain (➤ 186)

Fontana dell'Acqua Paola, Via Garibaldi: triumphal arch (1610–12, ➤ 102)

Fontana dell Naiadi, Piazza della Repubblica: art nouveau nymph with sea creatures (1901)

Fontana dei Quattro Fiumi by Bernini (➤ 90)

Fontana della Barcaccia (➤ 137)

Quattro Fontane, Via Quattro Fontane: four baroque fountains at an intersection

Finding Your Feet

First Two Hours

Fiumicino Airport

Rome has two airports, the International Airport Leonardo da Vinci, better known as Fiumicino, and the smaller Ciampino Airport and they are 32km (19 miles) and 18km (11 miles) respectively from the city centre. International flight information (arrivals/*arrivi* and departures/*partenze*), tel: 06 6 59 51 or www.adr.it.

■ Fiumicino Airport (open daily 24 hours) has **four terminals**. Terminal 1 handles domestic flights; 2, flights from the European Schengen countries; 3, international flights from countries outside the Schengen area and some intercontinental flights; 4, flights operated by American Airlines, United Airlines, Continental, Delta, US Airways and El Al. The terminals are on two levels; arrivals are on the lower floors, departures on the floor above.

■ Avoid taxi and hotel touts in the airport, Rome's taxis are white and usually have the number of the company are on the car door.

Getting to Central Rome by Public Transport

■ The easiest and fastest way to get from Fiumicino airport to the city centre is the **express rail service Leonardo da Vinci** to Rome's main railway station, Stazione Termini (for information on onward travel from Termini, ➤ 32). The airport train station is eight minutes walk from the main international terminal – there is a lift and a glass covered walkway from the main terminal building. Alternatively you can walk across the square in front of the arrivals hall and take the lift.

■ **Tickets for the express rail service** (€14) can be bought from automatic machines in the arrivals terminal and on the station concourse, or from a small ticket office (daily 7:48–2:30, 2:48–9:30) and adjoining "Tabacchi & Giornali" newsagents on the right of the tracks as you face the platforms. Consider buying a second ticket for your return journey, as there can be long queues at Stazione Termini.

■ Tickets must be **validated** in the machines at the entrances to the platforms before boarding the train. Failure to validate your ticket may result in a heavy fine.

■ **Express trains** depart at regular intervals between 6:38am and 11:38pm with departures at 8 and 38 minutes past the hour. The journey time to Termini is just over 30 minutes. Be sure to board the right train, as departures from the airport station also link (roughly every 20 minutes) to four other Rome stations: Ostiense, Tuscolana, Tiburtina and Trastevere. The journey time is longer, around 50 minutes, but costs about half the price of the express train. Tickets can be bought from the same sources as tickets for the express trains (see above).

■ In addition to the **Leonardo da Vinci** express train hour, a **Terravision bus service** runs approximately every 30 minutes (5:40am–9:45pm) from outside the arrivals hall (Terminal 3) to Termini (Via Marsala, 29, in front of the TerraCafé) and back. Journey time is about 70 minutes with four stops; tickets (€6) can be bought on-board or online (€4; www.terravision.it).

■ **At night** the Cotral bus service (www.cotralspa.it) runs from 12:30am to 5am between Fiumicino Airport, Termini and Tiburtina. Tickets can be bought tobacco shops (€5) or from the driver (€7).

Getting to Central Rome by Taxi

Taxis from the airport to the city centre are expensive, and the Roman *tassisti* have a very bad reputation. The so-called fix prices (which the city of Rome negotiates every year with the drivers) are not a set price, but are graded according to location. Budget at least €50 for the 45 minute journey to the centre are around, but it can often take considerably longer because of heavy traffic. **Supplements** are charged on Sundays, public holidays, for journeys between 10pm and 7am, and for each individual item of luggage. All current supplements should be posted on a list inside the cab. And do not hesitate to call the number and complain, if the price is exorbitant.

■ To take a taxi to the city centre wait in line at the taxi rank outside the arrivals hall. Taxi drivers ignore those who try to flag down a taxi from the roadside. You can also make a **telephonic booking** with, for example, Taxi Roma (tel: 06 35 70; SMS 36 66 73 00 00; www.3570.it), or Società La Capitale Radio Taxi (tel: 06 49 94).

■ **Limousine services** can be booked at dedicated desks in the arrivals hall. These cost about the same or a little more than taxis that wait outside, and have the advantage that you know exactly how much you're paying before setting off. They are also usually more comfortable.

Car Rental

The major car rental companies (*autonoleggio*) such as Hertz, Sixt, Avis and Europcar all have offices at Fiumicino Airport. Their desks are located in car park C, which is linked to the arrivals hall via a lift and a glass pedestrian bridge (about eight minutes walk). The rental cars are a few minutes away in the same car park. The earlier you book, the cheaper the rates.

Ciampino Airport

Many charter flights and a few European low-cost scheduled flights use Ciampino, Rome's second airport (tel: 06 6 59 51; www.adr.it), which lies about 18km (11 miles) southeast of the centre. There are few tourist facilities at the airport, so it is a good idea to get some euros before you arrive.

Getting to the City Centre

■ Ciampino has no rail links with central Rome and the easiest way into the city is by **taxi**, which costs about €35.

■ **Buses** are operated by Cotral (www.cotralspa.it), Atral-Lazio (www.atrallazio.com), Terravision (www.terravision.eu) and SIT (www.sitbusshuttle.it); between them, they offer half-hourly departures. You can buy tickets (€4–€5) online, inside the arrivals terminal or on-board.

■ Easyjet and Ryanair operate their own **shuttle service** from Ciampino to Termini. Passengers can buy return tickets (€4) for this coach service at the exit from arrivals (tel: 06 97 61 06 32; www.terravision.eu).

Arriving by Car

All roads lead to Rome. The route is itself is not difficult, but as a rule visitors to the Eternal City find driving very stressful. In theory the city centre has restricted traffic access from 7am–7pm and after 10pm, but few Romans abide by the rule. Parking is limited, so the locals park their beloved *macchina* everywhere – on the church steps, on the pavements, double or even triple parked.

Finding Your Feet

- The approach from the north (from Florence) is via the Autostrada del Sole and the Grande Raccordo Anulare (GRA), the **ring road** that circles Rome. Follow the *Roma Centro* signs otherwise you may end up in the outskirts.
- Despite the restricted traffic access in the city centre, as a tourist you are allowed to drive to your hotel where you should immediately park your car in the **hotel car park** (when you make your booking ask about *parcheggio del albergo*) or look for one of the few **car parks** such as the Parcheggio Villa Borghese, Via del Galoppatoio, 33, www.sabait.it, where you can park for about €18 per day.

Arriving by Train
- Most national and international train services arrive at **Stazione Termini** railway station (5am–midnight. Information, tel: 06 89 20 21 or 06 48 47 54 75 from outside Italy; www.trenitalia.com).
- Some long-distance services, and services arriving at night, terminate at **Ostiense** or **Tiburtina** stations.

From Termini Station to Your Hotel
Termini lies on the eastern side of central Rome so it is best to take a taxi if your hotel is in the heart of the old city. Only the small hotels and hostels in the Monti district are within walking distance of the Stazione Termini.
- The station is a haven for **pickpockets**, so it is vital to keep a close watch on your luggage and valuables at all times.
- Never accept offers from any hotel tout, private taxi or money changers who approach you.
- **Taxis** depart from immediately outside the front of the station building – do not exit using the side entrances off the central concourse and walkway. Be aware that queues for taxis are often long.

Tourist Information
The Thursday supplement of *La Repubblica* newspaper and the weekly magazine *Roma c'e* have listings for the theatre, cinema, nightclubs and restaurants.

Websites
The following websites are useful sources of general tourist information about Rome:
- An excellent and comprehensive tourist information website is **www.060608.it** it covers all aspect of a trip to Rome, including important cultural advice and event details.
- **www.romaturismo.it** with links to accommodation, city tours, airport transfers, and the like.
- **www.romeinformation.info** with sightseeing tips and more.

Archeologia Card
The Archeologia Card (valid for 7 days, €27.50 or €17.50 for EU citizens 18–25 years of age) gives admission to the Colosseo, Palatino, Palazzo Altemps, Palazzo Massimo alle Terme, Crypta Balbi, Terme di Diocleziano, Terme di Caracalla, Mausoleo di Cecilia Metella and the Villa dei Quintili on the Via Appia Antica. The card is available from the respective museums.

- **www.vatican.va** is the official website of the Vatican offering everything you need to know about the Pope, his audiences, the Vatican State and the Vatican Museums, the largest art collection in the world.
- **www.capitolium.org** is the official site of the Forums with up-to-date information about the renovations.

Tourist Information Sites

The city has Tourist Information Sites (Punti Informativi Turistici, PIT) that offer maps, information about events and the Roma Pass (➤ below) that gives three days free bus and Metro travel, as well as admission to two museums of your choice www.romapass.it.

There are sites at the both Fiumicino and Ciampino airports, at Termini railway station (Via Giolitti, 24), at Castel Sant' Angelo (Piazza Pia), Corso (Via Minghetti), Via dei Fori Imperiali (opposite the entrance to the Roman Forum), Piazza Cinque Lune (near Piazza Navona) and Via Nazionale (Palazzo degli Esposizioni).

Getting Around

Much of central Rome is small enough to explore on foot and it is the easiest way to get around to most of the sights, but you will probably need to use taxis or public transport at some point during your visit, especially to reach the more interesting outlying sights and for excursions from the city.

Bus and Metro

The city's red-grey **Metro buses** depart from the main bus station on the large Piazza Cinquecento in front of Stazione Termini. However, the huge network (servicing 5 million residents) can be daunting for visitors, and finding the right destination and the exact point of departure can be very confusing. At peak times the buses are often overcrowded with little space for cumbersome luggage. Bear in mind that rides in the Roman traffic always take longer than intended, making it hard to stick to any schedule.

- Tourists and pickpockets use the same buses to all the main attractions. Be especially careful on the popular **bus 64** and the **express bus 40** (with fewer stops) from Stazione Termini to the Vatican!
- The faster option is to take the underground Metro, there are only two lines (Metro A and B) which intersect at Stazione Termini. **Metro A** runs from Battistini to Anagnina (a suburb in the south-east towards Castelli Romani) while **Metro B** goes from EUR-Laurentina to Rebibbia (with a new branch B1 to Piazza Bologna). The service runs from Mon–Fri 5:30–11:30pm, Sat 5:30am–12:30am. The barriers and steep escalators are impossible to negotiate with heavy or cumbersome luggage.
- You can purchase the official Roma Metro bus **timetable** from the ATAC office (Piazza Cinquecento) and from tobacconists (*tabacchi*) for €6.

Tickets

Bus and Metro tickets (single or 10) are available from the ATAC office. A **BIT** (*biglietto integrato a tempo*) single ticket is €1.50 and is valid for 75 minutes from time of validation. A day ticket costs €6, a three-day ticket €16.50.

Finding Your Feet

The integrated three-day **Roma Pass** for €34 is very popular with weekend tourists. It includes a map, is valid for the entire transport network and gives free admission to two museums of your choice – no queues – but excludes the Vatican Museums. It also provides discounts for other museums and exhibitions. The Roma Pass is available at all the tourist information kiosks and ATAC offices, for example in front of Stazione Termini and at Fiumicino Airport (www.romapass.it).

Bus Routes 116, 117, 118, 119

The best routes are those running the small ATAC electric buses that only cost €1.50 each way.

Bus 116 goes from the Villa Borghese (Porta Pinciana) via Via Veneto, Piazza del Parlamento, Corso Vittorio Emanuele, Campo de' Fiori to the leafy Janiculum Hill.

Bus 117 goes from Piazza del Popolo via Piazza Venezia, Via dei Fori Imperiali, Colosseo to the Basilica San Giovanni in Laterano.

Bus 118 departs from Piazzale Ostiense and goes via the Aventine and the Terme di Caracalla to Via Appia.

Bus 119 goes from Piazza Augusto Imperatore via the Pantheon, Campo de' Fiori, Via del Corso, Piazza Navona to Piazza di Spagna (Mon–Fri 8–9, Sat 8–midnight).

Other useful bus routes:

23 San Paolo–Ostiense–Piazza Risorgimento (for the Vatican Museums)

40 Termini–San Pietro. Express with fewer stops than the 64

60 (Express) Largo Pugliese–Via Nomentana–Piazza Venezia–Stazione Ostiense

62 Piazza Bologna–Piazza Venezia–Porta Pia (San Pietro)

64 Termini–Piazza Venezia–Corso Vittorio Emanuele II–San Pietro

75 Termini–Foro Romano–Colosseo

80 (Express) Piazza Vimercati–Corso Trieste–Via Veneto–Piazza San Silvestro

81 Piazza Venezia–San Pietro–Piazza Risorgimento (for Vatican Museums)

Archeobus

The green double-decker bus service to the Via Appia Antica only runs Fri, Sat, Sun. Departures are from 9–4:30 every 30 minutes from Piazza Cinquecento (Stazione Termini). There are 12 hop on /hop off points along the way to the Christian catacombs and the Via Appia Antica. Tickets cost €12 and are valid for two days. They are also offered in combination with the red double-decker Linea 110 bus city tour for €25 (www.archeobus.it).

A cheap alternative (€1.50) to get to the Via Appia Antica is the public bus 218 (from S. Giovanni in Laterano) or bus 118 (from Piazzale Ostiense).

Line 110 – Red Double-decker

Daily 8:30–8:30 every 15 minutes from Piazza Cinquecento (Termini). Hop on/hop off city tour of all the main sights, 48 hour ticket €20 or a day ticket €15.

Stops: Colosseo, Circo Massimo, Bocca della Verità, Vaticano, Fontana di Trevi. Combined ticket with Archeobus / Linea 110, €25 valid for 2 days (www.trambusopen.com)

Rome Open Tour – Green Double-decker

Daily 9– 8 every 20 minutes from Piazza Cinquecento (Stazione Termini), 11 stops in the city centre, day ticket €15 (www.romeopen tour.com).

Roma Cristiana – Saint Peter's Route

The yellow double-decker bus route goes to the main Christian churches and landmarks such as the Colosseum, Piazza Navona and Santa Maria in Trastevere. Daily except Sunday and Wednesday morning (no traffic during the Pope's audiences) about every half hour. Departures at 9am from Piazza Cinquecento (Stazione Termini) or 9:30am from Via Conciliazione (San Pietro) until 6:30pm. €20 for a day, €22 for 2 days (www.romacristiana.com).

Bicycles, Vespas, Segways and Mopeds

If you want to flit the through Rome's traffic on a Vespa – like Gregory Peck and Audrey Hepburn in the classic film *Roman Holiday* – you can rent a scooter at, for example, **BiciBaci**, Via Viminale 5, Metro A and B: Termini, 8–8, www.bicibaci.com, or at **Spagna Rent**, Vicolo del Bottino, 8, exit Metro A: Spagna, 9–7, tel: 06 3 22 52 40, or **Roma Rent**, Vicolo dei Bavari 7a, near Campo de' Fiori, tel: 06 68 95 55. You must be over 21 and a passport and credit card are required. But beware, traffic is busy and the roads are full of potholes.

■ A more eco-friendly option is to hire a bicycle, rickshaw or electric bike from Ronconi at the entrance to Villa Borghese.

■ A 3-hour guided **Segway Tour** costs about €75, www.rome-by-segway.com.

■ The city of Rome has a **bike-sharing scheme**, with 10 pick-up points across the centre, but the bureaucratic registration (also available at the tourist kiosks) is not particularly tourist friendly.

Accommodation

Travellers to Rome are all after A Room with a View, preferably one where they can see the dome of St Peter's from their hotel bed. This expensive wish can only be fulfilled from the luxurious Hotel Hassler Medici, high above the Spanish Steps. In most hotels you are better off with a room facing the courtyard, una camera tranquilla al cortile – no view, but nice and quiet.

Hotel categories are a bit of a gamble in Rome and the one- to five-star grades do not always guarantee a corresponding quality in amenities. Although fast feedback on the internet has led to a certain standardization, you do need to be prepared for some surprises: dingy rooms, tiny bathrooms, showers with no curtain, tepid morning coffee, substandard tea bags, the nightly buzz of mopeds, and sometimes staff who could be far or more accommodating.

It is best to have a laid-back approach to your accommodation in Rome; after all there are other things to offset any inconveniences, such as the grandeur of a marble and stucco entrance hall, a picturesque courtyard or perhaps a magnificent view from the top floor. They should more than compensate for a broken lift or leaky tap. Especially in the noisy, bustling *centro storico*, the old adage applies: location, location, location. Even if the hotel is a little shabby the area will make up for it with romantic night-time strolls to all the attractions right on your doorstep.

Breakfast

Hotel breakfasts in Rome have improved enormously in recent years but if yours is still poor, do as the Romans do and go to the nearest bar where for an excellent cappuccino and a fresh pastry *(cornetti)*.

Parking

The historic centre is closed to through traffic from 7–7 and after 10pm but this does not mean that there is any less noise, there is still heavy traffic from the local residents. As a tourist, you may drive to your hotel and unload your luggage but you must then immediately move your car to the hotel's reserved parking and leave it there until your departure.

Prices

The pricing system of the **hotels** is often misleading – although the tough internet competition has improved this – and while room rates must by law be displayed in the reception, the prices are net. There are then surcharges such as 19% VAT, breakfast, WiFi, and even air conditioning in the hot summer months.

Hotel rates in Rome are similar to those in London and Paris. The financial crisis has meant that some hotels offer *offerte speciali*, internet specials for online bookings. But on the whole finding a double room for under €100 is still a rarity in the city centre. As a result many tourists opt for a **bed and breakfast** where the rate is €70–150 for a double room. There are also numerous **monasteries** and **convents** that offer couples accommodation (from €35 per person, for details see www.monastery stays.com) however, most are outside of the city centre. For younger tourists there are plenty of **hostel** options in the trendy Monti district, some are so hip that they do not even have a door sign and can only be booked online (from €20 per person).

Reservation Agencies

If you haven't reserved a room, then *on no account* accept rooms from touts at the airport or railway station. Instead, contact **Enjoy Rome**, Via Marghera 8A (tel: 06 4 45 18 43; www.enjoyrome.com), which operates a free room-finding service. Or try the free **Hotel Reservation Service** (tel: 06 6 99 10 00; www.hotelreservation.it, 7am–10pm) at Fiumicino, Ciampino and Termini.

Budget Accommodation

Camping Village Flaminio: A green camping area in northern Rome, with swimming pool and bungalows. Via Flaminia Nuova, 821; tel: 06 3 33 26 04; www.villageflaminio.com.

Casa Internazionale delle Donne: International Women's hostel Orsa Maggiore ("Great Bear") is housed in a former convent boarding school in Trastevere. Via San Francesco Sales, 1a/Via Lungara; tel: 06 6 89 37 53; www.foresteriaorsa.altervista.org.

Accommodation

Youth Hostel: Ostello del Foro Olimpico (Viale delle Olimpiadi, 61; tel: 06 3 23 62 67; www.ostellionline.org).
YWCA (Via Cesare Balbo, 4; tel: 06 4 88 04 60; www.ywca-ucdg.it). All welcome.
Hostel Sandy (Via Cavour, 136; tel: 06 4 88 45 85; www.sandyhostel.com). Dorm hostel-type accommodation.
Suore Pie Operaie (Via di Torre Argentina, 76; tel: 06 6 86 12 54). Centrally located, women only. Booking essential.
Pensione Ottaviano Hostel: The oldest hostel in Rome, near the Vatican. Via Ottaviano, 6, tel: 06 39 73 81 38 www.pensioneottaviano.com

---

Accommodation Prices

Price categories below are for a double *(una matrimoniale)* or twin *(una camera doppia)* room for one night, and are given for guidance only. Seasonal variations may apply, with more reasonable rates in winter.

€ under €120   **€€** €120–€250   **€€€** over €250

Albergo Cesàri €€

Opened in 1787, the three-star Cesari has been in business long enough to get things right, and latterly has maintained its standards through the efficiency of its staff and regular renovation – the last major overhaul was in 1999. It also has the bonus of a quiet, central position in a hard-to-find little street between the Pantheon and Via del Corso. The 47 rooms are comfortable with modern decorative touches, as well as TVs and air conditioning.
➕ 202 B1 ✉ Via di Pietra, 89/a
☎ 06 6 74 97 01; www.albergocesari.it

Grande Hotel de la Minerva €€€

The Minerva does not yet have the cachet of Rome's other five-star hotels, but none of its upmarket rivals can claim such a central position – behind the Pantheon and church of Santa Maria sopra Minerva. The hotel enjoyed a makeover that has improved still further the 135 rooms and suites and public areas. Service is excellent, the facilities are the equal of – and often superior to – similarly starred hotels, and little can beat the prospect as you step from the hotel's front door.

➕ 202 B1 ✉ Piazza della Minerva, 69
☎ 06 69 52 01; www.hotel-invest.com

Hotel Aberdeen €

Set in a wonderfully quiet location just off the Via Nazionale, this is the perfect place to relax after a busy day sightseeing. The transport links from here to all the main sights are excellent, though it's a little far from the *centro storico*. Breakfast buffet is served in a frescoed room.
➕ 203 E2 ✉ Via Firenze, 48
☎ 06 4 82 39 20; www.hotelaberdeen.com

Hotel Accademia €€   *Insider Tip*

If you're looking for a combination of modern design and historic surroundings, then the Accademia, near the Fontana di Trevi (▶ 124), is a good find. The building has retained its period exterior and has a patio. Inside, the rooms have the clean and minimalist lines of an up-to-the-minute boutique hotel. Owned by a small group, Travelroma, the other hotels (▶ website) are also worth considering.
➕ 202 C2 ✉ Piazza Accademia di San Luca, 74 ☎ 06 7 69 92 26 07;
www.accademiahotel.com

Finding Your Feet

Hotel Bramante €€

The Mariani family have been welcoming pilgrims and tourists to their hotel since 1873, when they converted this old palazzo, once the home of the architect Domenico Fontana, who came to Rome in 1563, into a hotel. Quietly set on a cobbled street, just a few minutes' walk from Basilica di San Pietro (➤ 154), the 16 rooms are all a good size, and furnished traditionally with restrained elegance. Breakfast is excellent and there's a small courtyard.

➕ 204 C4 ✉ Viccolo delle Pallini, 24
☎ 06 68 80 64 26; www.hotelbramante.com

Hotel Eden €€€

The five-star Eden ranks as one of the top three Roman hotels – which are all characterized by their traditional style – but here the atmosphere is far more relaxed. It's been an exclusive favourite among celebrities for more than a century, attracting European royalty and film stars. There are 110 rooms and eleven suites. Most rooms are enormous with marble bathrooms and beautifully antiques. La Terrazza restaurant is also superb, with spectacular views from the terrace – perfect for a romantic dinner. The Eden remains one of the top hotels in the world.

➕ 202 D3 ✉ Via Ludovisi, 49
☎ 06 47 81 21; www.edenroma.com

Hotel Fontanella Borghese €€

A hospitable welcome awaits you at this Roman-style, comfortable hotel, attractively situated on the upper floors of a 16th-century palazzo and close to Piazza di Spagna (➤ 136). Walk through the courtyard to discover a modern hotel with traditional style. Half of the rooms have bathrooms with tubs, and half have showers. The staff are exceptionally helpful and friendly, and the good public areas make a stay here a truly enjoyable and Roman experience.

➕ 202 B2 ✉ Largo Fontanella Borghese, 84
☎ 06 68 80 95 04; www.fontanellaborghese.com

Hotel Navona €

Never mind that this hotel only has a one-star rating, it is part of Rome's history, as parts of the building were built over the ancient Baths of Agrippa, which date back to the first century ad, and the English Romantic poets Keats and Shelley once occupied the top floor. Plus, its position is unbeatable – one minute from Piazza Navona. Set in a quiet side street away from the hustle and bustle, the vast majority of its 21 rooms have been renovated to a standard that makes a nonsense of its lowly star rating. The owners are a friendly Italo-Australian couple who make light of any communication problems. The only drawbacks are breakfast (take it in a nearby bar instead), the air conditioning, which commands a hefty supplement, and credit cards are not accepted. If the hotel is full, the owners may suggest you stay in the smarter, co-owned and slightly more expensive Zanardelli hotel just north of Piazza Navona.

➕ 202 A1 ✉ Via dei Sediari, 8
☎ 06 6 86 42 03; www.hotelnavona.com

Hotel Piazza di Spagna €€

The three-star Piazza di Spagna is not on the piazza, but in a quiet side street nearby. The attractive old building is covered in creeper. Its 20 rooms are not enormous, but the facilities are good: all rooms have air conditioning, a TV and telephone, and a bathroom. The location, especially if you intend to do a lot of shopping, could not- be better.

➕ 202 B2 ✉ Via Mario de' Fiori, 61
☎ 06 6 79 64 12; www.hotelpiazzadispagna.it

Hotel Relais de l'Opera €€

This elegant, small mid-range hotel is located in the trendy Monti district, with many restaurants, cafés and small shops. The Teatro dell'Opera, the Fontana di Trevi, the Basilica of Santa Maria Maggiore, the Foro Romano and Piazza Venezia are all nearby.

➕ 208 C5 ✉ Via Palermo, 36
☎ 06 39 26 64 10 74; www.relaisdelopera.com

Hotel Ripa €€€

Fans of sleek minimalism will be thrilled to find a hotel for the 21st century in the heart of the Trastevere district (➤ 101). Streamlined public areas give a taste of the bedrooms, where some might say style takes precedence over comfort. Classy and cool, this hotel will appeal to the discerning traveller.

➕ 206 C2 ✉ Via degli Orti di Trastevere, 1
☎ 06 5 86 11; www.ripahotel.com

ider Hotel San Francesco €€

The San Francesco in Trastevere is a good base from which to explore Rome. This comfortable hotel, which offers excellent value for money, has traditionally furnished rooms with white walls and rich textiles. The breakfast buffet is generous, but the big bonus is the rooftop terrace, where you can enjoy a drink while looking over the rooftops to the trees on the Janiculum.

➕ 206 C3 ✉ Via Iacopa de' Settesoli, 7
☎ 06 58 30 00 51; www.hotelsanfrancesco.net

Hotel Scalinata di Spagna €€€

What you pay for this three-star hotel might buy you a bigger room elsewhere, but it would take a considerable sum to purchase a setting quite as romantic – the hotel sits at the top of the Spanish Steps looking down over Keats' house and the Piazza di Spagna. It has a beautiful staircase and a small roof garden.

➕ 202 C3 ✉ Piazza Trinità dei Monti, 17
☎ 06 6 79 30 06; www.hotelscalinata.com

Hotel Teatro di Pompeo €€/€€€

In Rome you walk through history, but in this three-star hotel you can sleep in it as well. On a quiet square east of Campo de' Fiori, the hotel occupies the site of the ancient Theatre of Pompey, which dates from the first century BC. Parts of the original building can still be seen in the remarkable rough-stone vaulted dining room and elsewhere. History aside, this is a pleasant hotel thanks to a welcoming owner, modest size – just 13 rooms – and the charm of many of the rooms: the attic rooms with their beamed ceilings and terracotta floors are among the best.

➕ 205 F3 ✉ Largo del Pallaro, 8
☎ 06 68 30 01 70; www.hotelteatrodipompeo.it

Hotel Teatropace 33 €€/€€€

Location, location, location goes hand in hand with peace and quiet at this charming hotel, close to the iconic Piazza Navona (➤ 88), one of Rome's loveliest squares. The apricot-coloured washed building dates from 1585 and access to the upstairs rooms is by a beautiful, shallow-stepped, stone spiral staircase. As often in Rome, rooms are on the small side, but they're well designed to make the most of the space, and the marble-appointed bathrooms (mainly with showers) are state-of-the-art. Order breakfast the night before and it's brought to your room.

➕ 202 A1 ✉ Via del Teatro Pace, 33
☎ 06 6 87 90 75; www.hotelteatropace.com

Hotel Trastevere €

The friendly two-star Trastevere is the best of a handful of hotels in the lively and atmospheric Trastevere district (➤ 101). Though the 20 rooms are small, they are well-appointed with modern bathrooms, terracotta floors and wood panelling. There are also four private apartments with kitchens available, which are good value if there are more than two of you or if you are staying more than a few nights. It can be noisy later in the evenings.

➕ 206 C3 ✉ Via Luciano Manara, 24
☎ 06 5 81 47 13; www.hoteltrastevere.net

Food and Drink

Eating out is one of Rome's great pleasures. The city has a huge range of restaurants, from humble trattorias and traditional dining rooms to sleek and expensive contemporary eateries, and there are plenty of places where you can get inexpensive snacks, pizzas and sandwiches. In summer – as an extra bonus – it's often possible to eat outside.

- Don't be put off by Rome's hearty specialities, many of which require a strong stomach (➤ 20), because most restaurants offer a broad range of **familiar Italian dishes**, which will delight most palates.
- Differences between types of restaurants in Italy are becoming increasingly blurred. An ***osteria*** was once the humblest type of eating place, but now tends to describe new and unstuffy restaurants serving simple, often innovative, food in relaxed surroundings. Anywhere described as a ***pizzerie*** is likely to be even simpler; it will often serve a few pastas, salads and other dishes as well as pizzas. A ***trattoria*** is the general name for a traditional and unpretentious restaurant, while ***un ristorante*** is usually smarter and more expensive. A smart and expensive restaurant in Rome, more than most cities, does not guarantee good food; often you can eat well in the humblest places.
- For most of the eating places listed in this guide it is well worth trying to **reserve**, the exception being pizzerias, which rarely take reservations. For more popular restaurants you may need to reserve a few days in advance.
- Restaurant **menus** are usually broken down into a **number of courses**; these begin with *antipasti* (hors d'oeuvres), followed by *il primo* (pasta, gnocchi, risotto or soup) and *il secondo* (meat or fish). Vegetables *(il contorno)* or salad *(insalata)* are usually served separately from the *secondo*. For dessert you can choose between *il dolce* (sweet), *formaggio* (cheese) and *frutta* (fruit). Puddings are often disappointing. You're not obliged to wade through all the courses on the menu, and none but the top-ranking restaurants should mind if you just have a salad and a plate of pasta, especially at lunch.

Roman Cuisine

Traditional Roman cuisine is *cucina povera*, which literally translates as "poor kitchen" where many dishes are made from the most humble of ingredients by thrifty housewives – and yet are still very tasty. In the booming 1980s and 1990s dishes made from offal or hearty vegetable soups were hard to find in Roman trattorias however, thanks to the Slow Food movement regional cuisine has made a comeback.

In the Testaccio district, site of the city's ancient rubbish heap and old slaughterhouse, there are numerous trattorias (also expensive ones such as Checchino dal 1887) that serve classics dishes like *pasta fagioli*, pasta with beans or *pagliata*, unweaned calf intestines with penne pasta. *Abbacchio alla scottadito*, lamb roasted with rosemary potatoes, or *porchetta*, suckling pig with crackling, are all an integral part of Roman celebrations. You should also try some excellently prepared *carciofi alla giudia*, fried artichokes, especially in the old Jewish Ghetto.

Food and Drink

- Romans take **lunch** *(il pranzo)* from 1pm and **dinner** *(la cena)* from 8pm. The famous long Roman lunch followed by a lengthy siesta is largely a thing of the past, except on Sunday, which is still an excuse for a big traditional lunchtime meal.

- **Service** *(servizio)* and *pane e coperto* (bread and cover charge) may bump prices up in all restaurants. Both should be itemized on the bill. If a service charge is not included, then you should **tip** at your discretion up to about 15 per cent. If the service is included, then an additional 5–10 per cent will suffice.

- The **bill** *(il conto)* should be a properly printed receipt. It is best to request a proper bill *(una ricevuta fiscale)*.

Culinary highlights at a glance
To sample the best that Rome has to offer, try the following places:
Tazza d'Oro (➤ 96) for coffee
Il Gelato di San Crispino (➤ 144) for ice cream
Leonina (➤ 79) for pizza by the slice
Agata e Romeo (➤ 142) or **Les Étoiles** (➤ 174) for a romantic meal
Bar della Pace (➤ 114), **Ar Galletto** (➤ 113) or **Antica Fabbrica del Cioccolato SAID** (➤ 144) for people-watching

---

Eating Cheaply

- Many restaurants, especially around Termini railway station, offer a set-price **tourist menu** *(un menù turistico)*, but the food is often poor.

- Keep costs down by drinking **house wine** *(vino della casa)*, usually a good white Frascati or similar, available in a quarter-litre (around a half-pint) carafe *(un quartino)* or half-litre (around 1 pint) jug *(mezzo litro)*.

- Most bars offer **sandwiches** *(tramezzini)*, which are invariably made from the blandest white bread with crusts removed. Far better are *panini*, or filled rolls, which you can often have heated *(riscaldato)*.

- **Pizza** by the slice *(pizza al taglio)* is often sold from tiny hole-in-the-wall bakeries, but check the quality of the topping; in the worst places it amounts to no more than a smear of tomato.

- Drink your coffee at the counter – it often costs three times if you sit at a table.

- A *pasticceria* specializes in **cakes** and pastries.

- A *torrefazione* is a bar that also **roasts coffee** for retail sale.

What to Drink

- The first drink of the day is generally **coffee** (➤ 42), usually a cappuccino accompanied by a sweet croissant *(un cornetto)*. After lunch or dinner, Italians always drink an espresso, *never* cappuccino.

- **Tea** *(un tè nero)* still exotic for most Italians and it is no wonder as the quality of the tea bags rather poor. When they do drink it they take it with lemon *(un tè al limone)* and without milk. If you want tea with milk, ask specifically for *un tè con latte* – sometimes you may have to insist on *latte freddo* (cold milk).

- **Mineral water** *(acqua minerale)* is widely available, either fizzy *(acqua gassata)* or still *(acqua non gassata)*. If you want a glass of water ask for *un bicchiere d'acqua*. If you prefer free tap water, ask for a *bicchiere d'acqua dal rubinetto* or *acqua normale*.

Finding Your Feet

- **At the table** Italians usually drink a light, dry house wine (*vino sfuso/ vino de la casa*), which are good and inexpensive. In Rome popular white wines come from towns such as Frascati in the nearby Castelli Romani wine region, while red wines often come from Tuscany or Piedmont.
- Bottled **fruit juice** (*un succo di frutta*) is often drunk at breakfast. Freshly squeezed juice is *una spremuta* of either orange (*una spremuta d'arancia*), grapefruit (… *di pompelmo*) or lemon (…*di limone*). Lemon Soda (the brand name), a bitter lemon drink, is another good soft drink.
- **Beer** (*birra*) is lager, but darker-style beer (*birra scura*, *nera* or *rossa*) may be available. For draft beer ask for *birra alla spina*. Good Italian brands are Peroni or Nastro Azzurro. Beer is traditionally enjoyed with pizza.
- **Aperitifs** include fortified wines such as Martini, Cinzano and Campari. Note that Campari Soda comes mixed in a bottle; for the real thing ask for *un bitter Campari*. You'll often see people drinking an orange-coloured aperitif – this is Aperol or the non-alcoholic Crodino. Prosecco, a white sparkling wine from northeast Italy is another popular *aperitivo*. Gin and tonic is *gin e tonica*.
- After-dinner **digestifs** include brandy (Vecchia Romagna is the best brand), *limoncello* (lemon liqueur), or *amaro*, literally "bitter". The best-known brand being the very bitter Fernet Branca; a good and less demanding brand is Averna. Romans may also have *grappa* after a meal, a strong clear *eau de vie*, or sweeter drinks such as the almond-flavoured Amaretto or aniseed-flavoured Sambuca (sometimes served with an added coffee bean).

Further Information
The following websites are useful for the latest information on restaurants:

www.gamberorosso.it – easy-to-use site of the Italian wine guide, with an excellent selection of restaurants

www.foodinrome.com – an informative, easy-to-use site with a good restaurant selection, updated weekly

www.060608.it – main tourism site with more than 2,200 restaurant listings

---

Coffee Essentials
- **un espresso** (or, more colloquially, **un caffè**) – an espresso coffee (short and black)
- **una doppia** – double espresso
- **un lungo** – espresso with a little more water than usual
- **un macchiato** – espresso with a dash of milk
- **un caffè corretto** – espresso with a dash of whisky or other liqueur
- **un cappuccino** – espresso with added frothed milk
- **un caffè latte** – cappuccino with more milk and no froth
- **un americano** – espresso with hot water to make a long coffee drink
- **un caffè Hag** – decaffeinated coffee
- **un caffè freddo** – iced coffee. It is usually served with sugar already added. Ask for *un amaro* if you want it without sugar.
- **un cappuccino freddo** – iced cappuccino

Shopping

Rome is the showroom of the Italian fashion – even if it is created elsewhere – and all the finest designer shops, from Armani to Zegna, are in the dignified old palazzi in the triangle between Via del Corso, Via del Babuino and the elegant Via Condotti, with the side streets Via Borgognona and Via delle Carrozze (▶ 145).

■ **Less expensive clothes and shoe shops** line several key streets, notably the northern pedestrian zone of the Via del Corso – which you'll find packed with shoppers on Saturdays – Via del Tritone and Via Nazionale. Shoes and clothes generally are good buys, as are food, wine, accessories such as gloves, leather goods, luxury items and fine antiques.

■ Other streets have their own specialities: **antiques and art galleries**, for example, on Via dei Coronari, Via Giulia, Via del Babuino, Via del Monserrato and Via Margutta; paper and wickerwork on Via Monterone; religious ephemera and clothing on Via dei Cestari. Via del Governo Vecchio or Via dei Banchi Nuovi, for example, are dotted with second-hand stores, jewellers and small artisans' workshops.

■ Rome remains a city of small shops and boutiques where malls and department stores play only a minor role. That is with the exception of the **Galleria Alberto Sordi**, the belle époque arcade on Via del Corso that has elegant cafés, exquisite shops and the Feltrinelli bookstore.

■ The city has several fine **markets**, notably the picturesque **Campo de' Fiori** (▶ 86), the **Nuovo Mercato Esquilino**, housed in a converted barracks on Via Lamarmora near **Piazza Vittorio Emanuele** (this is central Rome's main market, open Monday to Saturday 10am–6pm), and the famous Sunday flea market at **Porta Portese** southwest of the centre near Porta Sublicio in Trastevere. Porta Portese is reputedly the largest flea market in Europe, with around 4,000 stalls selling anything and everything, from antiques to cheap junk. It becomes extremely crowded by mid-morning, so try to arrive early (it finishes at 2pm). 👪 Children and teens will love the colourful diversity. Beware of pickpockets.

■ Most food **shopping** is still done in tiny neighbourhood shops known as *alimentari*. These sell everything from olive oil and pasta to basic toiletries. They usually have a delicatessen counter, where you can have a fresh sandwich *(panino)* made up from the meats and cheeses that are on display.

■ Rome **shop assistants** have a reputation for aloofness, especially in smarter boutiques. If they pretend you don't exist, ignore them or politely ask for help: the phrase is "Mi può aiutare, per favore?"

■ Don't be tempted to bargain – **prices are fixed**. Prices may drop in sales *(saldi)*.

Opening Times

■ In the **city centre**, opening times are Monday to Saturday 9–7 or 8pm. The long 1–4pm lunch break is mostly a thing of the past. Nowadays it is *orario continuo*, open all day.

■ The vast majority of shops are **closed on Sundays and Monday morning**. Many food shops close on Thursday afternoon in winter and Saturday afternoon in summer.

■ **In August many stores close** completely for weeks at a time *(chiuso per ferie* is the telltale sign – closed for holidays).

Entertainment

Rome's cultural scene was transformed in 2002 with the opening of the Auditorium Parco della Musica, a world-class venue that offers a staggering range of music and the performing arts. The city is also noted for music festivals – often staged in beautiful churches and palazzi. The Testaccio district, with its nightclubs, jazz clubs, and other venues is a popular nightlife area.

Information

- Information about most events and performing arts can be obtained from the main visitor centre and information kiosks around the city (➤ 33).
- The main **listings** magazine is *roma c'è* (www.romace.it), an invaluable weekly publication with details of classical and other musical events, theatre, dance, opera, nightclubs, current museum and gallery opening times, shopping, restaurants and much more. It also has a summary of key events and galleries in English at the back. It can be obtained from most newspaper stands and bookstores. The English-language *Wanted in Rome* (www.wantedinrome.com) is published every other Wednesday.
- If you read some Italian, listings can be found in *Time Out Roma* (issued on Thursday); *Trovaroma*, a "what's on" insert in the Thursday editon of *La Repubblica* newspaper; or daily editions of newspapers such as *Il Messaggero* (which has a detailed listings supplement, *Metro*, published on Thursdays).

Tickets

Rome does still not have any good electronic ticket sales facilities, and while the **www.060808.it** site has event information you will still be obliged to queue at the individual box offices before a performance. You can try your luck with a ticket agency such as **Orbis** (Piazza dell'Esquilino, 37; tel: 06 47 44 77 6; Mon–Sat 9:30–1, 4–7:30). Tickets for some classical, jazz and other concerts are also available from Ricordi music stores, of which there are five, and from **Hello Ticket** (toll-free in Italy: 8 00 90 70 80; www.helloticket.it). Tickets for the Auditorium-Parco della Musica can be booked online.

Nightclubs

- Where nightclubs are concerned, be aware that a popular club one year can lose its following or re-emerge with a facelift and new name by the next.
- Long-established **gay bars and clubs** include L'Alibi (➤ 118). Other clubs such as Piper (➤ 148) often have gay nights.
- For most clubs **admission prices** are high, but entry often includes your first drink. For tax and other reasons, some clubs or bars define them-selves as private clubs, which in practice means you have to fill out a (usually free) membership card. Remember, too, that many clubs close during summer or move to outdoor or seaside locations beyond the city.

Classical Music

Especially during Rome's summer festival, Estate Romana, there are concerts, operas and ballets (for listing: info kiosks, the *roma c'e* magazine and www.060808.it) in the concert halls of the Auditorium Parco della Musica as well as in many churches and palazzi courtyards.

The Ancient City

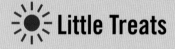 Little Treats

A genuine emperor and the replica

Newlyweds have their pictures taken on
the piazza in front of the **equestrian statue
of Emperor Marcus Aurelius** (► 50). The original
is in the Capitoline Museums.

Monument with spectacular views

Enjoy the views from the roof terraces of the
Monumento a Vittorio Emanuele II (► 50).

Take a break from the hustle and bustle

A few steps from the Colosseum is the
inviting the little park of **Colle Oppio** (► 76),
ideal for a rest or picnic.

The Ancient City

Getting Your Bearings

What remains of ancient Rome is not confined to a single area of the modern city. Buildings and monuments from the era of the Roman Empire and earlier are scattered far and wide, yet the heart of the old city – around the Capitoline, Palatine and Esquiline hills – still boasts the largest present-day concentration of ancient monuments.

This area makes an excellent point from which to start your visit, placing into context much of what you'll see elsewhere in the city. The itinerary starts where Rome itself probably started, on the Capitoline Hill, close to the busy Piazza Venezia. This piazza is the hub of the modern city; roads lead off from here to the four points of the compass: Via del Corso to the north and Piazza del Popolo; Corso Vittorio Emanuele II to the west and the Basilica di San Pietro; Via IV Novembre to the east and Stazione Termini; and Via dei Fori Imperiali to the south and the Colosseo. The Capitoline Hill, however, was the early focus of the ancient city. From its slopes you can look over and then explore the open spaces of the Foro Romano (Roman Forum), the social, political and mercantile heart of the old Roman Empire. From here it's only a few steps to

Getting Your Bearings

the Colosseo, the greatest of all ancient Roman monuments, and then on to a quieter residential area and your first church, San Clemente, a fascinating historical hybrid which contains a beautiful medieval interior, the remains of an older fifth-century church, and the partially excavated ruins of a second century Roman temple.

Just a few minutes' walk away stands San Giovanni in Laterano, Rome's cathedral church, and among the most important churches in the city after St Peter's. And if you still have some time, retrace your steps to the Capitoline Hill and explore the Capitoline Museums, which are filled with masterpieces from the Roman era.

TOP 10

⭐ Capitolino ➤ 50
⭐ Foro Romano ➤ 52
⭐ Colosseo ➤ 60

Don't Miss

⓫ San Clemente ➤ 67
⓬ San Giovanni in
   Laterano ➤ 70

At Your Leisure

⓭ Piazza Venezia ➤ 72
⓮ Musei Capitolini ➤ 73
⓯ Colonna Traiana ➤ 73
⓰ Fori Imperiali ➤ 74
⓱ San Pietro in Vincoli ➤ 75
⓲ Colle Oppio ➤ 76
⓳ Santi Quattro Coronati ➤ 76
⓴ Museo d'Arte Orientale ➤ 77

Perfect Days in

The Perfect Day

If you're not quite sure where to begin your travels, this itinerary recommends a practical and enjoyable day out, taking in some of ancient Rome's best places to see. For more information see the main entries (➤ 50–77).

🕘 9:00am
Begin the day by walking to busy **🔞 Piazza Venezia** (➤ 72), taking time to admire the colossal Monumento a Vittorio Emanuele II and **🔟 Colonna Traiana** (➤ 73). Then climb the shallow ramp of steps near the piazza's southwest corner to the ⭐**Capitolino** (Piazza del Campidoglio, ➤ 50).

🕤 9:30am
Explore the church of **Santa Maria in Aracoeli** (➤ 51) and admire the view from the terraces of the Monumento a Vittorio Emanuele II. From the Piazza del Campidoglio take the small lane to the left of the city hall past the bronze Capitoline Wolf statue and admire the view down on to the Foro Romano.

🕙 10:00am
Go down the steps to the main entrance to the ⭐**Foro Romano** (ill. below, ➤ 52), one of the world's most historic ruins.

🕛 12:00pm
Emerge close to the ⭐**Colosseo** (ill. right, ➤ 60) and **Arco di Costantino** (➤ 64). You can visit them now or after lunch. You could have a snack lunch in **Cavour 313** wine bar (➤ 78), one of the cafés east of the Colosseo, a meal in **Il Bocconcino** (➤ 78), or buy provisions in Via Cavour and head for the Colle Oppio.

🕑 2:00pm
By now the queues to the Colosseum should have eased – time to view the famous monument from within and pose for a photograph (about €2) with one of the "gladiators".

🕞 3:30pm
Walk a short distance on Via di San Giovanni in Laterano to **⓫ San Clemente** (➤ 67). This unique church offers a journey through time: from the church above (12th century, with magnificent gold mosaics), down to the simple lower church

(4th century). And below that, a temple to the Persian god Mithra and a Roman house dating back to Caesar's era.

4:30pm

Make your way along Via dei Santi Coronati, a quiet side street, to visit the church 19 **Santi Quattro Coronati** (➤ 76), before continuing toward the soaring San Giovanni in Laterano, the cathedral church of Rome and one of the most important places of worship in the city.

5:30pm

Explore 12 **San Giovanni in Laterano** (➤ 70), not forgetting its ancient baptistery and cloister, the latter graced with countless superbly decorated columns. Then take a bus or the Metro A (San Giovanni) if you don't want to retrace your steps to the Colosseo and Piazza Venezia.

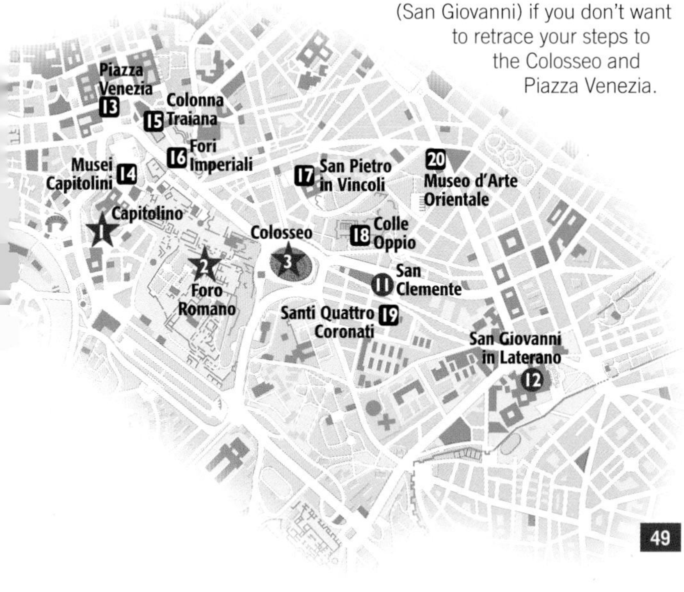

★ Capitolino

The Capitoline Hill, is the smallest but most important of Rome's original Seven Hills. Home to Bronze Age tribes as early as the 14th century BC, it formed the city's birthplace, eventually becoming the hub of its military, religious and political life. Its history, position and many sights make it the perfect introduction to the ancient city.

Today, much of the Capitolino has been obscured by the **Monumento a Vittorio Emanuele II**, the huge white edifice that dominates **Piazza Venezia** (▶ 72). In the earliest times, however, the hill had two distinct crests: one to the north, which was known as the *Arx*, or Citadel, and is now the site of the church of **Santa Maria in Aracoeli**; and one to the south, known as the *Capitolium*, which is now largely given over to magnificent palaces such as the Palazzo dei Conservatori.

Between the two lay the *Asylum*, an area reputedly created by Romulus as a place of sanctuary, the aim being to attract refugees to the fledgling city. Today this area is occupied by **Piazza del Campidoglio**, a square largely laid out by Michelangelo and bounded by Rome's town hall, the Palazzo Senatorio (to the rear), and the **Musei Capitolini**, or Capitoline Museums, to either side (▶ 73).

View over the Piazza del Campidoglio toward the statue of Emperor Marcus Aurelius from Palazzo Senatorio

Piazza d'Araocoeli

Ignore the steps to **Santa Maria in Aracoeli** – there's an easier entrance to the church in the piazza above – and climb the shallow stepped ramp (1536), or *cordonata*, in front of you. This was designed by Michelangelo for the triumphal entry of Emperor Charles V into Rome, and is crowned by two huge Roman statues of Castor and Pollux placed here in 1583. At the heart of the piazza stands a copy of a famous equestrian statue of Emperor Marcus Aurelius – the original is in the Palazzo Nuovo on your left, part of the Capitoline Museums (the rest of the museum is in the Palazzo dei Conservatori on your right).

Fresco of the *Life of San Bernardino* in the Chapel of St Bernardino of Siena, Santa Maria in Aracoeli

Head for the space between the Palazzo Nuovo and Palazzo Senatorio, where you'll find steps on the left into **Santa Maria in Aracoeli** (and the entrance to the Monumento a Vittorio Emanuele II, ► 72), a church already considered ancient when it was first recorded in AD574. The church is filled with chandeliers, ancient columns and a beautifully decorated ceiling. It also contains frescoes on the *Life of San Bernardino* (1486) by the Umbrian artist Pinturicchio (in the first chapel of the right, or south, aisle), and the *Tomb of Luca Savelli* (1287), attributed to the Florentine sculptor Arnolfo di Cambio (left side of the south transept).

TAKING A BREAK

The Capitoline Museums have a café (entrance on the lane to the right of Palazzo dei Conservatori), as does the terrace of the Monumento a Vittorio Emanuele II.
Santa Maria in Aracoeli

➕ 207 E5 ✉ Piazza d'Aracoeli ☎ 06 69 76 38 39
🕐 May–Sep daily 9–12:30, 3–6:30; Oct–April 9–12:30, 2:30–5:30
🍴 Cafés in Capitoline Museums and on terraces of Monumento a Vittorio Emanuele II 🚇 Colosseo 🚌 40, 44, 46, 60, 63, 64, 70, 75, 81, 85, 87, 175 and all other services to Piazza Venezia 💰 Free

INSIDER INFO

- Be sure to walk through the passages to the left and right of the Palazzo Senatorio for views over the Foro Romano (Roman Forum, ► 52).
- It is not worth visiting the **Monumento a Vittorio Emanuele II** (tel: 06 6 99 17 18), the entrance to which is rather hidden at the top of the steps that also give access to Santa Maria in Aracoeli. Instead go down the short corridor to emerge on the monument's colossal terraces, with superb views of the Fori Imperiali, and an excellent café (daily 9:30–5:30; 4:30 in winter; glass lift to the roof: €7).

★2 Foro Romano

The Foro Romano (Roman Forum) was the heart of the Roman Empire for almost 1,000 years. Today, its once mighty ensemble of majestic buildings has been reduced almost to nothing, yet the surviving ruins provide a romantic setting in which you can still catch a glimpse of the glory that was Rome.

Exploring the Forum

When exploring the Forum, it's essential to remember the site's 3,000-year history, and the degree to which monuments over this period were built, rebuilt, moved, destroyed, adapted, plundered and used as a living area before it was left to fall into wistful ruin. Only a handful of structures, therefore, such as the **Arco di Settimio Severo** (▶ 54) or the **Basilica di Massenzio** hint at their original size or layout.

If monuments are all you seek, you'll probably leave disappointed, or at best bemused by the jumble of stones and columns. The trick here is to enjoy the beauty and romance of such ruins, and appreciate their historical associations: after all, you are literally walking in the foot-steps of Julius Caesar, Nero, Caligula, Claudius, Hadrian and countless other resonant names from antiquity.

Marsh to Majesty

The Forum was not Rome's original heart – that honour probably went to a fortress hamlet on the more easily de-fended Capitoline Hill to the northwest. The future hub of the empire actually began life as the *Velabrum*, a marshy inlet of the Tiber between the Capitoline and Palatine hills. This was the area that featured in the myth of Romulus and Remus (▶ 11), for it was here that the twins were found and suckled by the She-Wolf, and here that Romulus – according to legend – founded Rome in 753BC.

During the Iron Age, the area probably served as a local cemetery and later as a meeting place, common land and rubbish tip for the shepherds and other inhabitants of these early settlements. In the 5th/6th century BC, Tarquinius, the Etruscan fifth King of Rome, ordered the construction of the *cloaca massima*, the sewer system that drained the swamps that today run below the Forum. The meant that the area could be used not only for shops and houses, but also temples, courts, basilicas and the other great buildings of state. Successive emperors and consuls vied with one another to leave ever-grander memorials to their military and political achievements. This state of affairs continued until about the second century ad, when a grow-ing shortage of space meant that political power followed the emperors to their new palaces on the Palatino, or Palatine Hill. Trade and commerce, meanwhile, moved to the Mercati di Traiano (▶ 74), while new building projects

The remains of the Temple of Castor and Pollux at the Foro Romano

were diverted to the nearby Fori Imperiali, or Imperial Fora
(➤74).

    After the fall of Rome in the 5th century the site declined
swiftly; many of the monuments tumbled, and the stone
was plundered to build Rome's medieval churches and
palaces. By the 16th century the Forum was little more
than an overgrown meadow. Excavations began around
1803, but remain far from complete. Major excavations
to explore previously untouched ground around the Curia
and Argiletum began in 1996.

Inside the Forum

You enter the Forum alongside the **Arco di Settimio Severo**,
a huge arch raised in AD203 to mark the tenth year of the
reign of Emperor Septimius Severus. It also commemorated
the minor military victories of his sons, Geta and Caracalla,
hence the battle scenes depicted in the large marble reliefs.
To the left and a little in front of the arch, a line of stones

The Ancient City

HILL OF PALACES

The Palatino, or Palatine Hill (left), which rises above the Forum to the south, is one of Rome's Seven Hills. Sometimes called Rome's Beverly Hills, the area contains ruins of grand palaces built after the first century BC by the city's rich and powerful (the word "palace" comes from Palatino). You come here not so much for monuments – the ruins are even more confusing than those of the Forum – but to enjoy the area's gardens, shady walks, fountains, small museum, orange groves and pretty views over the Forum. It's a charming, atmospheric place, the perfect way to spend a couple of relaxing hours during the hottest part of the day.

indicates the remains of the **Rostra**, or orator's platform, where Mark Antony reputedly made his "Friends, Romans, countrymen" speech after the assassination of Julius Caesar. The platform took its name from the bronze prows (rostra), from ships that were captured by the Romans in battle, which decorated it. They have given their name to the speaker's "rostrum" ever since.

The eight-columned **Tempio di Saturno** (Temple of Saturn) to the south is one of the Forum's oldest temples – it dates from around 497BC – perhaps because Saturn, a god of agriculture, was one of Rome's most venerated gods from earliest times: the ancient Romans believed the city's initial prosperity and power were based on its agricultural prowess.

Walking away from the Capitoline Hill, you pass the **Basilica Giulia** on your right, begun by Julius Caesar in 54BC to complement the Basilica Aemilia opposite. The nearby **Tempio di Castore e Polluce**, or Temple of Castor and Pollux, was supervised by the city's *equites*, or knights, and was home to the Empire's weights and measures standards. To its south is the infrequently open **Santa Maria Antiqua**, the Forum's most important Christian building: it was converted from an earlier pagan monument in the sixth century.

Right: View from the Foro Romano toward the Palatino, which is remarkable for its tranquil gardens as much as its ruins

Below: Detail of a battle scene on the Arch of Septimius Severus in the Foro Romano

Along the Via Sacra

Cutting through the Forum is the **Via Sacra**, once the Forum's principal thoroughfare and the route taken by victorious generals and emperors parading the spoils of war. On your left as you walk along the surviving flagstones are the ruins of the Basilica Aemilia, built in 179BC as a business and moneylending centre. The large brick building ahead and to the right is

The Ancient City

the much restored Curia, or Senate House, probably completed by Augustus in 28BC, when it was the meeting place of Rome's 300 or so senators.

The area to the Curia's right is the **Argiletum**, the site of a now-vanished temple that once held a statue of Janus, the two-faced god. Its twin doors were kept open in times of war and closed in times of peace: in 1,000 years, it is said, they were closed on only three occasions. In front of the Curia is the **Lapis Niger**, or Black Stone, a black marble slab which marks the site of a sanctuary to the god Vulcan. A staircase leads to a chamber beneath the shrine, where you'll see a headstone inscribed in Latin dating from the sixth century BC (the oldest example ever found). Modern scholars believe the inscription warns against profaning the sacred site.

Temples and the Vestal Virgins

The **Tempio di Antonino e Faustina**, built in AD141 by Emperor Antoninus to honour his wife, Faustina, is beyond the Curia. It makes a good introduction to the site, mainly because it is so well preserved, its survival due to its consecration as a church in the 11th century. Some of the oldest graves ever found in Rome were uncovered nearby.

Beyond this point and the Temple of Castor and Pollux are the **Tempio di Vesta** and **Atrium Vestae**, respectively the Temple and House of the Vestal Virgins. It was in the temple that the Vestal Virgins tended Rome's sacred flame, a symbol of the city's continuity.

Part of the **Basilica di Massenzio** (begun AD306), beyond the Atrium on the left, is one of the Forum's most impressive

Most visitors to Rome are drawn to the romantic remains of the Foro Romano

Tempio di Antonino e Faustina

monuments: in its day it would have been still more awe-inspiring, for what remains is only a single aisle of what was once a 100m (110-yard) nave. Remarkably, only one of what originally must have been dozens of columns from the basilica still survives, and now it stands in front of Santa Maria Maggiore (➤ 130).

The Arco di Tito

The Forum's last major monument before the Colosseo is the **Arco di Tito**, Rome's oldest triumphal arch, built in AD81 by Emperor Domitian to honour Titus (Tito), his brother and predecessor as emperor. Titus' most famous victory was over the Jews in AD70, and the arch's beautiful reliefs depict a series of scenes of the emperor's triumphal return to Rome with spoils from the campaign.

TAKING A BREAK

There are no places for refreshments inside the Forum: the nearest cafés are to be found off Piazza del Campidoglio (➤ 51), the grid of streets east of the Colosseo, or in Via Cavour. 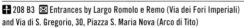 (➤ 78) a pleasant *enoteca* (wine bar).

Insider Tip

🔢 208 B3 ✉ Entrances by Largo Romolo e Remo (Via dei Fori Imperiali) and Via di S. Gregorio, 30, Piazza S. Maria Nova (Arco di Tito)
🕐 Daily 9am until one hour before sunset
🚇 Colosseo 🚌 75, 85, 117, 175, 810, 850 to Via dei Fori Imperiali
🎟 €12. Combined two-day ticket is also valid for the Palatino and Colosseo

---

INSIDER INFO

- Before exploring the Foro Romano, **enjoy an overview of the site** from the steps and terraces on the rear eastern side of the Campidoglio. Steps from the balconies lead down to one of the Forum entrances alongside the Arco di Settimio Severo.
- Avoid visiting the Forum in the heat of the afternoon as there is little shade on the site – but there are some fountains with refreshing drinking water.
- If you only have **limited time** to spend, the most significant among the ruins (and sites definitely not to be missed) are the Curia, Arco di Settimio Severo, Tempio di Vesta and Basilica di Massenzio.

The Heart of the Roman Empire

Today the ancient centre of Rome, from the Roman Forum, to the Colosseum and the Via Appia, is one huge archaeological park.

The remains of the **7** Arco di Settimio Severo are a testimony to its former grandeur

1 Arco di Tito: The 15.4m (50.5 feet) high and 13.5m (44 feet) wide structure is Rome's oldest triumphal arch.

2 Atrium Vestae: The House of the Vestal Virgins complex consisted of a large central atrium, with the living quarters of the guardians who tended the sacred flame symbolizing Rome's continuity. Today the outline, with base and pedestals for the honorary statues, are clearly visible while the preserved statues are exhibited in various Roman museums.

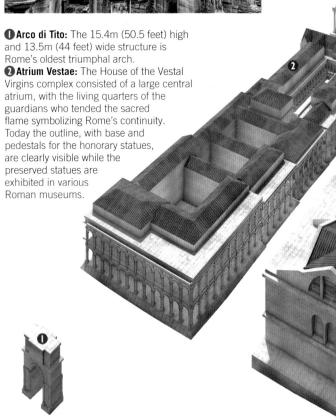

❸ Tempio di Castore e Polluce:
Reconstructed under Tiberius in the
1st century; all that remains of the temple
are three 12m (39 feet) tall Corinthian
columns supporting part of an entablature
of the temple.

❹ Basilica Giulia: Only the foundations and
some column pieces remain of the original
101m (331 feet) long and 49m (160 feet)
wide civil law courts.

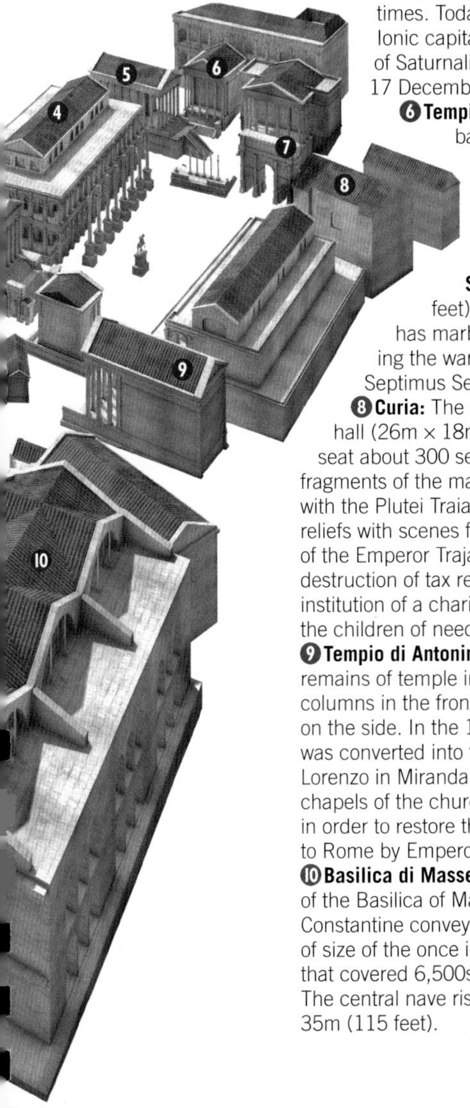

❺ Tempio di Saturno: The temple was
destroyed by fire and rebuilt many
times. Today eight columns with
Ionic capitals remain. The feast
of Saturnalia was celebrated on
17 December at the temple.

❻ Tempio di Concordia: Dating
back to the Republican
era, only the foundation
remains remain of the
once richly decorated
Temple of Concord.

**❼ Arco di Settimio
Severo:** The 2m (69
feet) high triumphal arch
has marble reliefs commemorat-
ing the wars led by Emperor
Septimus Severus.

❽ Curia: The original Senate meeting
hall (26m × 18m; 85ft × 60ft) could
seat about 300 senators. Today some
fragments of the marble floor remain along
with the Plutei Traiani, two large marble
reliefs with scenes from the political life
of the Emperor Trajan. To the left, the
destruction of tax records, to the right, the
institution of a charitable organisation for
the children of needy families (alimenta).

❾ Tempio di Antonino e Faustina: The
remains of temple include six Corinthian
columns in the front and several pillars
on the side. In the 12th century the temple
was converted into the church of San
Lorenzo in Miranda. In 1536 the side
chapels of the church were demolished
in order to restore the temple for the visit
to Rome by Emperor Charles V.

❿ Basilica di Massenzio: The remains
of the Basilica of Maxentius and
Constantine convey a good impression
of size of the once imposing building
that covered 6,500sq m (699,000sq ft).
The central nave rises to a height of
35m (115 feet).

☆3 Colosseo

It is with good reason that the Colosseum – symbol of classical Rome, which was built in AD80 in a record time of only eight years – was included as one of the Seven New Wonders of the World.

First Impressions

To grasp the Colosseo's scale you need to admire it from afar. The best place for an overview is the **Colle Oppio** (► 76), a park to the northeast of the monument, or the belvedere (Largo Agnes) immediately above the Colosseo Metro station exit (best reached from Via Cavour via Via del Colosseo or up the steps just to the right of the Metro as you face the station exit). The more usual viewpoint – the open ground to the amphitheatre's west, alongside the flank of the **Foro Romano** (► 52) – is less satisfactory. The entrance to the monument's upper levels is nearby, and from here you can walk around a part of the exterior, well away from the roaring traffic; you can also admire the **Arco di Costantino** from the same point (► 64, panel).

From the ancient past to the present – the Colosseo continues to host major events

Early Days

The massive building project of the Colosseo was begun around AD72 by Emperor Vespasian. Its inspiration was the Teatro di Marcello and its site had previously been used for an artificial lake annexed to Nero's palatial Domus Aurea, or Golden House. The area's marshy conditions proved problematic, and required the laying of enormous drains – many of which still survive – and the creation of immense foundations. The costs of building the monument were met by the spoils of war, in this case the Romans' triumph over the Jews in AD70, which realized 50 tonnes of gold and silver from the temple of Jerusalem alone. Jewish slaves captured in the campaign provided the labour force.

By the time of Vespasian's death in AD79, the monument had been completed to its third tier. Additions were made by Vespasian's son, Titus, who inaugurated the Colosseo in AD80 with celebrations that saw the slaughter of 5,000 animals and 100 days of festivities.

The completed structure was an architectural triumph. Its simple design has provided a model for stadiums to this day, with **tiered seating** and 80 exits, or *vomitoria*, which allowed huge crowds – estimates of the Colosseo's capacity range from 50,000 to 73,000

(Continued on page 64)

The Blueprint for Modern Stadiums

The world's largest ancient amphitheatre may be preserved enough to impressively illustrate its original state but the structure also reflects the traumas of its history: fires, earthquakes, neglect and traffic pollution have all left their mark.

The Colosseum is also an impressive sight from a distance

❶ Facade: The arcades of the outer walls are framed by half-columns with capitals of the Doric order on the first floor, the Ionic on the second and the Corinthian order on the third floor. The fourth floor has rectangular window openings.

❷ Arcades: The 80 entrance arcades on the ground lead to a sophisticated system of stairways and corridors, which guided the mass of spectators. The numbers above the entrances corresponded to those on the pottery shards used as admission tickets.

❸ Cavea: The 57m (187 feet) auditorium has two semicircles opposite each other with five rows of seats where allocation was depended on social status. The first tier of broad steps (with seating) was for the imperial court and senators, the eight marble steps of the second tier were for the nobility, while the wooden seats in the third and fourth tier were reserved for the common people. Admission was free.

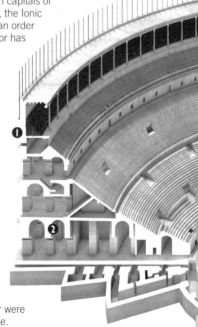

Underneath the wooden floor of the arena were chambers that housed the equipment for the games, the animal cages and chambers for the gladiators. It is likely that there were lifts up to the arena

4 Oval: The centre of the arena itself is a large oval 86m (287 feet) long and 54m (177 feet) wide. The arena hosted gladiatorial events, animal hunts and theatre performances. The oval shape made it possible for spectators to watch several fights at the same time.

5 Underground structure: Although the little remains of the passageways and chambers beneath the oval it is still possible to get a good idea of the layout.

6 Velaria: The top floor of the Colosseum had supports for masts that held up huge sailcloth awnings to shade the spectators from the sun or rain.

The four-tier facade was made out of 100,000m³ (3,500,000ft³) of travertine stone and 300 tons of iron and was 50m (164 feet) high

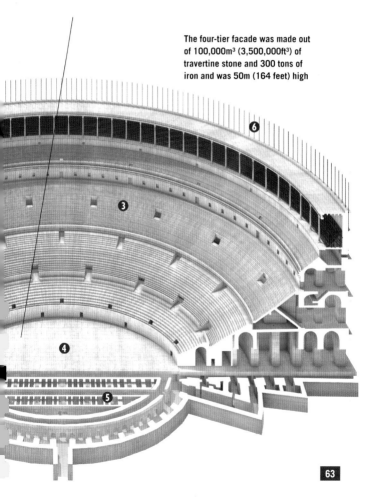

The Ancient City

people – to leave the stadium in minutes. Above the seating, a vast sailcloth roof, or *velarium*, could be pulled into place by sailors of the Imperial fleets to shade spectators from the elements. It was supported by 240 wooden masts, the supports and sockets for which you can still see in a ring below the structure's uppermost cornice.

Inside the Colosseo

Inside, much of the original seating and flooring have disappeared. A major fire in AD217 devastated the upper levels and wooden arena (*arena* means sand, which covered the stage area). Other fires and earthquakes over the next 400 years further damaged the structure. By the sixth century the arena was being used as workshops and a cemetery; by 1320 the entire south side of the monument had collapsed. This and other parts of the

Many of the sculptural reliefs on the Arco di Costantino were lifted from older monuments and then remodelled to fit their new home

ARCO DI COSTANTINO

In any other context, the Arch of Constantine (AD315) would be a major monument. Being overshadowed by the Colosseum, it is often ignored in favour of its neighbour. A triumphal arch like the Arco di Tito (▶ 57) and Arco di Settimio Severo in the Foro Romano (▶ 53), it was raised to commemorate the triumph of Emperor Constantine over Maxentius, his imperial rival, at the Battle of Milvian Bridge (AD312) just north of Rome. It is the city's largest and best-preserved arch, and one of the last major monuments built in ancient Rome. Most of its materials were pilfered from other buildings. These included many of the sculptural reliefs, notably the eight reliefs framing the inscription, which portray scenes of an emperor at war or engaged in civic duties. They were probably removed from a monument raised to celebrate victories by Marcus Aurelius in AD176. Wherever the face of Aurelius appeared, masons simply recarved the reliefs to portray Constantine.

The same happened in the arch's central passage, where the two main reliefs show scenes carved during the reigns of Domitian or Trajan. With a little judicious recarving and relabelling (*Fundator quietis* – "founder of calm"), the panels were altered to show Constantine riding into battle against the barbarians (on the monument's west side) and being crowned by the figure of Victory.

Stone from the Colosseo was plundered to build many of Rome's churches and palaces

building were then ransacked for building stone, most of which found its way into churches, roads, wharves and palaces such as the Palazzo Venezia and Palazzo Barberini. The desecration ceased in 1744, when Pope Benedict XIV consecrated the site in memory of the Christians who had supposedly been martyred there.

Contrary to popular myth, however, few if any Christians were killed in the Colosseo, whose primary function was to stage gladiatorial and other games. Today, you can look down on the **maze of tunnels and shafts** that lay under the stage, the means by which the games' animals, gladiators and other protagonists were brought to the stage from distant pens. Clever plumbing, it's said, also meant the stage area could be flooded to present mock sea battles.

The Spectators, the Emperor and the Sport

Spectators were rigidly segregated by status and sex, and they were expected to dress specially for the occasion. The emperor and Vestal Virgins faced each other at the lowest levels in special boxes. Alongside them, on wide platforms, sat the senators, all of whom were expected to dress in white togas and bring their own chairs (bisellia). Above them sat the knights and aristocrats, then came the ordinary Roman citizens (plebeians) and finally – some 40m (130 feet) up and 50m (165 feet) from the stage – the women, slaves and poor (though few women, by all accounts, ventured to the games). Some groups had separate sections, notably soldiers, scribes and heralds, and some were banned altogether, namely gravediggers, actors and retired gladiators. A special official, or *designator*, kept everyone in their rightful place.

The doomed men greeted their ruler with the famous words "*Ave Caesar morituri te salutant*", and emperors and spectators then often had control over a protagonist's destiny. A wounded man could appeal for mercy by raising a finger on his left hand; the wave of a handkerchief would then indicate a reprieve, while the sinister and still-familiar downturned thumb meant death.

TAKING A BREAK

Avoid the expensive cafés and bars in the monument's immediate vicinity. Instead, try **Via Cavour** or the streets off **Via di San Giovanni in Laterano**. Try **Café Café** (➤ 78) for a snack lunch or **Il Bocconcino** (➤ 78) for a meal.

✚ 208 C3

✉ Piazza del Colosseo, Via dei Fori Imperiali

☎ 06 06 08; 06 39 96 77 00; online booking at www.pierreci.it

🕓 Interior: April–Aug daily 8:30–7:15; Sep 8:30–7; Oct 8:30–6:30; Nov to mid-Feb 8:30–4:30; mid-Feb to mid-March 8:30–5; mid-March to end March 8:30–5:30

🚇 Colosseo ⬛ 30B, 75, 85, 87, 117, 175, 186

💶 €12. Combined two-day ticket is also valid for the Palatino and Colosseo

The floodlit Colosseo at night is one of Rome's unmissable sights

INSIDER INFO

- Return to the Colosseo after **nightfall**, to see the monument floodlit.
- Climb to the monument's **upper tiers** for a proper idea of the structure's size and the complexity of the tunnels below the stage area.
- If you're tired of all the bustling crowds and the traffic, walk to the nearby Colle Oppio park (➤ 76).
- The Colosseo's "gladiators" often expect to be paid if you photograph them.
- Once you've climbed up to the first tier, there's plenty of information on the Colosseo in the shape of a **permanent exhibition**, complete with excellent information in English, devoted to the Flavian dynasty, of which Vespasian was the founder. Fascinating insights are to be found in the displays of artefacts, which were found during excavations, such as gaming pieces used by members of the crowd to pass the time between contests, lost hairpins, combs and trinkets, and remnants of Roman lunch boxes and flasks that the spectators used to hold their picnics.

⓫ San Clemente

San Clemente has a deceptively plain exterior, but step inside and you will be taken on a fascinating journey through time. The church has the finest medieval interior in Rome – complete with some sublime frescoes and mosaics – and remnants of earlier places of worship from the Roman era. A site that spans 2,000 years of religious observance.

The *Triumph of the Cross* above the high altar dates from the 12th century. The 12 sheep and 12 doves symbolize the Apostles

San Clemente divides into three sections, stacked one on top of the other: a 12th-century church above a fourth- or fifth-century church, which sits on a late second-century Mithraic temple. The church alone would be worth a special visit for the vivid mosaic, the *Triumph of the Cross* in the apse, but the two lower structures also make the complex a must. The simple lower church (4th century), dedicated to the 4th pope, St Clement (AD88–97), with traces of ancient frescoes, and yet further below, the temple for the Persian sun god Mithras, where the Roman legionaries paid homage with the blood of slain bulls.

Note that you enter the main church via a side door on Via di San Giovanni in Laterano, though the main entrance is occasionally open.

Medieval Interior

The main body of the church at ground level was built between 1108 and 1184 to replace the church that now lies beneath it, which was destroyed by Norman raiders in 1084. Inside, it retains Rome's finest medieval interior,

The Ancient City

most of the city's churches having been modified in the baroque age – only Santa Maria in Cosmedin (➤ 185) rivals San Clemente.

The highlights are many. Among the paintings, pride of place goes to a Renaissance **fresco cycle** of the *Life of St Catherine* (1428), one of only a handful of works by the influential Umbrian artist Masolino da Panicale (it's in the rear left aisle chapel, to your right as you enter).

Among the **mosaics**, the star turn is the 12th-century *Triumph of the Cross*, which forms a majestic swathe of colour across the apse. Scholars think its design was based on that of a similar mosaic that was lost when the earlier church was destroyed in the 11th century. The work is full of detail and incident: note in particular the 12 doves on the cross and the 12 sheep below, symbols of the Apostles. The imposing 14th-century tabernacle below and to the right is by the Florentine sculptor Arnolfo di Cambio.

The marble-panelled walls of the **choir screen** (fifth–ninth century) dominate the **nave**. Such screens were a typical feature of early medieval churches but are now rare. Many of the panels were salvaged from the earlier church, while various columns originally hailed from the Foro Traiano (Trajan's Forum) in the Fori Imperiali (➤ 74).

The Temple and Excavations

Steps accessed from the rear right-hand (south) side of the church lead down to what remains of the earlier church, the existence of which was only discovered in 1857. The remains here are relatively scant.

More is to be gained by dropping down yet another level, where there are the remains of two Roman-era buildings, parts of which are still only partially excavated. Almost the first thing you encounter is the cast of a **Mithraic altar**. Mithraism was a popular Roman cult that survived into the Christian era. The bull was one of Mithraism's main

The interior of the 12th-century church

symbols, hence the beast portrayed on the altar being killed by the god Mithras, along with the figures of torch-bearers and a snake, a symbol of regeneration. The cult was finally suppressed in AD392.

A Roman House and Warehouse

This subterranean area of the church also includes part of a **Roman house** in which a *mithraem*, or place of worship, had been installed in the central room, probably toward the end of the second century. Such temples were meant to replicate Mithras' cave, so doors would have been blocked or narrowed to a slit to allow sunlight to strike the cult's icons and images.

Christ and Our Lady, detail of the medieval frescoes that adorn the apse of San Clemente

The house itself is much older, archaeologists having discovered date-stamps corresponding to the reign of Domitian (AD90–96) on the steps of the ancient staircase.

The layout of the second structure here corresponds in part to that of a *horrea*, or warehouse, and may well have been a granary, although some early theories suggest it could have been the site of workshops belonging to the Imperial Mint, the *Moneta Caesaris*. Newer theories suggest the site contains two buildings, one being commercial premises, the other a house built over these premises which belonged to a wealthy Roman Christian. This Christian, so the theory goes, went by the name of Clemente, and founded a church on the site dedicated to his saintly namesake.

TAKING A BREAK

There are many small bars on **Via di San Giovanni in Laterano** and adjoining streets where you can stop for a coffee, a drink or a quick bite to eat.

✚ 209 D3 ✉ Via di San Giovanni in Laterano
☎ 06 7 74 00 21; www.basilicasanclemente.com
🕐 Church and excavations: Mon–Sat 9–12:30, 3–6, Sun 12–6; closed during services 🚇 Colosseo 🚌 75, 85, 87, 117, 175 to Piazza del Colosseo or 85, 117, 850 to Via di San Giovanni in Laterano 💶 Church: free. Excavations: €5

INSIDER INFO

If the main door of the upper church is open, try to look outside at the *quadroporticus*, the distinctive square colonnaded courtyard that fronts the main facade. Such courtyards were once common features of early Roman basilica churches – rectangular churches with simple naves and no transepts – but are now rare.

⑫ San Giovanni in Laterano

San Giovanni in Laterano, not St Peter's, is the cathedral church of Rome; St Peter's lies in the Vatican, a separate sovereign state. Even without its exalted status, however, this great church would be worth visiting, both for its soaring facade and the beauty of its interior, cloister and baptistery.

Badly damaged by a bomb blast in 1993, the Roman Catholic 'Mother of all Churches' was immediately restored. San Giovanni in Laterano has venerable origins. It was in a Roman palace on the site, where Constantine, the first Christian emperor, met Pope Miltiades in 313, and here that Constantine raised the city's first officially sanctioned church (over what had been the barracks of his personal guard). From earliest times it housed the *cathedra*, or throne, of the Bishop of Rome. The church's importance continued for centuries – for example, popes were crowned here until the 19th century. During this time, the original church was destroyed by the Vandals, and subsequent churches were replaced or restored following fires and earthquakes. In the portico at the foot of the immense facade (built in 1735) stands an **ancient**

Baroque architect Francesco Borromini remodelled much of San Giovanni's sumptuous interior

San Giovanni in Laterano

Baroque statues of saints adorn San Giovanni's facade

statue of Constantine, while to its right are the church's magnificent **main bronze doors**, which were brought from the Curia, or Senate House, in the Foro Romano (➤52).

The Interior and Baptistery

The church's restrained **interior** (1646–50) is largely the work of the baroque architect Borromini, who thoughtfully retained the nave's earlier gold-hued and beautifully **ornate ceiling**. The ceiling aside, you shouldn't miss the **papal altar and canopy** (begun in 1367) at the main crossing, where, until latterly, only a pope could officiate. It reputedly holds the skulls of saints Peter and Paul, and part of a table that is said to have been used by St Peter.

San Giovanni's real glory is its **cloister** (1215–32), entered from the south side of the church (left), a tranquil corner with dozens of variously shaped columns, many adorned with exquisite Cosmati work (an intricate inlay of beautiful coloured stones and marbles).

Outside the church to its rear – you need to exit the building and bear left – is Constantine's San Giovanni in Fonte, or **Baptistery of St John**. Some of the building has been altered over the years, but significant older parts survive, notably the fifth-century mosaic in the north apse and the Chapel of St John (461–68), which preserves its original doors. Opposite is the **Scala Santa**, or Holy Staircase, which leads directly into the Santa Santorum, the private chapel of the popes. The staircase was reputedly removed from Pontius Pilate's palace by St Helena in the 5th century and brought to Rome. Many pilgrims climb them on their knees in order to receive a plenary indulgence from their sins.

➕ 209 E2 ✉ Piazza di San Giovanni in Laterano
☎ 06 69 88 64 33; www.vatican.va. Scala Santa: 06 7 72 66 41
🕐 Church: daily 7–6:45. Cloister: daily 9–6. Baptistery: daily 7:30–12:30, 4–6:30. Scala Santa: daily 6:30–12, 3–6
🚇 San Giovanni 🚌 3, 16, 81, 85, 87, 117, 218, 360, 590, 650, 714, 810, 850
💷 Church, Scala Santa: free. Baptistery, Cloister: €3

INSIDER INFO

- While visiting San Giovanni you might wish to visit the **flea market** (Mon–Fri 8:30–1:30, Sat 8:30–6) held along nearby Via Sannio, a right turn just through Porta San Giovanni.
- If you baulk at the long walk back to the city centre from San Giovanni, consider taking the Metro from nearby Giovanni Metro station (just beyond Porta San Giovanni).

Insider Tip

At Your Leisure

🔟 Piazza Venezia

Piazza Venezia is the key to central Rome, a huge square from which some of the city's major streets strike off to the four points of the compass. But while you will probably pass through the piazza several times, it is not a place with many important things to see – save for the huge white edifice on its southern flank, the **Monumento a Vittorio Emanuele II**.

This magnificent marble monolith, built between 1885 and 1911, commemorates the unification of Italy and the country's first king, Vittorio Emanuele. It is also called the *Altare della Patria*, or Altar of the Nation – the tomb of Italy's Unknown Soldier is here – but Romans know it as the "typewriter" or "wedding cake" after its huge marble tiers. Its terraces (➤ 50) offer superb views of the surrounding area.

On the square's west side stands the Palazzo Venezia (1451), which for 200 years between 1594 and 1797 was the property of the Venetian Republic – hence its name and the name of the square. The palazzo is known for the balcony from which Mussolini once harangued crowds in the square below – the dictator kept an office in the building – and for the underrated **Museo del Palazzo Venezia**, used for temporary exhibitions and noted for its permanent collection of medieval paintings, textiles, ceramics, jewellery and other decorative arts. If it's open, you should also look into **San Marco**, a church best known for its beautiful gilt ceiling and magnificent ninth-century apse mosaic.
➕ 207 E5

Museo del Palazzo Venezia
➕ 199 E5 ✉ Via del Plebiscito, 118
☎ 06 69 99 43 88; www.ticketeria.it
🕐 Tue–Sun 8:30–7:30 (hours vary for temporary exhibitions)
🍴 Cafés in Via delle Botteghe Oscure
🚇 Cavour 🚌 All services to Piazza Venezia
💶 Museum: €5

Fragments of a massive statue of the Emperor Constantine I in the courtyard of the Palazzo dei Conservatori

14 Musei Capitolini

On the left (north) side of Piazza del Campidoglio stands the **Palazzo Nuovo**, whose inner courtyard contains the Roman statue of a river god, *Marforio*, a particular favourite with photographers.

As you explore the two floors of the palace, you will find that it contains many beautiful antique sculptures, the highlights of which are the *Dying Gaul* and the *Capitoline Venus*, both Roman copies of Greek originals.

Across the piazza, and linked to the Palazzo Nuovo by an underpass, is the **Palazzo dei Conservatori**, which houses the rest of the museum's impressive collections. Star of the show, and housed in a stunning modern space, the Esedra, within the palazzo, is the celebrated equestrian statue of Marcus Aurelius (AD161–80). It originally stood in the piazza outside but was brought inside after restoration for safekeeping (▶50; the statue outside is a copy). It is the only such statue to survive from this period, and throughout the Middle Ages was repeatedly referred to by artists and writers. It forms part of the nucleus of the museum, founded in 1471 by Pope Sixtus IV.

Other galleries here contain the Spinario (a first-century bronze of a boy removing a thorn from his foot), the famous She-Wolf statue, symbol of Rome, an Etruscan bronze dating from the fifth century BC and paintings by Caravaggio, Veronese, Tintoretto and Bellini.

Some 400 of the museum's sculptures have been relocated to **Centrale Montemartini**, a converted power station at Via Ostiense 106 (south of the city).

Remains of the superb Temple of Minerva at the Forum of Nerva, Fori Imperiali

🕂 207 E4 ✉ Piazza del Campidoglio, 1
☎ 06 06 08; www.museicapitolini.org
🕐 Tue–Sun 9–8 (last entry 7pm)
🍴 Café on the roof terrace of the museum
🚇 Colosseo 🚌 All services to Piazza Venezia
🎫 €13; combined ticket with Centrale Montemartini: €15

15 Colonna Traiana

Trajan's Column rises as a lonely, majestic sentinel from the ruins of Trajan's Forum. Built in AD113, it was raised to mark two victorious military campaigns over the Dacians, who lived in what is now Romania.

The Ancient City

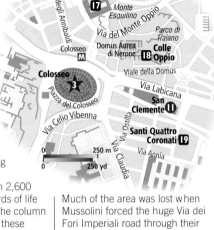

Like triumphal arches, such columns were typical of Roman victory monuments, and likewise also invariably contained friezes and reliefs recording details of a campaign's battles and events. Here, the reliefs run in a remarkable spiral – more than 200m (650 feet) of exquisitely carved marble, containing a continuous 155-scene sequence with more than 2,600 figures portrayed two-thirds of life size. The importance of the column is in the intense detail of these scenes, detail which has allowed scholars to learn much about the Roman military machine.

One reason for the column's survival is that it formed the bell tower of a Christian church, San Nicola de Columna. When the church was demolished the ancient monument was saved thanks to Renaissance popes who appreciated art, such as Julius II. The structure comprises 29 vast drums of marble – eight for the base, nineteen for the column and two for the summit pedestal. Inside is a spiral staircase carved from the solid stone, a miracle of Roman engineering, but a miracle withheld from public view, for the column can only be admired from the outside. The figure crowning the summit is St Peter, added in 1588, replacing a bronze statue of Trajan, whose ashes once resided in a golden urn at the column's base.

✚ 199 F5 ⊠ Via dei Fori Imperiali
🚇 Cavour 🚌 Services to Piazza Venezia

16 Fori Imperiali

The Imperial Fora comprise five fora built when lack of space in the old Foro Romano (➤ 52) forced emperors, from Julius Caesar onward, to look elsewhere for a site for their grandiose architectural schemes.

Much of the area was lost when Mussolini forced the huge Via dei Fori Imperiali road through their heart in the 1930s. Recently cars and scooters were banned from a section of the busy street around the Colosseum, as an experimental forerunner to a pedestrian zone. However, as buses, taxis and bicycles are still allowed, traffic chaos is inevitable.

The best approach to the Fori Imperiali though, is to concentrate on the stunningly restored **Foro Traiano**, which houses the Museo dei Fori Imperiali and is home to the **Colonna Traiana** (➤ 73). Opened in 2007 after a massive clean-up job, the complex includes the forum itself and the towering remains of the **Mercati di Traiano** (Trajan's Market) behind. From the entrance on Via IV Novembre, you can walk through the Great Hall, past beautifully lit marbles, to the terrace above the Great Hemicycle, built in AD107. Stairs lead down through the different levels of this market, passing more than 150 Roman shops and offices, many with their doorjambs still showing the fitments for their night shutters. East of the Great Hall, you can access Via Biberatica, an ancient street lined with shops and bars.

Alongside Trajan's Forum to the right is the **Foro di Augusto** (begun

in 42BC), part of an immense building project initiated by Augustus,
whose most striking ruins are the
remains of the Temple of Mars Ultor.
Across the road lie the scant remains of the Foro de Cesare, or
Caesar's Forum, the first of the
Imperial Fora, built by Julius Caesar
in 54–46BC. There is even less to
see of the remaining fora: the Foro
di Nerva (AD96–98), whose best
surviving relic is a frieze on the colonnade on the corner of Via Cavour
and Via dei Fori Imperiali, and the
Foro di Vespasiano (AD71–75), also
known as the Foro della Pace,
whose former library contains the
church of Santi Cosma e Damiano.

Mercati di Traiano
➕ 200 B4 ✉ Via IV Novembre, 94 ☎ 06 06 08;
www.mercatiditraiano.it 🕐 Daily 9–7
🚇 Cavour 🚌 40, 64, 70, 170 🎟 €6.50

⒘ San Pietro in Vincoli
It takes only a couple of minutes
to walk to this church from the
Colosseum, and only a little longer
to see its main attraction – an imposing **statue of Moses** (1503–13),
one of Michelangelo's sculptural
masterpieces. The statue was
conceived as part of a 42-figure
ensemble designed to adorn the
tomb of Pope Julius II, one of
Michelangelo's principal patrons.
In the event the project was never

Michelangelo's masterpiece in San Pietro
in Vincoli depicts Moses receiving the
Ten Commandments

ST PETER'S CHAINS
San Pietro in Vincoli was built in 432,
reputedly on the site where St Peter was
condemned to death during the persecutions of Nero. The church takes its
name from the highly venerated chains
(vincoli) that you see in a casket under
the main altar. There are actually two
sets of chains: one is believed to have
been used to bind Peter in Jerusalem,
the other thought to have been used
to shackle him in Rome's Mamertine
prison. When the two were eventually
united they miraculously fused together.

---

realized, although it would torment
Michelangelo for much of his life –
he referred to it as this "tragedy of
a tomb". Instead he was distracted
by other works such as the Sistine
Chapel (➤ 166) – another Julius
commission – and then after Julius'
death deprived of funds by popes
who saw little glory in funding their
predecessor's obsession.

The statue of *Moses* hints at what
might have been, a monumental
figure captured at the moment
he receives the tablet of the Ten
Commandments (shown here under
his right arm). Michelangelo left a
famous signature in the statue's
beard – his profile – and gave Moses
a wonderfully equivocal expression
as he watches the Israelites dance
around the golden calf, his look
of divine illumination at receiving
the tablets mixed with fury at his
people's faithlessness and idolatry.

Note, too, the figure's horns,
which represent beams of light,
features ascribed to Moses in the
iconography of many medieval paintings and sculptures. The main flank-
ing statues are also by Michelangelo,

and represent Rachel and Leah, symbols of the active and contemplative life. The other figures are the work of Michelangelo's pupils.

➕ 208 C4 ✉ Piazza di San Pietro in Vincoli, 4a ☎ 06 97 84 49 50 🕐 Apr–Sep daily 8–12:30, 3:30–7; Oct–March 8–12:30, 3–6 🚇 Colosseo or Cavour 🚌 75 to Via Cavour or 75, 85, 87, 117, 175 or 186 to Piazza del Colosseo 🎫 Free

🔟8 Colle Oppio

The Colle Oppio is central Rome's most convenient park, a pretty area of grass, walkways, trees and archaeological remains spread over the slopes of the Esquiline Hill, one of the original Seven Hills. It is the perfect place to relax away from the hustle and bustle of the city, or for a picnic. It takes its name from one of the hill's two summits, the *Cispius*

> **OFF THE BEATEN TRACK**
> *Insider Tip*
> The little-known park of **Villa Celimontana** south of the Colosseo (entered from Via della Navicella) is a good place to escape from the rigours of sightseeing. The area around the park is also relatively quiet, with interesting churches, such as **Santa Maria in Domnica** and **Santo Stefano Rotondo**, and little lanes, such as Viale del Parco and Clivo di Scauro, which lead to Santi Giovanni e Paolo.

The superb interior of Santi Quattro Coronati, home to an enclosed order

and *Oppius*. Although just across the street from the Colosseum, it is little used by visitors, but locals make full use of its café and quiet corners, particularly on Sundays. The park's loveliest area of grass, only faintly shaded by slender palms, is the section right by the entrance across from the Colosseo.

The park makes a pleasant way to reach Santa Maria Maggiore (► 130) or Palazzo Massimo alle Terme (► 132), avoiding the busy Via Cavour and other roads. Avoid visiting the park at night.

➕ 209 D3 ✉ Via Labicana, 136 🚇 Colosseo

🔟9 Santi Quattro Coronati

The basilica of the Four Crowned Saints stands on the site of one of Rome's earliest churches and is now home to an enclosed order of Augustinian nuns – you'll have to ask them for the key to visit parts of the complex. It's dedicated to four Roman martyrs; take your pick as to whether they were Roman soldiers executed for refusing to pray before the statue of Esculapius, the god of healing, or stonemasons who refused to carve his statue – nobody knows for sure.

The first church was built in the fourth century and was burned down during the 1084 Norman sack. It was rebuilt as a fortified monastery, incorporating the apse from the original church; you can still see traces of this basilica-form structure. Inside, the church has one of the loveliest of Rome's cosmatesque floors and retains its matrimonium – the upstairs gallery where women sat during religious ceremonies.

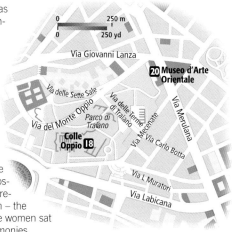

There's access to a secret **cloister**, complete with double columns and arches surrounding a flower-filled garden with a fountain. You can also take in the **oratory** outside the church (ring the bell and ask for the key), which contains a fresco cycle depicting the Donation of Constantine, an early Christian piece of propaganda, which claims that the Emperor Constantine gave the Pope authority over the West.

➕ 209 D3 ✉ Via Santi Coronati, 20 ☎ 06 70 47 54 27 🕐 Mon–Sat 9:30–12, 4–5:30; closed during services 🚌 85, 87, 117, 850 🎫 Free

🔟 Museo d'Arte Orientale

There is a spectacular wealth of artworks, pottery, jewellery and sculptures from the swathe of civilizations that runs from the Near to the Far East in this state museum, housed in the 19th-century **Palazzo Brancaccio**. The collection includes Chinese and Korean ceramics as well as some finds from archaeological digs in the Swat region of Pakistan.

➕ 209 D4 ✉ Via Merulana, 428 ☎ 06 46 97 48 32 🕐 Tue, Wed, Fri, 9–2; Thu, Sat, Sun 9–7:30 🚌 16, 360, 649, 714 🎫 €6

🏆 A JOURNEY THROUGH TIME FOR YOUNG AND OLD

Romaculta (tel: 33 87 60 74 70; www.romaculta.it/engl/main.html) also offer guided tours tailored for children between 6 and 14 years of age, such as the one that explores the so-called *statue parlanti* ("talking statues") of ancient Rome.

Kind parents will head for **Rewind Rome** (Via Capo d'Africa, 5; tel: 06 77 07 66 27; daily 9–7; €12), an interactive 3D experience that takes you back to AD310.

There is also the rather creepy **Mithaic temple** in the bowels of San Clemente (►67).

Where to...
Eat and Drink

Prices
Prices are for a starter and a main course excluding drinks:
€ under €30   €€ €30–€50   €€€ over €50

The area of Rome that embraces the Capitoline Hill, Colosseo and Foro Romano is almost entirely given over to monuments, and the number of restaurants is correspondingly small. Though most are aimed at tourists, there are a handful of good places in the side streets close to the main sights.

Antica Birreria "Peroni" €
Don't be tempted into the overpriced cafés or snack bars on Piazza Venezia. Instead, walk just round the corner to this *birreria*, or beer hall. The term is slightly misleading for what is more a large, pleasant bar and simple restaurant. You could just have a beer: it's worth a visit simply to admire the original art nouveau interior. Romans pack the place at lunchtime to take advantage of the inexpensive but well-prepared pasta. Service is canteen style; the seating is at simple wooden tables. The atmosphere is lively but not intimidating.
🚩 208 A5 ✉ Via di San Marcello, 19
☎ 06 6 79 53 10 🕐 Mon–Sat 12–12.
Closed 2 weeks in Aug

Insider Tip
Il Bocconcino €€
Simple surroundings and an accent on seasonal, regional produce are the hallmarks of this friendly trattoria, whose owners adhere to the principles of the Slow Food movement. The menu changes seasonally, but you can always expect high quality cured and fresh meat, excellent cheeses, home-made pasta, some vegetarian dishes and good puddings. Try the ravioli stuffed with spinach and ricotta followed by a grilled steak or rabbit casserole and vegetables fresh from the market. Service can be slow.
🚩 208 C3 ✉ Via Ostilia, 23
☎ 06 77 07 91 75 🕐 Daily 11–11

Café Café €
A tiny, one-room café-restaurant just seconds from the Colosseo with a cosy, ochre-coloured interior, Café Café serves good cold snacks, with one or two hot dishes daily. It is perfect for lunch, tea, coffee or a glass of wine.
🚩 209 D3 ✉ Via dei Santi Quattro (Coronati), 44
☎ 06 7 00 87 43 🕐 11am–1am. Closed Aug

Cavour 313 €
This popular and long-established wine bar is surprisingly little patronized by tourists despite being less than a minute's walk from the main entrance to the Foro Romano. First impressions inside are of rather plain and uninspiring wood-dominated decor, but don't be put off: the atmosphere is informal and friendly, the many good hot and cold snacks are well priced, and there's a selection of more than 500 wines.
🚩 208 C4 ✉ Via Cavour, 313 ☎ 06 6 78 54 96
🕐 Mon–Sat 12:30–2:30, 7:30–12:30; Sun 7:30pm–12:30pm (Oct–May only)

Insider Tip
Ciuri Ciuri €
Ten minutes' walk from the Colosseo (▶ 60) and less than five from San Clemente (▶ 67), this splendid Sicilian *gelateria* and bar is a wonderful place for a quick, inexpensive lunch. Here you'll find all the Sicilian specialities, *arancini* (deep-fried

rice balls stuffed with meat and cheese), deep-fried vegetables in batter, *iris*, a pastry stuffed with ricotta cheese, and tiny pizzas. The big draws, though, are the gelati and *pasticceria* (pastries), all made to Sicilian recipes. Now's your chance to try *cannoli*, a pastry tube stuffed with sweetened ricotta and candied fruit, *cassata*, the quintessential Sicilian cake, and some of the creamiest, richest ices you've ever sampled – try the *amarena* (morello cherry) served in a sweet roll.

✚ 209 D3 ✉ Via Labicana, 126–128
☎ 06 45 42 48 56; www.ciuri-ciuri.it
Ⓣ Tue–Sun 8am–11pm

Leonina €

You can tell that you are in the presence of something special by the regular long lines of customers outside Leonina. They are waiting for some of Rome's best *pizza al taglio*, or pizza by the slice. Prices for what is usually the most inexpensive of snacks are higher here than elsewhere, but then so is the quality of the pizza.

✚ 208 C4 ✉ Via Leonina, 84
☎ 06 4 82 77 44 Ⓣ Daily 8am–11pm

Luzzi €

For a real local and Roman trattoria experience, head for Luzzi, a good neighbourhood dive near San Clemente (▶67). It is packed inside and out (there are exterior tables all year round) with Romans enjoying basic favourites, such as good pizzas from the wood-fired oven, straightforward pasta dishes and simple *secondi*. It can be very busy, so come before 8pm to be sure of a table and get ready to enjoy the food and atmosphere.

✚ 209 D3 ✉ Via Celimontana, 1 (on corner of Via San Giovanni in Laterano) ☎ 06 7 09 63 32
Ⓣ Thu–Tue 12–3, 7–midnight.
   Closed 2 weeks in Aug

San Teodoro €€€

The time to eat at this decidedly upmarket restaurant is during the hot summer months, when tables spill out onto one of the neighbourhood's prettiest piazzas. The predominantly fish cooking covers a wide range of Italian cuisine, with some dishes, such as *minestra di broccoli* (broccoli ravioli served in fish broth) firmly rooted in *cucina Romana*, while other dishes are modern and imaginative fusions of seafood and crisp fresh vegetables. Leave room for some pudding because *pasticceria* and gelati are taken very seriously here.

✚ 207 E4 ✉ Via dei Fienili, 49–51
☎ 06 6 78 09 33 Ⓣ Mon–Sat 1–3:15, 8–11:30.
   Closed 3 weeks in Dec–Jan

Trattoria Morgana €€

This quintessentially Roman restaurant has been going since 1935, when an older wine bar was transformed into a popular neighbourhood eating house. So it remains today, packed with locals enjoying Roman specialities such as snails, tripe and oxtail. But you'll also find a good range of more usual dishes, which include home-made pasta, drippingly fresh mozzarella from Campania, grilled meat and a selection of fresh fish. The wine list offers a good choice of regional wines.

✚ 209 D3 ✉ Via Mecenate, 19–21
☎ 06 4 87 31 22 Ⓣ Tue–Sun 12:30–3, 7–11

Trattoria Sora Lella €€ *Insider Tip*

Sora Lella lies on Tiber Island between the Capitoline area and Trastevere district. It is worth the detour, as the accomplished, authentic Roman cooking is a cut above what you would expect of somewhere that affects the informal atmosphere (but not the prices) of a simple trattoria. Sora Lella was actually Elena Fabrizi, a popular Roman actress, and the restaurant was named in her honour by her son, Aldo Trabalza, after her death in 1993.

✚ 207 D4 ✉ Via di Ponte Quattro Capi, 16, Isola Tiberina ☎ 06 6 86 16 01
Ⓣ Daily 12:30–2:30, 8–10:45. Closed Aug

The Ancient City

Where to...
Shop

This is a sightseeing area rather than an area of the city for shoppers to visit with any great expectations, though you may stumble across the odd artisan's workshop, gallery, antiques shop or specialist store in the side streets off Via Cavour (the best hunting grounds are Via dei Serpenti, Via del Boschetto and Via Madonna dei Monti). One such is **La Bottega del Cioccolato,** a vivid red chocolate shop at Via Leonina, 82 (tel: 06 4 82 14 73; Mon–Sat 9:30–7:30).

Otherwise most of the shops in the streets around Rome's ancient monuments are local food and general stores for those who live around Via Cavour (by the Forum) and in the residential enclave between the Colosseo and San Giovanni in Laterano.

Where to...
Go Out

Ancient monuments and entertainment are seldom found together in Rome. One exception is the **Teatro dell'Opera** with its popular summer festival in the **Baths of Caracalla**, where the three Tenors (Domingo, Pavarotti and Carreras) celebrated their debut in 1992. There are operas such as *Il Pagliaccio*, *Cavalleria rusticana* or performances of the film music of the Italian composer Ennio Morricone. ✚ 208 C5; Biglietteria del Teatro dell'Opera; Piazza Beniamino Giglio, 1; tel: 06 4 81 70 03; Mon–Sat, 9–5.

 MUSIC & THEATRE

The **Teatro di Marcello** provides a summer venue for classical concerts organized by the **Associazione Il Tempietto** (Via Rodolfo Morandi, 3; tel: 06 87 13 15 90; www.tempietto. it). Between Nov and July the association's concerts move indoors to the church of **San Nicola in Carcere** (tel: 06 6 86 99 72), south of the Teatro at Via del Teatro di Marcello, 46. Tickets are available from both venues about two hours before each performance. **San Giovanni in Laterano** is one of only a handful of churches to maintain a choir and present a sung Mass. The church is also a good place to hear the superb Luca Blasi organ (usually played during and after the 10am Sunday Mass). Contact visitor centres or the church itself for further details. The tiny church of **San Teodoro** in Via San Teodoro on the Palatine Hill is also used as a concert venue by the choral association "Agimus", short for the **Associazione Giovanile Musicale** (tel: 06 32 11 10 01, www.agimus.it). Theatre and dance productions are held at the **Teatro Colosseo**, east of the Colosseo at Via Capo d'Africa, 5a (tel: 06 7 00 49 32).

NIGHTLIFE

This is not an area rich in nightlife. **Micca Club** (Via Pietro Micca, 7a, tel: 06 87 44 00 79; www.miccaclub. com; Thu–Tue 7pm–3am, closes for summer break) has opened on its fringes and has a programme ranging from burlesque shows to jazz concerts. A good place for a light meal or a late-night drink near Termini is the **Zest** bar in the modern Radisson Blu es. Hotel (Via Filippo Turati, 171, tel: 06 44 48 41, www. rome.radissonsas.com, 9am–1am). Alternatively, if you've been out late and need a drink or bite to eat, **La Base** at Via Cavour, 274 (tel: 06 4 74 06 59), which stays open until 4:30 every morning.

The Heart of Rome

 **Little Treats**

Even busier by night
After dark marvel at the floodlit
fountains and the street performers on
the **Piazza Navona** (➤ 88).

A dramatic spectacle when it rains
Visit the **Pantheon** (➤ 92) when it rains
and see how the water gushes through
the hole in the roof.

Tempting vegetables
The morning farmers' market in Piazza
San Cosimato in Trastevere (➤ 101)
is a feast for the eyes.

Getting Your Bearings

The heart of Rome – the area bounded by the curve of the Tiber in the west and Via del Corso in the east – is often described as "Renaissance Rome" or "Baroque Rome" or even "Medieval Rome". No description is quite right, for the area is a wonderful mixture of ancient monuments, churches, palaces, streets and squares that span 2,000 years of history.

The two-day itinerary in this chapter epitomizes this diversity perfectly, offering a superb amalgam of sights that cover Rome's rich history and artistic legacy. It will give you a real insight into the city's overlapping epochs. The area covered in the first day has an atmosphere and appearance all its own, thanks to its combination of tiny old cobbled streets, imposing Renaissance palaces, the occasional broad thoroughfare – Corso Vittorio Emanuele II is the axis around which the area hinges – and a sprinkling of larger or grander squares such as Campo de' Fiori and Piazza Navona. This is also an area where people live and work, and its artisans' work-shops, neighbourhood shops and busy markets create the atmos-phere of a village rather than a capital city.

It is also scattered with rem-nants of Imperial Rome, among them the Pantheon, which rivals the Foro Romano and the Colosseo, as well as a marvellous museum of antiquities, the Palazzo Altemps.

Two of Rome's most distinctive districts are also encompassed in this chapter. The medieval Jewish Ghetto, a web of streets just beyond Lungotevere di Cenci on the north-ern banks of the Tiber, is a mostly residential enclave of peaceful streets and small squares, with a handful of more traditional restau-rants and shops. Across the river lies Trastevere, a self-contained corner of the city, filled with pic-turesque old streets and squares. It retains much of its old working-class character – despite the fact that its appearance has made it one of Rome's main restaurant districts. This is a good place to explore by day or in the evening, though it has relatively few church-es, museums and monuments.

View of Rome through trees of the Botanical Garden located in Trastevere

TOP 10

⭐ Campo de' Fiori ➤ 86
⭐ Piazza Navona ➤ 88
⭐ Pantheon ➤ 92

Don't Miss

㉑ Palazzo Altemps ➤ 97
㉒ Trastevere ➤ 101

At Your Leisure

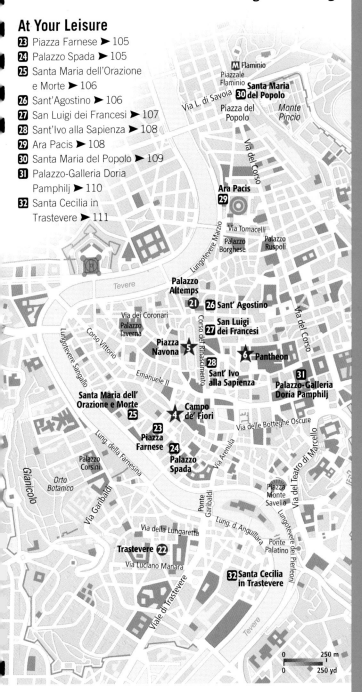

Two Perfect Days

If you're not quite sure where to begin your travels, this itinerary recommends a practical and enjoyable two days exploring the Heart of Rome, taking in some of the best places to see. For more information see the main entries (➤ 86–112).

Day 1

Morning
Breakfast in ☆**Campo de' Fiori** (➤ 86), before exploring its wonderfully evocative morning food and flower market. Next, head off to **23 Piazza Farnese** (➤ 105), the Via Giulia – one of Rome's most elegant streets – and (perhaps) visit the small **24 Palazzo Spada** art gallery (➤ 105).

Walk back to ☆**Piazza Navona** (ill. left, ➤ 88), a baroque show-piece second only to St Peter's, meander the side streets off the square – notably

Via della Pace – and stop for a coffee in one of its cafés.

Just north and east of Piazza Navona lie the churches of **26 Sant'Agostino** (➤ 106) home to a Raphael fresco and **27 San Luigi dei Francesi** (➤ 107), graced with three major paintings by Caravaggio.

Lunch
Try **Cul de Sac** or **Bar della Pace** (➤ 114) if you only want a snack lunch, **La Carbonara** (➤ 113) for an inexpensive meal al fresco, or indulge at **Ar Galletto** (➤ 113).

Afternoon

Visit **㉑ Palazzo Altemps** (➤ 97), where some of the greatest classical Roman sculpture is on display. Then make your way to the ☆ **Pantheon** (➤ 92), the most perfectly preserved of all Rome's ancient monuments.

Spend the rest of the afternoon exploring **Via del Corso**, one of the main shopping streets, and the streets to its west. Alternatively, visit the **㉙ Ara Pacis** (➤ 108), a Roman monument covered in intricate marble reliefs, and explore the art-filled church of **㉚ Santa Maria del Popolo** (➤ 109).

Day 2

Morning

Allow an hour or so to see the rich collection of paintings at the **㉛ Palazzo-Galleria Doria Pamphilj** (➤ 110); its state apartments typify the magnificent scale on which the aristocratic Roman families lived. Walk to Trastevere by way of **Santa Maria in Cosmedin** and Rome's oldest Jewish **Ghetto** (➤ 184). Alternatively, take tram 8 from Largo Argentina.

Lunch

You can take lunch in any number of places on your walk to, or around, Trastevere: try **Alle Fratte di Trastevere** (➤ 113).

Afternoon

Spend time simply exploring **㉒ Trastevere's** pretty streets and squares (ill. below, ➤ 101), before making your way to **Santa Maria in Trastevere** (➤ 102), which is usually open all day. Trastevere has plenty of stylish places to eat, so you may wish to extend the day and stay in the area for dinner without returning to your hotel. Do this either by walking up to the **Gianicolo** (➤ 96) to enjoy good views over the city, or by visiting the church of **㉜ Santa Cecilia in Trastevere** (➤ 111).

⭐4 Campo de' Fiori

Campo de' Fiori (Field of Flowers) is a place you will probably return to more than once during your stay. One of Rome's prettiest piazzas, it is the site of a wonderful outdoor market, with picturesque palaces and houses providing the backdrop for a colourful medley of stalls selling fruit, flowers and fish.

Take time to wander around these stalls and enjoy the street life: the redoubtable Roman matriarchs trimming vegetables, the fishmonger bawling his wares, and the local house-wives driving a hard bargain with knowing stallholders. When you have had your fill of sights, sounds and smells, pick one of the small cafés around the square and watch proceedings over a cappuccino.

In its earliest days the square really was a field of flowers: until the Middle Ages it formed a meadow that fringed the first-century BC Theatre of Pompey. Then it was built over and quickly became a bustling focus of city life. All manner of famous names were associated with the surrounding district: Lucrezia Borgia was born locally, her brother Cesare was assassinated nearby, and the artist Caravaggio murdered a rival after losing a tennis match in the square. Lucrezia's father, Alessandro, better known as Pope Alexander VI, would also have been familiar with the area, for one of his mistresses, Vanozza Cattenei, ran some of the inns and brothels for which the district became celebrated.

Today, there's relatively little to see here apart from the market and the **statue of Giordano Bruno** at its heart (▶ Insider Info). However, be sure to explore some of

The market at Campo de' Fiori is one of Rome's prettiest

The Campo is a popular place to meet at night

the characterful surrounding streets, notably **Via dei Cappellari** (Street of the Hatters, ➤ 187), a lane filled with boutiques and small shops. Also walk the short distance to Piazza Farnese to admire the square and its palace (➤ 105), and then continue to Via Giulia, one of Rome's most exclusive residential streets, to look at the church of Santa Maria dell'Orazione e Morte (➤ 106).

TAKING A BREAK

The Campo is full of small cafés and restaurants: one of the nicest is the **Caffè Farnese** (Via dei Baullari, 106–7) just off the square on the corner with the grander Piazza Farnese. One of the best places for lunch or dinner is the old-fashioned **Ar Galletto** (➤ 113), a few steps off the square.

➕ 205 E3 ⊠ Piazza Campo de' Fiori 🚌 40, 46, 62, 64 to Corso Vittorio Emanuele II or H, tram 8, 63, 271, 780 to Via Arenula

INSIDER INFO

- The Campo's cafés make a perfect – and pricey – place for a coffee break; the market is also at its least crowded early on (it runs daily except Sunday from about 6am to 2pm).
- As in any busy part of the city, be sure to keep a tight grip on your valuables.
- The Campo is also popular at night: the **Vineria Reggio** wine bar (No 15) and the American-run **Sloppy Sam's** (No 10) in the piazza's eastern corner are among the liveliest bars.

In more detail At the heart of Campo de' Fiori stands a cowled and rather **ominous-looking statue**, easily missed amid the debris of the market. This depicts Giordano Bruno, a 16th-century humanist and scholar who was burned at the stake on this spot in 1600 for the crime of heresy. His secular outlook suits the square, which to this day remains unusual among Roman piazzas in having no church.

★ Piazza Navona

None of Rome's many squares is as grand or theatrical as Piazza Navona. The magnificent piazza, one of the city's baroque show-pieces, is dominated by three fountains, a ring of ochre-coloured buildings – many hung with flowers in the summer – and an almost constant throng of visitors, artists and stallholders.

You will probably be tempted back here many times during your visit, although whether your budget will stretch to too many drinks at the piazza's pretty but expensive cafés is another matter. You don't need to spend money, however, simply to enjoy the area, which is an **irresistibly atmospheric** place for meeting and people-watching at most times of the day and night.

The piazza's distinctive elliptical shape betrays its origins, for the square corresponds almost exactly to the **outline of the racetrack** and stadium built on the site by Emperor Domitian in AD86. This was known as the *Circus Agonalis*,

Street traders and artists contribute to Piazza Navona's lively atmosphere

a name which by the Middle Ages had been modified to *in agone* and the dialect *n 'agone* before arriving at the present "Navona".

All manner of activities took place here over and above games and races, not least the martyrdom of Sant'Agnese (Saint Agatha), a 13-year-old girl killed in AD304 for her refusal to renounce her Christian beliefs and marry a pagan. She was thrown into a brothel close to the stadium, then paraded naked in the Circus, only for her nakedness to be covered by the miraculous growth of her hair.

The Church of Sant'Agnese in Agone

The simple oratory eventually built on the site of her death was superseded by the present church of **Sant'Agnese in Agone** (www.santagneseinagone.org, Mon–Sat 9:30–12:30, 3:30–7, Sun 10–1, 4–7) on the piazza's western edge in the mid-17th century. One of the architects involved in the church was Borromini, the great but troubled rival of Rome's other baroque superstar, Gian Lorenzo Bernini, who designed the piazza's central fountain, the **Fontana dei Quattro Fiumi** (1648), or Fountain of the Four Rivers.

The fountain's four major statues represent the four rivers of Paradise – the Nile, Ganges, Plate and Danube, and the four known corners of the world – Africa, Asia, Europe and America. Note the dove on the top of the obelisk, a symbol of Pope Innocent X Pamphilj, who commissioned the work.

Pope Innocent was also responsible for other major changes to the square, notably the creation of the Palazzo Pamphilj (now the Brazilian Embassy) for his beloved sister-in-law Olimpia. These changes largely put an end to the horse racing, jousting and bullfights that had taken place in the square for much of the Middle Ages. At times the piazza was also flooded, allowing the city's aristocrats to be pulled around the resultant artificial lake in gilded carriages, an echo of the so-called *naumachia*, the mock seabattles staged by the ancient Romans under similar circumstances.

TAKING A BREAK

Most of the piazza's cafés are much of a muchness, though those on its eastern flanks enjoy a little more sun. Two of the best-known bars are **Caffè Bernini** (No 44) and **I Tre Scalini** (► 114), the latter celebrated for its sensational chocolate chip ice cream *(tartufo)*.

Insider Tip

Bernini's Fontana dei Quattro Fiumi lies at the heart of the piazza

➕ 205 F3
✉ Piazza Navona
🚇 Spagna 🚌 30, 70, 81, 87, 116, 492, 628 to Corso del Rinascimento or 40, 46, 62, 64 to Corso Vittorio Emanuele II

INSIDER INFO

- Be warned that drinks at cafés around Piazza Navona are some of the most pricey in the city, but you can sit at your table as long as you wish.
- Most visitors overlook Piazza Navona's two lesser fountains. At the piazza's northern end stands the **Fontana del Nettuno**, or Fountain of Neptune, which shows the marine god grappling with a sea serpent. At the southern end is Giacomo della Porta's **Fontana del Moro** (1575), or Fountain of the Moor, whose central figure – despite the fountain's name – is actually another marine god: the erroneous name probably comes from the name of the sculptor, Antonio Mori, who added the dolphin from a design by Bernini.
- Since the baroque era Rome has had so-called *statue parlanti* ("talking statues") where anonymous satirical notes are hung around the necks of certain statues. One such example is near the Piazza Navona: **Pasquino** is still used by the Romans today to vent against policies.

Insider Tip

In more detail An often-told tale relates how Bernini deliberately designed one of the statues on his central fountain so that it appeared to be shielding its eyes or recoiling in horror at Sant'Agnese, the church of his great rival, Borromini.

It's a nice story, but in truth the fountain was created before the church. In fact, the Nile hides its eyes, because its source was undiscovered when the statue was carved.

★6 Pantheon

The Pantheon is the closest you'll come to a magnificent Roman building. One of Europe's best-preserved ancient buildings, its majestic outlines have remained almost unchanged despite the passage of almost 2,000 years. No other monument presents such a vivid picture of how Rome would have looked in its ancient heyday.

The first sight of the Pantheon is one of many people's most memorable moments. The initial impact of the building is further reinforced when you move closer, for only then does the building's colossal scale become clear – few stone columns, in Rome or elsewhere, are quite as monolithic as the Pantheon's **massive pillars**. The building itself does not take long to admire, however – inside or out – for there's little specific to see, which means your best bet is to take in the former temple from the sanctuary of an outdoor café table in **Piazza della Rotonda**.

The Pantheon, one of Europe's best-preserved ancient buildings

Imperial Design
The Pantheon you see today was built by Emperor Hadrian between AD118 and 125. It largely superseded two previous temples on the site, the first having been built some 150 years earlier between 27 and 25BC by Marcus Agrippa, the son-in-law of Emperor Augustus. This structure was damaged by a **momentous fire** that swept through Rome in AD80. A second temple, built by Emperor Domitian, suffered a similar fiery fate when it was **struck by lightning** in AD110.

Given this history, the large dedication picked out in bronze letters across the building's facade is puzzling, for it alludes to Marcus Agrippa: *M. AGRIPPA L. F. COS TERTIUM FECIT* (Marcus Agrippa, son of Lucius, made this in his third consulship). This apparent anomaly is evidence of Hadrian's modesty, for he habitually retained the name of a building's original dedicatee on the monument.

Subsequent rulers were less modest, as you can see from the faint two-line inscription below in much smaller letters: *pantheum vetustate corruptum cum omni cultu restituerunt* ("with every refinement they restored the

ORIGIN OF THE NAME
For so great a building it is remarkable that no one really knows why it is called the Pantheon. The term comes from the Greek and means "all the gods", but there is no record of any such cult elsewhere in Rome. Some theories suggest it was devoted to the 12 Olympian gods of ancient Greece, others that it was not a temple at all in the accepted sense, but rather a place where rulers would glorify themselves by appearing in the company of statues of the gods.

Pantheon

Pantheon, worn by age"). This refers to renovations supposedly made by emperors Severus and Caracalla in AD202, which, however, never took place

Hadrian's involvement was confirmed in 1892, when archaeologists – who until then associated the building with Agrippa – found that many of the Pantheon's bricks contained the Emperor's personal seal. Hadrian's involvement probably included the building's design, the squares and circles of which created a structure of near-architectural perfection.

Temple to Church
Plenty of Roman buildings shared the Pantheon's mixed fortunes, but few survived the passage of time in such pristine form. The reason for its excellent condition is that it became a Christian church in AD608, when Rome's then ruler, the Byzantine emperor Phocas, presented the building to Pope Boniface IV. This was the first time a temple constructed for pagan rites had been **converted into a church** – worship in such temples had previously been banned – and the change brought with it the ruling that to remove even a single stone from the site constituted a mortal sin.

Not all the building survived unscathed, however, as you'll see from the **porch's exterior walls**, which were

The Heart of Rome

once largely clad in white marble. The main body of the building to the rear was simply faced in stucco, a cheap way of imitating marble. Better preserved than the cladding are the **huge columns**, most of which are fashioned from Egyptian granite, together with their capitals and bases, which were carved from finest Greek Pentelic marble. Even here, though, certain contingencies had to be made: one column, for example, was brought from Emperor Domitian's villa in Castelgandolfo in the hills above Rome in 1626; two more – needed to replace damaged pillars – came from the Baths of Nero in 1666.

BON APPÉTIT!
Among the treasures lost from the Pantheon over the centuries is a statue of Venus that once stood outside Agrippa's original version of the temple. The statue was celebrated for the earrings with which it was adorned, made by cutting in half a pearl that Cleopatra left uneaten after a famous bet she made with Mark Antony that she could spend 10 million *sesterces* on a single meal.

Damage was not always accidental, however. Sometimes it was inflicted, most notably when Emperor Constans II plundered the bronze gilding that covered many surfaces in 663–67: most of it found its way to Constantinople and was melted down and re-formed into coins. Something similar happened in 1626, when Pope Urban VIII was persuaded by Bernini, the celebrated architect and sculptor, to remove the ancient bronze gilding from the portico's wooden beams. Some 200 tonnes of metal were removed, most of which went to make Bernini's huge *baldacchino*, or altar canopy, in St Peter's (► 154). Enough metal was left over, it is said, to provide Urban with 80 new cannon for the Castel Sant'Angelo (► 172).

Dome and Interior

Walking into the interior usually produces a double take in visitors, for looking up at the great **coffered dome** reveals a 9m (30-foot) hole, or *oculus*, in the middle of the ceiling.

The interior walls of the Pantheon are clad in marble

Pantheon

The Pantheon's dome is one of the marvels of Roman engineering. It becomes progressively thinner and uses lighter materials toward its top

This was a deliberate part of Hadrian's design, intended to allow those inside the building a direct contemplation of the heavens. It is also a dramatic source of light, casting a powerful beam of sunlight into the marble-clad interior on sunny days and providing a glimpse of the beautiful starlit sky on clear evenings. On startling occasions, it also allows in birds and rain.

The dome is the Pantheon's greatest glory, measuring 43.3m (142 feet) in diameter – greater than the dome of St Peter's – exactly the same as the height of the building from floor to *oculus* (a perfect sphere would fit in the interior). This was the world's largest concrete dome until 1958, when it was superseded by the vaulted roof of the Center of New Industries and Technologies in Paris.

The dome's distinctive **coffering**, or *lacunas*, was made by pouring material into moulds, just one of the cupola's many engineering subtleties. What you can't see is the way in which the dome's skin becomes thinner as it

The Heart of Rome

approaches its apex so reducing its overall weight. Neither can you see the way in which progressively lighter materials were used: concrete and travertine at the base, volcanic tufa midway up, and featherlight pumice close to the *oculus*.

Horse-drawn carriage on the Piazza della Rotonda, outside the Pantheon

Lower down, little of the **marble veneer** you see on the walls is original, although it is thought to correspond closely to Hadrian's original decorative scheme. Much of the pavement, however, although extensively repaired, is believed to be original. Around the walls are seven alternating rectangular and semicircular niches, originally designed to hold statues, but now given over in part to the **tombs of the Savoy kings** of Italy's monarchy (1870–1946). The third niche on the left contains the **tomb of the painter Raphael** (1483–1520), who was exhumed in 1833 and reburied here in an ancient Roman sarcophagus.

TAKING A BREAK

The **Tazza d'Oro** café (Via degli Orfani, 84; tel: 06 6 78 97 92, closed Sun) just off Piazza della Rotonda is considered by many to serve the best coffee in Rome.

➕ 205 F3 ✉ Piazza della Rotonda ☎ 06 68 30 02 30 🕐 Mon–Sat 8:30–7:30, Sun 9–6, holidays 9–1; Mass Sat 5pm, Sun 10:30am and 4:30pm
🚇 Spagna 🚌 116 to Piazza della Rotonda, or 30, 40, 46, 62, 63, 64, 70, 81, 87 to Largo di Torre Argentina 🎟 Free

INSIDER INFO

- The Pantheon is sometimes **closed on Sunday afternoon**.
- The Pantheon is a church and **entrance is free**.
- The Pantheon can be seen quickly and easily in conjunction with two other smaller sights: the Caravaggio paintings in **San Luigi dei Francesi** (➤ 107) and the Gothic church of **Santa Maria sopra Minerva**, founded in the eighth century over a Roman temple to Minerva. Outside the church, look out for Bernini's elephant statue supporting an ancient Egyptian obelisk. Inside, be sure to see the frescoes of the *Annunciation* and *Assumption* by Filippino Lippi (in the Cappella Carafa in the right, or south, transept), the statue of *The Redeemer* by Michelangelo to the left of the high altar, and the tomb of Fra Angelico, patron saint of painters, who is buried in a passage at the end of the north (left) nave.

In more detail The date on which the Pantheon was consecrated as a church – 1 November, 608 – is interesting, for it marked the beginning of All Saints' Day, or the Day of the Dead. The church was christened and dedicated to Santa Maria ad Martyres, the Virgin and the Christian Martyrs and countless martyrs' bones and relics were brought here from catacombs around the city to mark the event.

㉑ Palazzo Altemps

The Palazzo Altemps and its sister gallery, the Palazzo Massimo alle Terme (► 132), form the magnificent setting for the cream of Rome's state-owned antiquities. The Roman sculptures here are some of the city's finest, and are displayed in a beautifully restored Renaissance palace.

The Palazzo Altemps was begun around 1477, but took its name from Cardinal Marco Sittico Altemps, its owner after 1568. Altemps was a collector of antiquities, and would

Busts of the Caesars line the beautiful painted loggia of the Palazzo Altemps

The Heart of Rome

have been pleased at what has become of his palace, for it now houses some of the most sublime sculptures of the classical age. These sculptures form part of the collection of the **Museo Nazionale Romano**, whose exhibits were split between several new homes at the end of the 1990s.

The central courtyard of the Palazzo Altemps adorned with sculptures

The Palace and its Exhibits

Spread over two floors, and unlike many similar museums, this one won't dull your senses with endless rows of busts. Everything here is outstanding, with only a handful of exhibits in each room – some rooms have just one or two sculptures – with the result that each masterpiece has the space it needs to shine. As an added bonus, the palace itself has some beautifully decorated and frescoed rooms and chambers, not least the small church of Sant'Aniceto and the stunning painted loggia on the first floor.

After a small medley of rooms around the ticket hall you walk into the palace's airy central courtyard, flanked at its top and bottom (north and south ends) by two statue-filled arcades. Start your exploration by turning left, but note that although the rooms are numbered and named on the gallery plan, their open-plan arrangement encourages you to wander among the exhibits at random.

Room 7, the Room of the Herms, houses the first of the gallery's major works, two first-century figures of **Apollo the Lyrist**, both from the Ludovisi collection, a major group of sculptures amassed by Ludovico Ludovisi, a Bolognese nephew of Pope Gregory XV. The collection – purchased by the Italian government in 1901 – forms the core of the Altemps' displays. Another work from the collection, the **Ludovisi Athena**, dominates Room 9, a statue distinguished by the finely carved tunic and the snake twisting to stare at the goddess. Room 14 contains a wonderful sculptural group portraying Dionysus and satyr with a panther, full of beautiful details such as Dionysus' ringleted hair and a bunch of grapes.

Gallery Highlights

The gallery's real stars are on the first floor. To reach them, cross back over the courtyard and climb the monumental staircase close to where you first entered. This will bring you to the south loggia, where you should hunt out a second-century **sarcophagus** embellished with scenes of Mars and Venus, significant because it was drawn and much admired by Renaissance artists such as Raphael and Mantegna.

In the next room (Room 20, the Cupboard Room), you come face to face with two sensational statues: the ***Ludovisi Orestes and Electra***, a first-century group by Menelaus (the artist's signature can be seen on the supporting plinth), and the ***Ludovisi Ares***, a seated figure (possibly Achilles) with sword and shield; the sculpture is probably a Roman copy of a Greek original and was restored by Bernini in 1622.

The gallery's finest works occupy the next room (Room 21, The Tale of Moses Room), which contains little more than two monolithic heads and a deceptively humble-looking relief. The heads are the ***Ludovisi Acrolith*** (left of the relief) and the ***Ludovisi Hera***. The latter was one of the most celebrated and admired busts of antiquity, and has been identified as an idealized portrait of Antonia Augusta, the mother of Emperor Claudius, who was deified by Claudius after her death and held up as an exemplar of domestic virtue and maternal duty.

Less striking, but more precious to scholars because of its unusual nature and probable age, is the central relief, the ***Ludovisi Throne***, discovered in 1887 in the grounds of the Villa Ludovis. Although some controversy surrounds the piece, most critics believe it is a fifth-century BC work brought to Rome from one of the Greek colonies in Calabria, southern Italy, after the Romans conquered much of the region in the third century BC. The scene portrayed on the front of the "throne" probably shows the birth and

Roman victory portrayed in the second-century AD *Grande Ludovisi Sarcophagus*

welcome to land of Aphrodite (literally "born of the foam"). Panels on the throne's sides show two young girls, both seated on folded cushions, one nude and playing a double-piped flute, the other clothed and sprinkling grains of incense from a box onto a brazier.

Magnificent Sculptures

Three further exceptional sculptures dominate the room (Room 29) at the end of the palace's west flank, a large salon with ornate fireplace once used for entertaining palace guests. At its heart stands the ***Gallic Soldier and His Wife Committing Suicide***, one of the most dramatic and visceral sculptures in Western art. It was found with the ***Dying Galatian*** statue, now in the Musei Capitolini (► 73), and probably belonged to a group of linked statues based on three bronzes commissioned by Attalus I, king of Pergamum, to commemorate his victory over the Galatians. The marble copies here and on the Capitolino were commissioned by Julius Caesar to celebrate his victory over the Gauls. Like the *Ludovisi Throne*, the statue was found during construction of the Villa Ludovisi on land that once belonged to Julius Caesar. Finally,

The sculpture *Gallic Soldier and His Wife Committing Suicide* is said to have been commissioned by Julius Caesar

don't miss the room's superb helmeted head of Mars and the ***Grande Ludovisi Sarcophagus***, a virtuoso sculpture portraying a battle scene divided into three: the victors at the top; the combatants at the centre; and the vanquished at the bottom.

TAKING A BREAK

Stop for a coffee at the pretty and popular **Bar della Pace** (► 114), just off Piazza Navona.

➕ 205 F4 ✉ Piazza di Sant'Apollinare, 46
☎ 06 39 96 77 00; www.pierreci.it (bookings)
🕐 Tue–Sun 9–7:45 🚌 30, 70, 81, 87, 116, 492 and 628 to Corso del Rinascimento
🎫 €7, three-day combined ticket including Palazzo Massimo, Crypta Balbi, and Terme di Diocleziano

INSIDER INFO

- If you come to Rome in winter, try to **visit the Palazzo Altemps after dark**: the superb lighting in the gallery adds immense drama to many of its superb sculptures, busts, statues and exhibits.
- Invest in the **gallery guide and plan** published by Electa-Soprintendenza Archeologica di Roma: it is beautifully illustrated and provides interesting background information about the main exhibits.

㉒ Trastevere

Trastevere means "over the Tevere", and refers to a quaint enclave of the city on the southern bank of the Tiber (Tevere), an area that until recently was both the most traditional part of central Rome and the heart of its eating and nightlife district. Although no longer at the cutting edge, its cobbled streets and tiny squares are still picturesque places to explore and eat, either by day or night.

Trastevere is full of small bars and restaurants

Trastevere has an increasing number of hotels, but if you're staying elsewhere, it's not far to walk from the rest of the city. The routes you would take from places like the Capitolino or Campo de' Fiori run through interesting parts of the city such as the Ghetto, the Isola Tiberina and the cluster of churches and temples around Piazza Bocca della Verità (► 184). If you want to conserve your energy and catch a bus, or the tram 8, there's plenty of choice, as Ponte Garibaldi, the main bridge linking the rest of Rome to Piazza Sonnino, one of Trastevere's main squares, is a major city thoroughfare.

As for what you should see, there are two main sights – the fine church of **Santa Maria in Trastevere** (► 102), the focus of the area's central square, and the **Villa Farnesina** (► 103), which contains rooms and ceilings adorned with frescoes by Raphael.

Lesser attractions include the **Orto Botanico** (► 103), but in the final resort, this is a place to explore and admire at random, particularly the web of streets sandwiched between Via Garibaldi and Viale di Trastevere.

Insider Tip

The Heart of Rome

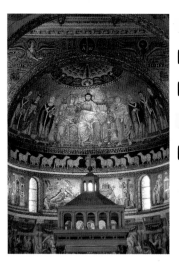

Santa Maria in Trastevere

The Piazza Santa Maria in Trastevere is a centre of Roman social life: kids playing football, old men chatting, lovers ca-noodling, though late at night the atmosphere becomes seedier. Even when there are no people to watch, you can simply enjoy the facade of the church that dominates the square. Santa Maria in Trastevere was reputedly founded in 222, which – if true – would make it one of the city's oldest churches. It is first properly documented in 337, when a church was begun here by Pope Julius I, on the site where it was believed that a miraculous fountain of oil had flowed on the day of Christ's birth.

The mosaic in the upper apse of Santa Maria in Trastevere depicts Christ and the Virgin enthroned

The present church dates from the 12th century, and was begun by Pope Innocent II, a member of a prominent local family. Its most arresting features are its **facade mosaics** – many Roman churches would have once been similarly decorated – which portray, among other things, the Virgin flanked by ten figures. Like the identity of the figures themselves, the identity of the mosaics' creator is not known, although Pietro Cavallini is a possible candidate, if only because he was responsible for many of the even more spectacular mosaics inside the church. For instance, Cavallini's hand can be seen in the lively mosaics of the lower apse (1290), which portray scenes from the Life of the Virgin. The scenes in the upper apse are earlier (1140), and are executed in a more old-fashioned Byzantine style.

Don't miss the church's lovely inlaid medieval pavement and the nave's ancient columns, the latter brought here from the **Terme di Caracalla**, where operas are performed today (➤ 80).

GIANICOLO

If you have the legs for a longer walk, then aim for the trees and greenery etched on the skyline above Trastevere. This is the Gianicolo, or Janiculum Hill, one of Rome's original "Seven Hills", and views over Rome from here make the climb worthwhile.

Walk up Via Garibaldi and look at the **Fontana dell'Acqua Paola** (1610–12), a monumental fountain created for Pope Paul V, and then see the late 15th-century church of **San Pietro in Montorio** at the top of Via Garibaldi, supposedly built over the spot on which St Peter was crucified (scholars believe he was actually martyred closer to the present-day site of the Vatican). In an adjoining courtyard stands the **Tempietto**, a tiny masterpiece of Renaissance architecture designed by Bramante, the architect partly responsible for the Basilica di San Pietro.

If you still have energy to burn, walk to the **Villa Doria Pamphilj** (➤ 110), Rome's largest park, a huge area of paths, pines, lakes and open spaces.

Villa Farnesina

From the church, walk northeast on Via della Scala and continue on Via della Lungara. At the end of the road is a beautiful Renaissance villa, built in 1511 for Agostino Chigi, a wealthy banker from Siena. Its highlight is the Loggia of Cupid and Psyche on the ground floor, adorned with frescoes painted by Raphael. It is believed that his model was the mistress of the villa's owner. Upstairs is the **Sala delle Prospettive**, a room entirely covered in frescoes containing views of Rome and clever trompe-l'oeil tricks of perspective. The adjoining room, formerly a bedchamber, contains vivid 16th-century frescoes by Sodoma.

A stone's throw from the villa you'll find the **Orto Botanico**, at the end of Via Corsini, a turn off Via della Lungara just

The steep walk up to San Pietro in Montorio, Trastevere

103

The Heart of Rome

south of the villa. Opened in 1883, its 12ha (30 acres) occupy the former gardens of the Palazzo Corsini, and spread up the slopes of the Gianicolo to the rear. It is famed for its palms and orchids, but is also a lovely place to take a shady time out from sightseeing.

TAKING A BREAK

The **Friends Art Café** (Piazza Trilussa, 34; tel: 06 58 16 11, daily 7:30am–2am) is a lively bar that serves everything from the morning cappuccino and *cornetto* (croissant) to after-dinner cocktails in surroundings of chrome and brightly coloured plastic.

Santa Maria in Trastevere

➕ 206 C4 ✉ Piazza Santa Maria in Trastevere
☎ 06 5 81 94 43 🕒 Daily 7:30am–8pm, but may close 12:30–3:30 in winter
🚌 23, 280, 780 💶 Free

16th-century frescoes in the Renaissance Villa Farnesina

Villa Farnesina

➕ 205 E2 ✉ Via della Lungara, 230 ☎ 06 68 02 73 97; www.villafarnesina.it; www.lincei.it 🕒 Mon–Sat 9–1 🚌 23, 780 and 280 to Lungotevere della Farnesina or H, 8, 630 and 780 to Viale di Trastevere 💶 €6

INSIDER INFO

- Try to see Santa Maria in Trastevere at night, when its facade and mosaics are usually **floodlit** to memorable effect.
- Trastevere is generally safe, but you should take care at night in the darker and more outlying streets.

Santa Maria in Trastevere lit up at night

At Your Leisure

23 Piazza Farnese

Piazza Farnese lies just a few steps from Campo de' Fiori, yet it's hard to think of two more contrasting Roman squares. While Campo de' Fiori is shabby and cramped, Piazza Farnese is broad and august, graced with elegant fountains, and unlike the Campo, which has no buildings of note, is dominated by the magnificent **Palazzo Farnese**. The palace, which has housed the French Embassy since 1871, is normally closed to the general public. The exterior was commissioned in 1515 by Cardinal Alessandro Farnese, later Pope Paul III. There are guided tours of the interior (book well in advance), giving you the chance to admire the magnificent ceiling frescoes by Annibale Caracci (1597–1603).

Much of the stone for the palace was pilfered from the Colosseo, and utilized here by the Tuscan architect Antonio da Sangallo the Younger. When Sangallo died in 1546 he was replaced on the project by Michelangelo, who designed much of the palace's cornice, many of the upper windows and the loggia. For one of Rome's grandest buildings, the French government pays the lowest rent in the city: set, before the advent of the euro, at one lira every 99 years. The Italians pay a similarly nominal sum for their embassy in Paris.

The **fountains** in the square were originally massive baths of Egyptian granite from the Terme di Caracalla. They were brought to the piazza in the 16th century by the Farnese family (look out for the carved lilies, the Farnese family symbol). They were turned into fountains in 1626.

🗺 202 E2–3 ✉ Piazza Farnese ⓘ Palazzo Farnese: Guided visits with Inventer Rome (by appointment only), www.inventerrome.com 🚌 40, 46, 62, 64, 916 to Corso Vittorio Emanuele II or H, 8, 63, 630, 780 to Via Arenula

24 Palazzo Spada

The Palazzo Spada was built for Cardinal Girolamo Capo di Ferro in 1548. Much of the building's charm derives from the facade, which is covered in beautifully patterned stucco work.

The second is an architectural *trompe-l'oeil* created in 1652 by the craftsman Francesco Borromini. It involves what appears to be a long columned corridor between two courtyards, which is in fact a passage a little under 9m (30 feet) long. The illusion is achieved by the deliberate narrowing of the corridor and foreshortening of the columns.

The third reason is to see its small, but very fine collection of paintings, among them works by Titian, Albrecht Dürer, Jan Brueghel the Elder and Guido Reni's portrait of his patron, Cardinal Bernardino Spada, who bought the palace in 1632.

🗺 197 F2 ✉ Piazza Capio di Ferro, 13 ☎ 06 6 83 24 09; www.galleriaborghese.it/spada ⓘ Tue–Sun 8:30–7:30 🍽 Cafés on the Campo de' Fiori and the Piazza Farnese 🚌 H, 8, 40, 46, 64, and other services to Via Arenula or Corso Vittorio Emanuele II 🎫 €5

The Heart of Rome

25 Santa Maria dell' Orazione e Morte

After looking at Piazza Farnese, walk along Via dei Farnesi. This soon brings you to **Via Giulia**, laid out by Pope Julius II between about 1503 and 1513, and still one of the city's most elegant and coveted residential thoroughfares. It's worth admiring, though perhaps not along its full length, for it runs for virtually 1km (0.6 miles) towards St Peter's.

Even if your itinerary doesn't take you down the street, devote a couple of minutes to the church on the junction of Via Giulia and Via dei Farnesi. Look for the unmistakable facade, decorated with stone skulls and, on the right side of the facade, looking down Via Giulia, the figure of a beaked bird – Osiris, the Egyptian god of death. A cheering inscription reads, in translation: "Me today, thee tomorrow". Santa Maria dell'Orazione e Morte (Our Lady of Oration and Death) was once the headquarters of a religious body known as the Compagnia della Buona Morte, or the "Company of the Good Death". Its charitable duties included collecting the unclaimed bodies of the poor and giving them a Christian burial. The corpses were stored in three tunnels running down to the Tiber, all but one of which were sealed up during construction of the river's modern embankment in the 19th century.

✚ 205 E2 ✉ Via Giulia
🕐 Sun 4–7pm 🚌 23, 63, 280

26 Sant'Agostino

The church of Sant'Agostino, built between 1479 and 1783, lies tucked away in the streets just north of Piazza Navona. The exterior is plain and unprepossessing, although the facade was one of the earliest Renaissance frontages in the city.

The elaborately painted ceiling of the church of Sant'Agostino

06

The interior, which was extravagantly refurbished in 1750, is that bit more promising, and holds some unlikely treasures for so modest a church. The first is a Michelangelo-influenced fresco of the Prophet Isaiah (1512) by Raphael, commissioned by a humanist scholar, Giovanni Goritz, as an adornment to his tomb (the painting is on the third pillar of the left, or north side, of the church).

The first chapel on the same side of the church features Caravaggio's *Madonna di Loreto* (1605). Turn around, and against the west wall – the wall with the entrance door – stands a statue by Jacopo Sansovino known as the *Madonna del Parto*, or *Madonna of Childbirth* (1521), much venerated by pregnant women or couples wanting a child.

🚻 194 A1 ✉ Piazza Sant'Agostino
☎ 06 68 80 19 62 🕐 Daily 7:30–12:30, 4–6:30
🍴 Cafés on the Piazza Navona
🚌 30, 70, 81, 87, 116, 492 and 628 to Corso del Rinascimento ✋ Free

27 San Luigi dei Francesi

The French national church in Rome (1518–89), is easily seen on the short walk between Piazza Navona and the Pantheon, and it is well worth stopping for the five minutes it takes to see its principal attractions: three superlative paintings by Caravaggio.

The paintings were Caravaggio's (► 26) first major Roman commission (1600–02), and all demonstrate

Detail of *The Martyrdom of St Matthew* by Caravaggio, in San Luigi dei Francesi

the dramatic handling of light and shade, or *chiaroscuro* (literally "clear and dark") for which Caravaggio was famed: *The Calling of St Matthew* (the saint hears God's summons while collecting taxes); *St Matthew and the Angel* (the altarpiece); and *The Martyrdom of St Matthew*.

🚻 202 A1 ✉ Piazza di San Luigi dei Francesi at the corner of Via Giustiniani and Via della Scrofa ☎ 06 68 82 82 71
🕐 Fri–Wed 10–12:30, Thu 10–12:30
🍴 Cafés on the Piazza Navona and the Piazza della Rotonda
🚌 30, 70, 81, 87, 116, 492 and 628 to Corso del Rinascimento ✋ Free

🚸 FUN AND GAMES IN THE CITY CENTRE

Children will probably enjoy looking around the **Campo de' Fiori** market (► 86) and watching the street performers in **Piazza Navona** (► 88). They'll also relish the ice cream at **I Tre Scalini** (► 114) or a trip to **Bertè** (Piazza Navona, 108; tel: 06 6 87 50 11; Tue–Sun 9–1, 3:30–7:30, Mon 3:30–7:30), one of Rome's oldest toy shops. **Legno e Fantasia** (Via del Governo Vecchio, 102; tel: 06 68 13 90 00; Tue–Sat 10–8, Sun 11–7) near Piazza Navona has wonderful wooden toys and puppets, as well as necklaces and bracelets. The **Orto Botanico** (Largo Cristina di Svezia, 24; tel: 06 49 91 71 07; March–Oct Mon–Sat 9–6:30, Nov–Feb Mon–Sat 9–5:30; €8, children aged 6–11 €4) is also the perfect place to take a shady break from all your sightseeing and provides plenty of playing space for children.

Insider Tip

Sant'Ivo alla Sapienza's spiral cupola was inspired by the sting of a bee

28 Sant'Ivo alla Sapienza

The fact that Sant'Ivo is rarely open matters little, for the church's main attraction is its extraordinary spiralling dome and lantern, the work of Borromini, a leading baroque architect and rival of Gian Lorenzo Bernini. Borromini received his commission from Pope Urban VIII, a member of the powerful Barberini family, and it is said the architect based his spiky and eccentric dome on the family's symbol, the bee, taking the bee's sting as his inspiration. You'll catch a glimpse of the dome if you walk from the Pantheon to Piazza Navona via Piazza Sant'Eustachio. For a closer look you need to enter the Palazzo della Sapienza, part of the papal university first founded in 1303.

🔹 202 A1 ✉ Corso del Rinascimento, 40 ☎ 06 68 649 87 🕐 Sun 9–12 🍴 Cafés on the Piazza Navona and the Piazza della Rotonda 🚌 30, 70, 81, 87, 116, 492 and 628 to Corso del Rinascimento 🎫 Free

29 Ara Pacis

There's no easy way to see this Roman monument, which lies in an isolated position near the Tiber and to the northeast of the Castel Sant'Angelo. It's well worth making a detour, however, for the **Altar of Peace** (13–9BC), now within architect Richard Meier's controversial modern pavilion (2006), contains some of the city's best-preserved Roman bas-reliefs.

Inside Tip

The altar was commissioned by Emperor Augustus to commemorate his military victories in France and Spain. The most striking and detailed of several sculpted friezes shows the procession that accompanied the altar's consecration, and includes the figures of Augustus, a number of high-ranking Roman officials and members of Augustus' family.

🔹 202 A2 ✉ Via di Ripetta ☎ 06 06 08; www.arapacis.it 🕐 Tue–Sun 9–7 🚌 224, 628, 926 to Passeggiata di Ripetta 🎫 €7.50

At Your Leisure

🞩 Santa Maria del Popolo

This church receives fewer visitors than it deserves, mainly because it lies on the northern fringe of the old city. Founded in the 11th century – allegedly over the tomb of Emperor Nero – it was much restored in later centuries by leading architects such as Bramante and Bernini. Inside the church, there are four outstanding artistic treasures worth seeing. The first is a series of frescoes (1485–89) behind the altar of the first chapel on the right (south) side by the Umbrian Renaissance painter Pinturicchio; the second is a pair of tombs (1505–07) in the choir by Andrea Sansovino; the third a pair of paintings by Caravaggio, *The Conversion of St Paul* and *Crucifixion of St Peter* (1601–02) in the first chapel of the left transept; and the fourth is the Cappella Chigi (1513), a chapel (second on the left, or north, side) commissioned by the wealthy Sienese banker Agostino Chigi. The last is noteworthy because virtually all of its component parts were designed by Raphael.

The Ara Pacis, a consecrated altar honouring Augustus' victories, with a relief depicting Tellus, the goddess of the earth and land

➕ 194 A4 ✉ Piazza del Popolo, 12
☎ 06 3 61 08 36
🕐 Mon–Sat 7–12, 4–7, Sun 7:30–1:30, 4:30–7:30
🚇 Flaminio 🚌 117, 119 to Piazza del Popolo
💶 Free

One of the ornate corridors within the Palazzo-Galleria Doria Pamphilj

🕮 Palazzo-Galleria Doria Pamphilj

You'd never imagine looking at the Palazzo Doria Pamphilj's blackened exterior that it contained a multitude of beautifully decorated rooms and galleries, the succession of which provides a sumptuous setting for one of Italy's most important private art collections. There's no shortage of great pictures in Rome, but what makes the Palazzo so appealing is its sheer beauty and the opportunity to see behind the scenes of a truly grand, private palace.

The Doria Pamphilj palace is one of Rome's largest, with countless rooms, five courtyards and four colossal staircases. Its size – in an age when the upkeep of such buildings is astronomical – is all the more remarkable given that it's still owned, and in part occupied, by the Doria Pamphilj family, headed today by two half-British siblings. This venerable papal dynasty was created when two families were united by marriage: the Doria, a Genoese merchant dynasty, and the Pamphili (or Pamphilj), a pillar of the Roman aristocracy.

From the entrance, climb the monumental stairway to the *piano nobile* and pick up one of the excellent multilingual audio guides (included in the ticket price), which will guide you round the palazzo, picking out highlights along the way; you should allow about 90 minutes for your visit. Five superbly decorated chambers, the state apartments, each more sumptuous than the last, open out one from the other. The ballroom, with its white and gold stucco decoration, mirrors and chandeliers is hung with figured silk. From here, you reach the private chapel, designed by Carlo Fontana in 1690, and the entrance to the picture galleries. These run round all four sides of the largest of the inner courtyards, and perfectly reflect 18th-century taste, with Flemish and Italian works hung alongside each other – the arrangement preferred by Prince Andrea Doria IV in 1760.

The collection's most famous work is Velazquez's **Portrait of Innocent X** (1650). A pope of notoriously weak character, Innocent is said to have remarked of the likeness that it was "too true, too true"; beside it stands Bernini's bust of Innocent, so that you can compare two different likenesses. Most of the greatest names of Italian art are also represented in the galleries, including Caravaggio's *Rest on*

the *Flight into Egypt* and the very beautiful *Magdalen*, Raphael's *Double Portrait* and Titian's dreamily seductive *Salome with Head of John the Baptist*. Other unmissable highlights include Filippo Lippi's *Annunciation* and Hans Memling's supremely pathetic *Pietà*.

➕ 199 E5 ✉ Via del Corso, 305
☎ 06 6 79 73 73; www.dopart.it 🕐 Daily 10–5
🚇 Barberini 🚌 60, 62 and all other services to Piazza Venezia 🎫 €11

32 Santa Cecilia in Trastevere

This church sits slightly west of Viale di Trastevere and the rest of Trastevere and can be included as part of a Trastevere stroll or a walk from the other side of the Tiber by way of the Isola Tiberina. Much of its appeal is wrapped up in the story of its dedicatee, St Cecilia, who is said to have lived here with her husband Valerio, a Roman patrician figure, in the fourth century. Valerio joined his chaste wife as a Christian, only to be rewarded with martyrdom. Cecilia's own martyrdom was protracted: attempts to scald and suffocate her failed, and she finally succumbed to three blows to her neck, but only after singing throughout her ordeal – one of the reasons why she is the patron saint of music.

The present church is a fascinating mixture of styles, ranging from the 12th-century portico to the grand 18th-century facade and chill baroque interior. Several fine works of art survived the years,

The Heart of Rome

notably a statue of St Cecilia by Stefano Maderno. The sculptor was apparently present when the saint's tomb was opened in 1599, her body having previously been moved from the catacombs outside the city on the orders of Pope Paschal I in the ninth century. Maderno made a drawing of her reputedly uncorrupt body, and in his statue clearly depicted the three cuts left by the Roman executioner's unsuccessful attempts to cut off Cecilia's head. Today, the saint's tomb is in the church's crypt which can be visited, along with excavations which reveal the remains of a Roman house.

Above the church's altar is a lovely Gothic **canopy** (*baldacchino*, 1293), the work of Arnolfo di Cambio. The apse is adorned with a beautiful and almost glowing ninth-century mosaic which shows Pope Paschal I presenting Cecilia and her husband Valerio to Christ. The cloister features celebrated frescoes of the *Last Judgement* (1293) by the Roman painter and

mosaicist Pietro Cavallini, a contemporary of Giotto.

✚ 199 D3 ⊠ Piazza di Santa Cecilia in Trastevere ☎ 06 5 89 92 89
🕐 Church: Mon–Sat 9:30–1, 4–6:30; Sun 11:30–12:30, 4–6:30. Cavallini frescoes: Mon–Sat 10:15–12:15, Sun 11:30–12:30. Excavations: daily 9:30–12:30, 4–6:30
🚌 56, 60, 75, 710, 780 💶 €2.50

Stefano Maderno's sculpture of St Cecilia, church of Santa Cecilia in Trastevere

Where to ...
Eat and Drink

Prices
Prices are for a starter and a main course excluding drinks:
€ under €30   €€ €30–€50   €€€ over €50

Alle Fratte di Trastevere €€
This wonderfully traditional Trastevere restaurant typifies everything that's best about a Roman family-run trattoria. It serves generous portions of freshly prepared seasonal and regional food. Dishes include *penne all' arrabbiata* and *spaghetti alla carbonara*, baked fish and veal escalopes with different sauces. Desserts are homemade, there are tables outside, service is brisk and friendly, the staff speak English and prices are very reasonable.
➕ 206 C3 ✉ Via delle Fratte di Trastevere, 49 ☎ 06 5 83 57 75
🕐 Mon, Tue, Thu–Sat 12:30–3, 6:30–11:30, Sun 12:30–3. Closed 2 weeks in Aug

Ar Galletto €€
Overlooking one of Rome's loveliest squares, this straightforward but stylish restaurant offers by far the best value for money of the restaurants on Piazza Farnese. Professionally and efficiently run, staples include a wonderful selection of vegetable antipasti such as *fiori di zucchi* (stuffed courgette flowers) and *puntarelle* (wild chicory shoots). Main courses range from Roman pasta specialties to grills and fish. The house white comes from the Alban hills, but it's worth perusing the wine list. Sit at one of the pretty tables outside in summer, right across from Palazzo Farnese.
➕ 205 E3 ✉ Vicolo del Gallo, 1 ☎ 06 6 86 17 14 🕐 Mon–Sat 12:15–3, 7:15–11. Closed 10 days in Aug

La Carbonara €/€€
This inviting restaurant is in a charming position on the Campo de' Fiori. The cuisine is simple, the prices quite high, but the view of the piazza...!
➕ 205 E3 ✉ Campo de' Fiori, 23 ☎ 06 6 86 47 83 🕐 Wed–Mon 12:15–3, 7–11:30. Closed 3 weeks in Aug

Da Francesco €
One of the most popular of the pizzerias near Piazza Navona (➤88), a cramped, quintessentially Roman eating house that serves some of the best paper-thin pizzas in the city. There is also an antipasto buffet to start with and the menu offers good, basic Roman *primi* and *secondi*. Factor in a jolly atmosphere, tables outside in summer and great value for money and you'll see why you may have to wait for a table.
➕ 205 E3 ✉ Piazza del Fico, 29 ☎ 06 6 86 40 09 🕐 Mon, Wed–Sun 12–3, 7–12:30; Tue 7–12:30

'Gusto €/€€
'Gusto's atmosphere and decor are chic and sophisticated but also informal. Downstairs in the busy split-level eatery you can sample pizzas, generous salads and other light meals (be prepared for lunchtime crowds), while upstairs in the restaurant there is a more ambitious and eclectic menu, combining Italian traditions and Eastern stir-fry cooking. Quality is good (rarely more), but you're here for the atmosphere as much as the food.
➕ 202 A3 ✉ Piazza Augusto Imperatore, 9 ☎ 06 3 22 62 73; www.gusto.it 🕐 1–3, 7:30–1

The Heart of Rome

Il Leoncino €

Other pizzerias in the city may be better known, but Il Leoncino, located just a couple of blocks west of Via del Corso, offers the authentic Roman pizzeria experience – and is likely to be busy with locals. Pizzas are made traditionally behind an old marble-topped bar and cooked in wood-fired ovens.

➕ 202 B2 ✉ Via del Leoncino, 28, off Piazza San Lorenzo in Lucina ☎ 06 6 86 77 57 🕐 Lunch: Mon, Tue, Thu–Fri 1–2:30. Dinner: Thu–Tue 6:30–12

Myosotis €€

The vivid modern dining rooms and light, innovative cooking at Myosotis are something of a departure from Rome's often rather traditional and decoratively uninspired restaurants. Service is amiable, the atmosphere relaxed and the prices reasonable. Menus change with the season, but almost always include Roman classics such as *spaghetti alla carbonara* and a selection of fish.

➕ 202 A1 ✉ Vicolo della Vaccarella, 3–5 ☎ 06 6 86 55 54 🕐 Mon–Sat 7:30pm–11pm. Closed 3 weeks in Aug

L'Osteria €€

Run by the same team as 'Gusto (▶ 113), this bustling restaurant on two levels applies the Spanish tapas approach to traditional trattoria cooking, so you can sample a wide range of dishes in the shape of tasters. Follow a few mouthfuls of *fritti* (deep-fried seafood or vegetables) with a couple of tastes of different pasta dishes, and then move on to traditional Roman meat dishes featuring offal. There's a great wine list that includes a good choice of wines by the glass.

➕ 202 A3 ✉ Via della Frezza, 16 ☎ 06 3 22 62 73 🕐 Daily 12:30–3:30, 7–1

Sora Margherita €

It's worth getting your head around the somewhat bizarre opening times to come here for a unique Roman experience. This hole-in-the-wall restaurant (find it by its number not some fancy sign) offers superlative Roman-Jewish cooking at bargain prices. The friendly welcome matches the quality of the food, such as *pasta e fagioli* (pasta and beans), and a mouth-watering *ossobuco* (veal shank). The wine is local, the napkins paper – no frills, just genuine Roman cooking.

➕ 207 D4 ✉ Piazza delle Cinque Scole, 30 ☎ 06 6 87 42 16 🕐 Oct–March Tue–Thu, Sun 12:30–3, Fri–Sat 12:30–3, 8–11:30; April–Sep Mon–Thu 12:30–3, Fri 12:30– 3, 8–11:30 (booking required)

Bar della Pace €

Frequent visitors to Rome may be cynical about this place just off Piazza Navona, but they still come back. By day, the bar is a pretty place for a coffee; by night it is one of the city's buzziest spots. The pizzeria-trattoria alongside is good.

➕ 205 E3 ✉ Via della Pace, 3–7 ☎ 06 6 86 12 16 🕐 Daily 9am–2am

Cul de Sac €

This wine bar, founded in 1968, close to Piazza Navona, serves a large selection of wines, as well as snacks – but no pasta dishes!

➕ 205 E3 ✉ Piazza Pasquino, 73 ☎ 06 68 80 10 94 🕐 Daily 12–4, 6–12:30

Il Goccetto €

An intimate and cosy wine bar close to Cul de Sac (see above), Il Goccetto takes its wine seriously. The setting, part of a grand medieval house, is lovely, with original frescoed ceilings.

➕ 205 E3 ✉ Via dei Banchi Vecchi, 14 ☎ 06 6 86 42 68 🕐 Mon–Sat 11:30–2, 7–11. Closed: 3 weeks in Aug, Sat lunch July and Aug

I Tre Scalini €

Bar on the Piazza Navona that has the best *tartufo* ice cream in Rome. It's perfect for a hot afternoon.

➕ 197 F3 ✉ Piazza Navona, 28–32 ☎ 06 68 80 19 96 🕐 Daily 9am–1am

Where to...
Shop

The heart of Rome is a large and varied area and the shopping opportunities here are correspondingly mixed and extensive. Small side streets often prove a happy hunting ground for specialities, notably Via dei Coronari (antiques), Via dei Giubbonari (second-hand clothing and shoes), Via Giulia (art and antiques), Via dei Cappellari (furniture), Via dei Sediari (religious ephemera), and Via del Governo Vecchio, Via dei Banchi Nuovi and Via dei Governo (gift shops, accessories, second-hand clothing and antiques). Although Trastevere also has its share of small craft, antiques and speciality shops, it is not a major shopping area; it does, however, have a large farmers' market in Piazza San Cosimato. The other main market in the area is at Campo de' Fiori (➤ 86).

BOOKS

Feltrinelli
Part of a large, modern nationwide chain, Feltrinelli stocks a good range of Italian and English-language titles. It also sells a wide selection of attractive cards, magazines and posters, as well as children's toys and games.
✉ Largo di Torre Argentina, 11
☎ 06 68 66 30 01
🕐 Mon–Fri 9–9, Sat 9am–10pm, Sun 10–9

Libreria del Viaggiatore
This book shop specializes in travel literature, maps and guides, and stocks a selection of foreign and English-language titles.
✉ Via del Pellegrino, 78
☎ 06 68 80 10 48
🕐 Tue–Sat 10–2, 4–8, Mon 4–8

CLOTHES

Arlette
Among the clothes shops that line this street near Piazza Navona, Arlette stands out for its relaxed, elegant and easy-to-wear women's clothes. Classic natural fabrics combine with good cuts to produce eminently desirable styles that have that Italian touch. They also sell accessories, such as scarves and bags.
✉ Via del Governo Vecchio, 49
☎ 06 6 88 06 8 37 🕐 Mon–Sat 10–8, Sun 12–7

Arsenale
Patrizia Pieroni shows her easy-to-wear and stylish collection in an airy white space; expect fashion with a distinctly boho twist, with great lines and a spread of colour and detail, as well as accessories.
✉ Via del Pellegrino, 172 ☎ 06 68 80 24 24
🕐 Tue–Sat 10–7, Mon 3–7

🧒 The Place for Kids
Quirky and colourful Italian children's clothes are on offer at this great little shop opposite the Pantheon, with frequently changing stock and a wide selection for boys and girls. Styles reflect what's what in the grown-up world with modern fabric and designs, and accessories, which will keep most children and their parents happy.
✉ Salita dei Crescenzi, 32 (Pantheon)
☎ 06 6 89 31 83 🕐 Mon–Sat 10–8

COSMETICS & TOILETRIES

Officina Profumo-Farmaceutico di Santa Maria di Novella
Insider Tip

This Roman outlet for a Florence-based shop sells a wide range of good quality cosmetics, soaps, herbal tinctures, natural sponges, perfumes, and other natural beauty products, the majority of which are made to traditional methods originally devised by Dominican monks.
✉ Corso del Rinascimento, 47
☎ 06 6 87 24 46 🕐 Mon–Sat 9:30–7:30

The Heart of Rome

FABRICS

Bassetti

Rows of fabrics fill this store, along with clothes and home furnishings. ✉ Corso Vittorio Emanuele II, 73 ☎ 06 6 89 23 26 🕙 Jul–Aug Tue–Sat 9–7:30, Mon 3:30–7; Sep–June Tue–Sat 9–1, 4–6, Mon 4–6

FOOD

Ai Monasteri

All the best products from Italian monasteries: natural cosmetics, health teas, organic honey, pickled mushrooms, chocolate, liqueurs and selected wines. Everything that has been prepared for many centuries by religious orders can be found in this very special shop at the northern end of Piazza Navona. ✉ Corso del Rinascimento, 72 ☎ 06 68 80 27 83 🕙 Mon–Wed, Fri–Sat 9–1, 4:30–7:30, Thu 9–1

Moriondo e Gariglio

This family-run concern makes and sells outstanding chocolate in all shapes, sizes and varieties. ✉ Via del Pie' di Marmo, 21–22 ☎ 06 6 99 08 56 🕙 Daily 9–7:30

Valzani

A long-established Trastevere institution celebrated for its cakes, chocolate, pastries and other sweet-toothed treats. ✉ Via del Moro, 37b ☎ 06 5 80 37 92 🕙 Mon, Tue 2–8, Wed–Sun 9:30–8

GIFTS

Aldo Fefe

This family business was started by bookbinder, Aldo Fefe, in 1932. The beautiful books, calendars, notebooks and boxes produced by the Fefe family make unique gifts. ✉ Via della Stelletta, 20b ☎ 06 68 80 35 85 🕙 Daily 9:30–1, 3:30–7:30

HOUSEHOLD

House & Kitchen

Looking for a Parmesan grater, salad bowl or a balsamic vinegar bottle stopper? Unlike Spazio Sette (➤ below), this traditional shop sells a full range of kitchen utensils – basic and exotic – and other household goods. ✉ Via del Plebiscito, 103 ☎ 06 69 92 01 67 🕙 Mon–Sat 9:30–8, Sun 10:30–2:30. Closed Sun in July and Aug

Ornamentum

Rome has several shops offering a beautiful range of furnishing and other fabrics, but none perhaps quite as sumptuous as Ornamentum on Via dei Coronari. This is the ultimate emporium for silks, damasks and other fabrics, as well as an enormous range of tassels, brocades and assorted furnishing accessories. ✉ Via dei Coronari, 227 ☎ 06 6 87 68 49 🕙 Tue–Fri 9–1, 4–7:30, Sat 9–1, Mon 4–7:30. Closed Aug

Spazio Sette

Old mixes with new at Spazio Sette, the city's best furniture, household and design store, where a huge range of consumer desirables are spread over three floors of a Renaissance palace complete with frescoed ceilings and a pretty courtyard garden. This is a truly Italian shopping experience. ✉ Via dei Barbieri, 7 ☎ 06 6 86 97 47 🕙 Tue–Sat 9:30–1, 3:30–7:30, Mon 3:30–7:30

STATIONERY

Il Papiro

Italian paper products make wonderful gifts to take home and add a little Italian elegance to any desk. This lovely shop sells desirable notebooks, photo albums, desk accessories and frames all made from superb Florentine figured and marbled paper in beautiful designs. This is also an excellent shop if you want to purchase pencils, stylish pens and multicoloured inks. ✉ Via del Pantheon, 50 ☎ 06 6 79 55 97 🕙 Mon–Sat 10–8, Sun 11–8

Where to...
Go Out

CLASSICAL MUSIC

One or two classical music organizations have their headquarters in
the centre of Rome (even if they
stage their concerts elsewhere).
One is the **Associazione Musicale
Romana** (AMR) on Via Gregorio VII
216 (tel: 06 39 36 63 22, 06 6 86
84 41; www.assmusrom.it), which
usually puts on **chamber concerts**
in spring and early summer; tickets
are obtainable from individual venues. Another organization is the
important **Oratorio del Gonfalone**
(tel: 06 6 87 59 52), which has its
own orchestra and choir who usually perform at the Oratorio del
Gonfalone in Via del Gonfalone, a
tiny street between Via Giulia and
Lungotevere Sangallo. It specializes
in hosting small chamber recitals,
but also presents concerts by visiting Italian ensembles.

Many of the city's major **church
music** concerts – usually per-formed
by visiting choirs – are staged in the
central **Sant'Ignazio**, a large church
in Piazza di Sant'Ignazio almost
midway between the Pantheon and
Via del Corso. Unfortunately, the
building has poor acoustics so the
seats in the rear are usually empty.
Contact visitor centres (► 32) for
details of forthcoming concerts, or
look for posters outside the church.
Recitals are usually free.

Several churches in the area offer
organ recitals, but you will need to
keep your eyes peeled for posters
in the local area advertising concerts. A good bet is **San Giovanni de'
Fiorentini** in Via Giulia where, at
afternoon Mass on Sunday, you
may be treated to the sound of
the church's wonderful late 17th-
century instrument being played.

The AMR (Associazione Musicale
Romana; ► left) generally organizes
an organ festival in the church during September.

NIGHTLIFE

Campo de' Fiori
Campo de' Fiori has become something of a focus for bars that come
into their own at nightfall. The place
that started the trend is the piazza's
gritty **La Vineria** (Campo de' Fiori,
15; tel: 06 68 80 32 68; Mon–Sat
8:30am–2am, Sun 5pm–1am), also
known as Da Giorgio, as authentic
a Roman wine bar as you could
hope for. It makes few concessions
to interior decoration – there is just
one plain bar – and the characters
who collect here can be colourful,
to say the least. The outside tables
are a favourite rendezvous on summer evenings. Almost immediately
alongside La Vineria is the **Drunken
Ship** (Campo de' Fiori, 20–21; tel:
06 68 30 05 35; daily 4pm–2am), a
boisterous and brash place much
favoured by young Romans and
foreign visitors alike. It serves mostly
beer rather than wine and is further
distinguished from its adjacent rival
by its bold design and the fact that
it has DJs and music most evenings:
happy hour usually runs from
about 5pm to 8pm.

Piazza Navona
For a somewhat calmer alternative
to the trendy and busy bars on
Campo de' Fiori, try **Cul de Sac**,
Il Goccetto (both ► 114) and the
perennially hip **Bar della Pace**
(► 114), the latter perhaps the
most popular place to hang out in
this part of Rome. For something
almost equally trendy but a little
less busy, wander round the corner
to **Bar del Fico** (Piazza del Fico,
26–28; tel: 06 6 86 52 05; Mon–Sat
9am–2am, Sun 6pm–2am). It is a
touch less expensive and in winter
has outdoor heating so you can
still sit outside.

Insider Tip

The Heart of Rome

Jonathan's Angels (Via della Fossa, 14; tel: 06 6 89 34 26; Mon–Fri 8pm–3am, Sat–Sun 6:30pm–3am), just off Piazza Navona, is a popular bar, decked out with candles and plenty of kitsch and overpowering paintings on the walls.

Also close to Piazza Navona is **Anima** (Via Santa Maria dell'Anima, 57; tel: 06 68 89 28 06; noon–4am), a small and welcoming bar and club with an eclectic music policy. A few minutes from the Pantheon is **Salotto 42** (Piazza di Pietra, 42; tel: 06 6 78 58 04; Tue–Sun 10am–2am), a cosy place for lunch or, later, cocktails in a stylish setting.

Piazza Venezia

Irish bars are big in many Italian cities, and Rome is no exception. One of the biggest and best in the city is **Trinity College**, housed near the Palazzo Doria Pamphilj over two floors of a beautiful Renaissance palace at Via del Collegio Romano, 6 (tel: 06 6 78 64 72; www.trinity-rome.com; noon–3am). Irish food is served along with the inevitable bottles of beer and stout.

Trastevere

In Trastevere, the best of the night-time bars and pubs is **Caffè della Scala** (Via della Scala, 4; tel: 06 5 80 36 10; www.caffedellascala.com; daily 5pm–2am), a big and bustling place for beer, wine by the glass, cocktails and light meals and snacks. It is definitely not the place for a quiet drink. For something quieter, try **Sacchetti** (Piazza San Cosimato, 61–2; tel: 06 5 81 53 74; Tue–Sun 6am–midnight), a family-run bar with tables outside. It serves delicious ice cream and home-made cakes and pastries.

Best of the live jazz and blues joints is long-established **Big Mama** (Vicolo San Francesco a Ripa, 18; tel: 06 5 81 25 51; www.bigmama.it; Oct–June Tue–Sat 9pm–1:30am). It describes itself, with some justification, as the "Home of Blues

in Rome", staging around 200 concerts a year. Stars of today and yesteryear perform alongside up-and-coming Italian musicians.

Testaccio

Though Trastevere is still lively at night and has many good bars and clubs, it is no longer as trendy as it was a few years ago. The axis of night-time action has now shifted to **Testaccio** and **Ostiense**, traditional working-class districts farther south. In summer the district buzzes with clubs, bars and outdoor venues, but it's peripheral to the city centre, so you'll need to take a bus or taxi to get there.

Venues of the moment change with some regularity, but you can always be sure to find something to suit your tastes. Two of the more permanent fixtures for live music and dancing are **Akab** (Via di Monte Testaccio, 69; tel: 06 57 25 05 85; www.akabcave.com; Tue–Sat 11pm–4am) and **Alpheus** (Via del Commercio 36, tel: 06 5 74 78 26, Fri–Sun 10:30pm–4am). **L'Alibi** (Via di Monte Testaccio, 40–7, tel: 06 5 74 34 48, Wed–Sun 11pm– 4:30am), a primarily (though not exclusively) gay club, is one of the most established and popular venues in the city.

CINEMA

If you're desperate to catch a film in its original language *(versione originale* or V*O)*, then head over to the **Nuovo Olimpia** (Via in Lucina 16G, tel: 06 6 86 10 68), a comfortable, two-screen cinema. It's an art-house-oriented venue run by the Circuito Cinema (www. circuitocinema.com).

Cult director Nanni Moretti owns his own cinema, **Nuovo Sacher** (Largo Ascianghi, 1; tel: 06 5 81 81 16; www.sacherfilm.eu), named after his passion for Sachertorte. In the summer, outdoor screenings.

Insider Tip

Northern Rome

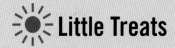 **Little Treats**

Trevi Fountain without the crowds
To have the magnificent **Fontana di Trevi**
(► 124) to yourself, get up early and arrive
between six and seven o'clock!

Go jogging amongst villas and museums
An attractive jogging path leads through the
Villa Borghese (► 126) park and gardens.

The young scene in Monti
The lanes around the beautiful **Piazza Santa
Maria Monti** (► 148) are full of old trattorias,
hip boutiques, ice cream parlours, bars and
hostels.

Getting Your Bearings

This chapter encompasses two contrasting areas of Rome. The first is around Termini, the city's main railway station, which you'd avoid were it not for a superb museum and major church; the second is around Piazza di Spagna, renowned for the Spanish Steps, full of wonderful streets, fantastic shops, memorable views, and compelling museums and galleries.

The mid 20th-century architecture of Termini railway station has its admirers, but in truth there is little in the area around the station – which is all traffic, cheap hotels and fast-food restaurants – to tempt you into staying longer than it takes to see the distinguished church of Santa Maria Maggiore and the magnificent collection of Roman statues, mosaics and wall paintings at Palazzo Massimo alle Terme.

Once your sightseeing in this part of the city is finished, you could catch the Metro A from Termini to Spagna station to visit Piazza di Spagna, a means of avoiding a mostly un-interesting and far from pretty 19th-century part of the city. Alternatively, you could walk from the Palazzo Massimo alle Terme towards Via Veneto, famous in the 1950s and 1960s as the focus of Rome's *dolce vita* days of hedonism and high living: today, sadly, it lives largely on its past reputation. You could also take in the works of art at Palazzo Barberini, as well as the interior of Santa Maria della Vittoria, home to a notorious Bernini sculpture.

By the time you reach the Fontana di Trevi, the most spectacular of the city's many fountains, you have re-entered Rome's old historic core and are close to its most exclusive shopping district, the grid of streets centred on Via Condotti. You could easily spend a couple of hours here window-shopping, perhaps followed by a lazy half-hour

La Fornarina by Raphael, a painting which many believed to be a portrait of his lover

people-watching in Piazza di Spagna. Literary pilgrims may want to visit the small museum on the piazza devoted to the poets Keats and Shelley.

Climb the Spanish Steps for views over Rome, and, if the weather's fine, walk northwest from Piazza di Spagna along Viale della Trinità dei Monti. This street offers fine views and leads into a more open part of the city, allowing you to strike into the Pincian Hill, and from there into the park and gardens of the Villa Borghese. A 1km (half-mile) walk through the park brings you to the Borghese gallery and museum, home to superb sculptures by Bernini and paintings by Caravaggio, Raphael and other major painters. If you don't want to walk, take a cab or bus 116 from Piazza di Spagna.

Getting Your Bearings

The Perfect Day

If you're not quite sure where to begin your travels, this itinerary recommends a practical and enjoyable day exploring Northern Rome, taking in some of the best places to see. For more information see the main entries (➤ 124–141).

⊕ 8:30am
Make your way to Piazza dei Cinquecento on foot, or by bus, Metro or taxi, and then walk the short distance to ㉝ **Santa Maria Maggiore** (➤ 130). Explore the magnificently decorated church, especially its mosaics, then visit the small nearby church of ㊱ **Santa Prassede** (➤ 138).

⊕ 9:15am
Walk to the ㉞ **Palazzo Massimo alle Terme** (➤ 132) and allow a couple of hours to explore the museum's superb collection of classical sculpture and rare Roman mosaics and wall paintings.

⊕ 11:00am
Walk west toward Piazza di Spagna, perhaps stopping off en route to visit Santa Maria della Vittoria, home to Bernini's erotic sculpture of St Teresa, **Santa Maria della Concezione** with the remains of 4,000 Capuchin monks (➤ 139) and the ㊳ **Palazzo Barberini** (below, ➤ 139), to see works by Raphael, Caravaggio (➤ 26) and Titian.

⊕ 12:30pm
Make your way to the ★ **Fontana di Trevi** (➤ 124) and then continue north toward Via Condotti (right) and Piazza di Spagna.

⊕ 1:00pm
Stop for a snack or a leisurely lunch in the streets around the Fontana di Trevi and Piazza di Spagna.

🕑 2:00pm

After lunch you might stop for a coffee in the historic **Antico Caffè Greco** (➤ 144). Serious shoppers will want to spend plenty of time in the area around **Via Condotti** (➤ 149); others can visit the **39 Museo Keats-Shelley** (➤ 140). Everyone should walk to the top of the **35 Spanish Steps** (➤ 136) to admire the marvellous views of the city.

🕒 3:00pm

Meander through the parkland of the Villa Borghese to the **10 Museo e Galleria Borghese** (right, ➤ 128, ticket pre-booking is mandatory), one of Rome's greatest museums with masterpieces such as Bernini's *Pluto and Proserpina* (ill. below). If the walk is too far, take bus 116 or taxi from Piazza di Spagna.

🕔 5:30pm

After seeing the Galleria you'll be far from the city centre. You could walk west through the parkland of the Villa Borghese to **42 Museo Nazionale di Villa Giulia** (➤ 141) or catch the 52, 53, 910 or 116 bus (Piazzale Brasile) back to the city centre.

⭐Fontana di Trevi

The Fontana di Trevi (Trevi Fountain) is the most beautiful of Italy's many fountains. It is perhaps most famous for its tradition – throw a coin in the waters and you will return to Rome – and for actress Anita Ekberg's nocturnal visit in Federico Fellini's classic film, *La Dolce Vita*.

One of the Fontana di Trevi's main attractions is that you stumble across it almost by accident. There it is as you turn from one of the three streets that lend the fountain its name (*tre vie* means "three streets") into the small piazza, a sight Charles Dickens described as "silvery to the eye and ear".

The fountain's waters were originally provided by the *Acqua Vergine*, or *Aqua Virgo*, an aqueduct begun by Agrippa in 19BC to bring water to the city from the hills outside Rome. It took its name from the legend that it was a young girl *(vergine)* who showed the original spring to a group of Roman soldiers. Today, the fountain disgorges a colossal 80,000cu m (2.8 million cubic feet) of water daily; in its Roman heyday the aqueduct could carry over 100,000cu m (3.5 million cubic feet) an hour.

The floodlit Fontana di Trevi attracts crowds of admirers

Water Bounty

The first major fountain to take advantage of this watery bounty was built in 1453 by **Pope Niccolò V**, who financed the project with a tax on wine. This led irate Romans of the time to sneer that the pontiff had "taken our wine to give us water". The present fountain was begun by another pope, **Clement XII**, in 1732 – an inscription above the fountain's main arch records the fact – and inaugurated 30 years later by **Clement XIII**.

The *fontana's* designer – probably **Nicola Salvi** – came up with the novel idea of draping the fountain over the entire wall of the Palazzo Poli, thus adding to its monumental scale and dramatic impact. The fountain's central figure

The triton blowing into the conch represents calm seas represents **Neptune**, or Oceanus. In front stand two tritons (1759–62) by sculptor Pietro Bracci: the one on the left as you face the fountain represents the stormy sea (symbolized by the agitated horse), while the figure on the right blowing into a conch shell represents the sea in repose.

Few visitors can resist the temptation to **cast a coin into the waters**. The tradition echoes the practice of both the ancient Romans, who often threw coins into certain fountains to appease the gods, and early Christians, who would scatter coins onto the tomb of St Peter and other saints and martyrs.

TAKING A BREAK

For superlative ice cream head to **Il Gelato di San Crispino** (➤ 144). Alternatively, stop for a coffee at **Antico Caffè Greco** (➤ 144) – you'll pay a price to drink here as it is one of Rome's most historic cafés.

✚ 202 C1 ✉ Piazza di Trevi 🚇 Barberini 🚌 52, 53, 61, 62, 63, 71, 80, 95, 116, 119, 175, 492 and 630 to Via del Tritone 🎟 Free

INSIDER INFO

■ The coins that you, and many others, toss into the Trevi Fountain do not go to waste. Previously, the basin was plundered at night by young men. Today, city workers sweep the fountain and retrieve the euro, dollar and yen coins. Nearly one million euros a year is given to the Roman Catholic charity Caritas which runs food programmes, shelters for the homeless and other social projects.

■ The **figures in the rectangular niches** either side of Neptune are allegorical figures symbolizing **"Health"** (with a relief above it of the young girl showing soldiers the source of the Acqua Vergine's spring) and **"Abundance"** (with a relief depicting Agrippa approving the aqueduct's design). The figures above them represent the four seasons of the year.

★ ⑩ Museo e Galleria Borghese

The Borghese gallery and museum may be relatively small, but the quality of its paintings and sculptures – notably works by Bernini, Canova, Raphael and Caravaggio – make it one of the jewels of Rome's rich artistic crown.

Wealthy Roman prelates and aristocrats over the centuries often amassed **huge private art collections**, many of which were later sold, broken up or passed to the city or Italian state. The finest of all such collections was accumulated by Cardinal Scipione Borghese (1579–1633), a nephew of Camillo Borghese, later Pope Paul V. Many works were sold to the Louvre in Paris in 1807, mostly under pressure from Napoleon, whose sister, the infamous Paolina, was married to Prince Camillo Borghese. Nevertheless, the surviving exhibits – which were bequeathed to the state in 1902 – make this the finest gallery of its kind in Rome, its appeal enhanced by a lovely setting, the beautifully restored **Casino** (1613–15), or summer house, of the Villa Borghese.

The Collection

The collection is simply arranged over two floors and around some 20 **gloriously decorated rooms**, the lower floor being devoted mainly to sculpture, the upper floor to paintings. One of the gallery's most famous works greets you in the first room, Antonio Canova's erotic statue of **Paolina Borghese**, in the guise of **Venus** (ill. ▶ 128). This is one of the most sensual sculptures of the Borghese or any other gallery; so sensual, in fact,

The lavish interior of the Galleria, once the Casino of the Villa Borghese, has been beautifully restored

that Paolina's husband, Camillo Borghese, forbade anyone to see it after its completion – even Canova. Paolina was a willing and knowing model, who when asked how she could possibly have posed naked for the work is said to have replied "the studio was heated". The next room introduces the work of Gian Lorenzo Bernini, the presiding genius – with chief rival Borromini – of the baroque in Rome. The room's principal sculpture is a statue of *David* (1623–24) in the process of hurling his slingshot stone at Goliath, the face of which is said to be a self-portrait of the sculptor. It was commissioned by Scipione – the cardinal became one of Bernini's main patrons – who is said to have held a mirror for Bernini while he worked on the self-portrait.

Insider Tip

Room III contains what many consider Bernini's masterpiece, **Apollo and Daphne** (1622–25), which portrays the flight of Daphne from Apollo, capturing the moment Daphne turns herself into a laurel tree to escape the god. An equally bewitching work awaits you in Room IV, *Pluto and Proserpina* (1622), renowned for the detail of

Bernini's *David*, one of the gallery's principal works

Northern Rome

Pluto's hand grasping Proserpina's thigh (ill. ▶ 123) – rarely has the softness of flesh been so convincingly portrayed in stone. The following room contains a statue of a hermaphrodite, a Roman copy of a Greek original – you may already have seen a similar work in the Palazzo Massimo alle Terme (▶ 132). Room VI has more works by Bernini: *Aeneas and Anchises* (1613), probably carved by Bernini in collaboration with his father when he was just 15, and the much later allegorical work *Truth* (1652), which remains unfinished.

In Room VIII you find another Roman original, a celebrated second-century statue, a **Dancing Satyr**. The room is better known, however, for **several major works by Caravaggio**, many of which were snapped up by Scipione when they were turned down by others as too shocking. Caravaggio is said to have painted self-

Antonio Canova's erotic reclining statue of Paolina Borghese

portraits in at least two of the pictures – as the **Sick Bacchus** (*c.* 1593) and as Goliath in **David with the Head of Goliath** (1609–10). His best works here, though, are the **Madonna dei Palafrenieri** (1605–06), the **Boy with a Basket of Fruit** (1593–95) and his **St Jerome** (1605–06). There are many other paintings on the gallery's upper floor.

Among the finest is **Raphael's Deposition** (1507). Other paintings include works by Perugino, Andrea del Sarto, Correggio – the outstanding *Danaë* (1530–31) – Lorenzo Lotto, Bronzino, and Giovanni Bellini.

One of the best pictures in the last room is **Antonello da Messina's Portrait of a Man** (*c.* 1475), the prototype of this genre of portrait painting.

⊞ 203 D4
✉ Piazzale del Museo Borghese, 5
☎ 06 39 96 78 00; 06 3 28 10;
www.galleriaborghese.it
🕐 Tue–Sun 8:30–7:30
🍴 Gallery café
🚇 Spagna or Flaminio 🚌 52, 53
and 910 to Via Pinciana or 116 to
Viale del Museo Borghese
💶 €11

INSIDER INFO

Numbers of visitors to the Galleria Borghese are limited, so it's obligatory to **reserve your entry ticket** (tel: 06 8 41 39 79 or www.galleriaborghese.it and www.ticketeria.it; Mon–Fri 9–7, Sat 9–1).

In more detail One of the Galleria Borghese's most mysterious and out-standing paintings is Titian's beautiful and little-understood **Sacred and Profane Love** (1514). The artwork has several differing interpretations and analyses.

Some claim its subject is actually Venus and Medea or Heavenly and Earthly Love; most critics, though, think it is an allegory of spring, and was inspired by the same strange dream romance, *Hypnerotomachia di Polifilo*, which provided Bernini with the idea for his eccentric elephant statue outside Santa Maria sopra Minerva (► 96).

㉝ Santa Maria Maggiore

Santa Maria Maggiore is the most important – and possibly the oldest – of some 80 churches in Rome dedicated to the Virgin Mary. Its surroundings are not the prettiest in the city, but the richly decorated ancient basilica, with its magnificent coffered ceiling and sublime mosaics, is is one of the most sumptuous in Italy.

According to legend, the church was built after the Virgin appeared to Pope Liberius in a vision on 4 August 356 and told him to build a church on the spot where snow would fall the following day. Snow duly fell, despite the fact that it was the middle of summer, leading not only to the foundation of a church, but also to the instigation of a feast day – Our Lady of the Snow – on 5 August. In truth, the church was probably founded in the middle of the fifth century, on the ruins of a Roman building dating back to the first century, or earlier.

This building was probably a temple to Juno Lucina, a mother goddess, much revered by Roman women, and it is probably no accident that a pagan cult was replaced by its Christian equivalent: the new church was dedicated to the mother of Christ as *Santa Maria ad Praesepe* (St Mary of the Crib). The church's maternal link was further reinforced by relics of Christ's Holy Crib, fragments of which were enshrined beneath the high altar.

Obelisks and pillars stand sentinel outside the church's (usually closed) north and south entrances, one a Roman copy of an Egyptian obelisk (in Piazza dell'Esquilino) removed from the Mausoleo di Augusto, the other a column removed from the Basilica di Massenzio in the Foro Romano (➤ 56). The main south entrance is the usual entry point for visitors.

A sublimely rich mosaic, depicting the Coronation of the Virgin, decorates the apse

Glorious Additions

Much has been added to the church since the fifth century, not least its immense weight of decoration, but the original basilica-shaped plan survives, a design probably adapted directly from the site's earlier structure. Almost the first thing to strike you inside is the magnificent coffered **ceiling**, reputedly gilded with the first gold brought home by the Spanish conquistadors in the conquest of Mexico and Central America. The Spanish royal couple Ferdinand and Isabella are said to have given it to Pope Alexander VI (1492–1503) a member of the infamous Borgia family.

The colossal columns supporting the ceiling lead the eye upward to a superb 36-panel sequence of **mosaics**, fifth-century works portraying episodes from the lives of Moses, Isaac, Jacob and Abraham. A later, but equally magnificent mosaic (1295) depicting the Coronation of the Virgin swathes the apse, the area behind the high altar, the work of Jacopo Torriti. Complementary colourful mosaics adorn parts of the church floor, examples of Cosmati inlaid marble work dating from the middle of the 12th century. More 13th-century mosaics can be seen on guided tours to the basilica's loggia. Among the interior's most impressive additions are a pair of large facing chapels: the **Cappella Sistina** (on the right as you face the altar) and the **Cappella Paolina** (on the left), completed for popes Sixtus V and Paul V in 1587 and 1611 respectively.

A shrine beneath the high altar is believed to contain a relic of the Nativity of Jesus Christ

TAKING A BREAK

If you want a leisurely drink, the best advice is to continue on towards Piazza di Spagna. A recommendation is the **Monti Doc**(► 148)

➕ 203 E1–F1 ✉ Piazza di Santa Maria Maggiore and Piazza dell'Esquilino ☎ 06 69 88 68 00 🕐 Daily 7–7; times may vary 🚇 Termini or Cavour 🚌 5, 14, 16, 70, 71, 75, 84, 105 🎟 Free

INSIDER INFO

- Santa Maria Maggiore is in a relatively unappealing part of the city close to the Termini railway station, but can be easily combined with a visit to the nearby Palazzo Massimo alle Terme (► 132).
- Look out for the **tomb of Cardinal Consalvo Rodriguez** in the chapel to the rear right of the high altar as you face it. The cardinal died in 1299, and the tomb was completed soon after. Its sculptor is not known, but the beautiful inlaid marble is the work of Giovanni di Cosma, one of the family first responsible for this distinctive "Cosmati" decorative style.

㉞ Palazzo Massimo alle Terme

The Palazzo Massimo alle Terme houses part of the Museo Nazionale Romano, one of the world's greatest collections of ancient art. Among the city's newer museum spaces, it provides a magnificent showcase for some of the most beautiful sculptures, paintings and mosaics of the Roman age.

The Palazzo lies close to Rome's unlovely Termini station, but don't be put off, for once inside the superbly restored 19th-century building you're confronted by beauty at every turn. The gallery spreads over three floors: the first two levels (ground and first floor) are devoted largely to sculpture, the top (second floor) mostly to mosaics and a series of frescoed Roman rooms moved from sites around the city. Such painted rooms are extremely rare, most frescoes of this age having long been lost to the elements. They are also surprisingly beautiful, so leave enough time to do them justice.

The Collections

These mosaics and paintings distinguish the Palazzo Massimo from its sister museum, the Palazzo Altemps (► 86–89), which is smaller and devoted to sculpture, and in particular, to the superb sculptures of the Ludovisi collection.

The exquisitely detailed statue of Emperor Augustus

Beyond the ticket hall and vestibule, bear to your right for the first of the ground floor's eight rooms, which are arranged around the palace's interior central courtyard. Ahead of you, along the courtyard's right-hand side, runs a gallery – one of three – filled with portrait busts and statues that served as funerary or honorary monuments in the last years of the Republican era (the end of the second and beginning of the first century BC). Room I opens to the right, where the highlight among several busts and statues of upper-class Roman figures is the *General of Tivoli*. It was probably the work of a Greek sculptor and is thought to have been executed between 90 and 70BC, at a time when the Romans were conducting numerous military campaigns in Asia.

Palazzo Massimo alle Terme

The beautifully restored Palazzo Massimo alle Terme

Room III contains a collection of Roman coins, while the highlight of Room V is a virtuoso statue of **Emperor Augustus** – note the exquisite detail of the emperor's toga. Different in style, but no less compelling, is Room VII's statue of **Niobede**, one of the mythical daughters of Niobe murdered by Apollo and Artemis: the statue shows Niobede trying to remove an arrow shot by Artemis. Other rooms and galleries on this floor contain many more similarly outstanding sculptures, as well as small areas of wall painting that whet the appetite for the exhibits on the museum's top floor.

Sculptures on the first floor move chronologically through the Roman era, continuing the theme from the floor below in Room I with work from the era of the Flavian emperors (after AD69) – Vespasian, Titus and Domitian. The following rooms contain exhibits spanning 400 years.

Themed Rooms

Interspersed with these are rooms arranged by theme, notably Room VI, which is devoted to the idealized sports and other statues that once adorned ancient Rome's gymnasiums and sporting arenas. Here you'll find the gallery's most famous statue, the *Discobolo Lancellotti*, or **Lancellotti Discus-Thrower** (mid-second century ad), the finest of several Roman copies of a celebrated fifth-century BC Greek bronze original. This original was widely celebrated by classical writers as a perfect study of the human body in motion.

A very different, but equally beguiling statue resides in Room VII, devoted to gods and divinities, and shows *L'Ermafrodito Addormentato*, or **Sleeping Hermaphrodite** (second century ad). Like the Discus-Thrower, the sculpture is the best of several known copies made from a popular Greek original created some 400 years earlier.

Northern Rome

The statue's sensuous appearance made it a popular adornment for gardens and open spaces in the grand houses of private individuals. A far cruder statue, depicting a **masked actor in the guise of Papposileno**, is the most striking figure in Room IX, which is given over to the theatre and performing arts.

Much of your time in the gallery should be spent on the top floor. Its first highlight is Room II, which contains **exquisite wall paintings** removed from the **Villa di Livia**, owned by Livia Drusilla, the third wife of Emperor Augustus (who reigned 27BC–AD14). The murals portray a garden scene, with cypress, pine and oak trees, a botanical paradise full of the flowers and fruits that thrived in the Roman Campagna 2,000 years ago.

Insider Tip

Wall Paintings

From here, walk back through Room I and along the floor's right-hand (north) gallery to Rooms III to V. These contain **wall paintings** removed from the Villa Farnesina (➤103), uncovered in 1879. Probably from a villa originally built for the wedding of Augustus' daughter, Julia, these are the most important Roman paintings of their kind, and embrace several distinct styles, from traditional Greek-influenced landscapes and mythological scenes to Egyptian-style friezes and architectural motifs. You rarely see such paintings,

The unusual frescoes from the Villa di Livia are one of the collections on display on the top floor

Detail of an altar dedicated to Mars and Venus

making their delicacy, skill and sublime colouring all the more surprising and memorable. Much the same can be said of the many **mosaics** exhibited on this floor, whose beauty and detail are in marked contrast to later – and supposedly more sophisticated – medieval mosaics across the city.

TAKING A BREAK

Places to stop for a drink or snack on the Piazza della Repubblica are somewhat uninspiring, but walk a little farther to Via Vittorio Emanuele Orlando 75 and you'll find **Dagnino** (Galleria Esedra; tel: 06 4 81 86 60; daily 7am–10pm), a lovely old-fashioned pastry shop selling Sicilian specialities.

✚ 203 E1 ✉ Largo i Villa Peretti, 1 ☎ 06 39 96 77 00; www.archeoroma.beneculturali.it; online booking at www.pierreci.it
🕐 Tue–Sun 9–7:45 🚇 Termini 🚌 64 and all other services to Piazza dei Cinquecento, Repubblica 🎫 €7. Combined ticket (valid for three-days, also for Palazzo Altemps, Crypta Balbi, Terme di Diocleziano)

INSIDER INFO

- The gallery is not difficult to navigate, but the excellent **gallery guide** contains a good plan of each floor.
- The gallery shop has many beautiful gifts and books, so bring money and credit cards in case you're tempted.

In more detail The beauty of the Palazzo Massimo – unlike many galleries of antiquities – is that it's not crammed with endless rows of dull statues: quality rather than quantity has been its guiding principle. There are relatively few works, and each is well labelled and well presented.

㉟ Piazza di Spagna

The Piazza di Spagna is one of Rome's great outdoor salons, a beautiful square that dominates the city's most elegant shopping district and whose famous Spanish Steps provide a magnet for visitors at all hours of the day and night.

The **Spanish Steps** are the piazza's most celebrated sight. More properly known as the Scalinata della Trinità dei Monti, they comprise a majestic double staircase that cascades down the slopes of the Pincian Hill from the church of **Trinità dei Monti**. Built in 1723 the steps are a favoured meeting place for Romans and visitors alike. Eating and drinking are unfortunately prohibited, but flirting is always allowed.

Both the square and the steps take their name from the Palazzo di Spagna, built in the 17th century as the Spanish Embassy to the Holy See. Before that, part of the piazza was known as the Platea Trinitatis, after the Trinità church.

The Fontana della Barcaccia with the Spanish Steps and the church of Trinità dei Monti in the background

The English Ghetto
Many foreign visitors made the area their home during the 18th-century heyday of the Grand Tour. The English,

in particular, were passionate admirers, so much so that the district became known as the "English ghetto" and boasted a famous café, the Caffè degli Inglesi, a favourite drinking den for expatriates. That particular establishment is no more, but there are two other historic cafés on or near the square: **Babington's Tea Rooms** (to the left of the steps as you face them), founded in the late 19th century by two English spinsters, and the **Antico Caffè**

Greco in Via Condotti, founded in 1760 and patronized by the likes of Goethe, Casanova, Shelley, Byron, Baudelaire, Wagner and Liszt.

Another visitor to the area's cafés would probably have been John Keats, who lodged – and died – in a house to the right of the Spanish Steps. Today, the building is given over to a **museum** (➤ 140) devoted to Keats and other literary exiles.

At the foot of the Spanish Steps is the tiny **Fontana della Barcaccia**, literally the "Fountain of the Rotten (or Worthless) Barge". Its name derives from the centrepiece, a half-sunken boat with water spilling lazily from its sides; the fountain's low level and less than spectacular display are the result of the low pressure of the Acqua Vergine aqueduct (➤ 124) which feeds it. The baroque design – possibly based on an earlier Roman model – was probably a joint effort on the part of Pietro Bernini and his more famous son, Gian Lorenzo Bernini. It was commissioned in 1629 by Pope Urban VIII, a member of the Barberini family, whose sun and bee emblems adorn the stonework.

TAKING A BREAK

The former studio of the sculptor Antonio Canova is now the café **Atelier Canova Tadolini**, where you can enjoy a cappuccino or *aperitivo* between the plaster busts (Via del Babuino, 150; tel: 06 32 11 07 02; Mon–Sat 8–12:30, thereafter a restaurant).

Insider Tip

➕ 194 C3 ✉ Piazza di Spagna 🚌 119

INSIDER INFO

- Climb to the top of the Spanish Steps from Piazza di Spagna for **good views**. Watch for pickpockets if the square is crowded.
- The church of **Trinità dei Monti**, begun in 1502, has immense scenic appeal, but nothing inside that really merits a visit.

At Your Leisure

36 Santa Prassede

This tiny church, in a side street immediately south of Santa Maria Maggiore, is celebrated for its mosaics, in particular those of the Cappella di San Zeno, situated on the left near the church's entrance. The gold-encrusted chapel was commissioned in 822 by Pope Paschal I as his mother's mausoleum. The square halo of Theodora, Paschal's mother, in the mosaic left of the altar, indicates that she was still alive when the work was commissioned. Other mosaics on the church's triumphal arch portray Christ flanked by angels in a heavenly Jerusalem, while those in the apse depict saints Prassede and Pudenziana. Prassede is said to have witnessed the martyrdom of 24 Christians who were then hurled into a well (marked by a marble slab on the church's floor): the saint then miraculously soaked up their blood with a single sponge.

✚ 209 D4 ✉ Via Santa Prassede, 9a
☎ 06 4 88 24 56 ⏰ Mon–Sat 7:30–12, 4–6:30, Sun 8–12, 4–6 🚇 Termini 🚌 5, 14, 16, 70, 71, 75 and other services to Piazza dell'Esquilino 💶 Free

37 Museo Nazionale delle Paste Alimentari

If you love pasta, then you'll enjoy this museum. Close to the Fontana di Trevi it is one of Rome's more unusual museums, thanks to its unique theme – pasta. The displays in its 11 rooms cover every aspect of the delicious food, from its history, cooking techniques and place in art to a collection of pasta-making equipment, models, dietary tips and photographs of famous people enjoying Italy's national dish.

✚ 202 C1 ✉ Piazza Scanderberg, 117
☎ 06 6 99 11 20; www.museodellapasta.it

Pope Paschal I commissioned the gold mosaics that adorn the Cappella di San Zeno

🕐 9:30–5:30 🚇 Barberini 🚌 52, 53, 56, 60, 61, 62, 71, 80, 81, 95, 116 and 119 to Via del Tritone or Via del Corso 💶 €10

38 Palazzo Barberini

The Palazzo Barberini was begun in 1625 for Cardinal Francesco Barberini, a member of one of Rome's leading patrician families. A magnificent baroque building in its own right, it is also a major museum, housing the lion's share of the collection of the **Galleria Nazionale d'Arte Antica** (the rest resides across the Tiber in the Palazzo Corsini).

Recent restorations have seriously given back the Palazzo's wow factor, seen at its best in the palace's superb centrepiece, the **Gran Salone**, a vast and fantastically decorated room dominated by Pietro da Cortona's allegorical ceiling frescoes depicting *The Triumph of Divine Providence* (1633–39). Other paintings are displayed chronologically in a

The elaborate columns and railings of the boundary of the Palazzo Barberini

series of beautiful rooms, and include major works by Caravaggio, El Greco, Tintoretto, Titian and many more.

The most famous picture is Raphael'a *La Fornarina*. The work depicts the beautiful Margherita Luti, the Baroque artist's mistress, the daughter of a baker (*fornaio* in Italian), who lived in his house in Rome until his premature death in 1520. Other masterpieces in the gallery include

Northern Rome

Narcissus and Judith Beheading Holofernes by Caravaggio and Hans Holbein's portrait of the bloodthirsty King Henry VIII.

🔟 203 D2 ✉ Via Quattro Fontane, 13
☎ 0632 810; www.galleriaborghese.it/barberini; online booking at www.ticketeria.it
🕙 Tue–Sun 8:30–7:30 🚇 Barberini
🚌 52, 63, 116, 119, 175 and 630 🎫 €8

39 Museo Keats-Shelley

Literary pilgrims will enjoy this lovely old house to the right of the Spanish Steps, where the 25-year-old English poet John Keats died in 1821 having come to Rome to seek a cure for consumption. Since 1909, the house has been lovingly restored and preserved as a small literary museum and working library for scholars of Keats and his fellow English poet, Percy Bysshe Shelley, who also died in Italy, drowned off the Tuscan coast. The fusty rooms are filled with old books, pamphlets and manuscripts, as well as literary mementoes such as Keats' death mask, a lock of the poet's hair, part of Shelley's cheekbone, and a reliquary containing strands of John Milton's and Elizabeth Barrett Browning's hair.

🔟 202 C2 ✉ Piazza di Spagna, 26
☎ 06 6 78 42 35; www.keats-shelley-house.org
🕙 Mon–Fri 10–1, 2–6; Sat 11–2, 3–6 Spagna
🚌 117 and 119 to Piazza di Spagna 🎫 €5

40 MACRO

Contemporary art fans should head for Rome's newest space, the **Museo d'Arte Contemporaneo di Roma**, housed in a wonderfully imaginative conversion of an old brewery. This huge 10,000sq m (107,639sq ft) extension, designed by superstar architect Odile Decq, finally gives Rome a space that attracts big international names in the modern art world, as well as providing room for large-scale multimedia installations and young artists. It works with **MACRO Future**, another stunning space in an old slaughterhouse, the Mattatoio, in Testaccio, Rome's most vibrant late-night area.

🔟 203 F4 ✉ Via Nizza, 131 (corner of Via Cagliari) ☎ 06 6 71 07 04 00; www.museomacro.org 🕙 Tue–Sun 11–11, Sat 11–10 🚌 90 🎫 €12.50

MACRO Future

🔟 206 C1 ✉ Piazza Orazio Giustiniani, 4
☎ 06 6 71 07 04 00; www.macro.roma.museum
🕙 Tue–Sun 4pm–midnight 🚇 Laurentina
🚌 719 🎫 €6

41 Museo Carlo Bilotti

The billionaire Carlo Bilotti, an Italian-American perfume tycoon, converted this 17th-century *aranceria* (orangery), built for the Borghese, in 2006 as a showcase for his superlative collection of modern art.

His passion was de Chirico, and
22 works by this artist and other late
20th-century luminaries are displayed in the permanent collection,
along with a 1981 Warhol of his
wife and daughter.

➕ 194 C4 ✉ Viale Fiorello La Guardia
☎ 06 06 08; www.museocarlobilotti.it
🕐 Tue–Sun 10–4 🚌 52, 53, 95, 910 🎫 €8

🔢 Museo Nazionale Etrusco di Villa Giulia

The Villa Giulia, tucked away in
the northern reaches of the Villa
Borghese, is worth the journey if
you have a passion for the
Etruscans, for a large part of the
huge building is given over to the
art and artefacts of that mysterious
civilization. The collection is the
greatest of its type in the world, but
for too long has been neglected
and left to gather dust. Many of the

The Villa Giulia houses the largest
collection of Etruscan art in the world

rooms contain unexciting rows of
urns and other funerary sculpture.
More inspiring are many exquisite
pieces of gold and other jewellery,
some of the larger sculptures, and
the reconstructed Etruscan temple
in the extensive gardens.

➕ 202 B5 ✉ Piazzale di Villa Giulia, 9
☎ 06 3 22 65 71; reservations
06 82 46 20 or www.ticketeria.com
🕐 Tue–Sun 8:30–7:30
🚇 Flaminio 🚌 3, 19,
231, 926 🎫 €8

[Map: Villa Borghese area showing Museo Nazionale Etrusco di Villa Giulia, Galleria Nazionale d'Arte Moderna, Bioparco, Villa Strohl Fern, Villa Borghese, Museo e Galleria Borghese, Museo Carlo Bilotti, Villa Albani, MACRO, Corso d'Italia]

OFF THE BEATEN TRACK

San Lorenzo is Rome's lively student district, which extends around the medical faculties
of La Sapienza University. What was once a working-class area favoured by socialists
and communists, is today a fashionable neighbourhood.

Some cosy trattorias, such as the **TramTram** (▶ 144) and the literary meeting place
Pommidoro (▶ 143), where the poet Pier Paolo Pasolini once sat and philosophized
with the writer Alberto Moravia, are still very popular.

Around Piazza di Spagna, you can escape the crowds on **Via Margutta**, a pretty street
filled with commercial art galleries, or in the web of **old streets** between Piazza del
Parlamento and the ruins of the Mausoleo di Augusto, the circular mausoleum of the
Emperor Augustus.

Where to...
Eat and Drink

Prices
Prices are for a starter and a main course excluding drinks:
€ under €25   €€ €25–€40   €€€ over €40

Neither of the two main areas in and around Termini and Piazza di Spagna are known for their restaurants: Termini is too downbeat, Piazza di Spagna too full of shops and sights. Yet both areas have good places to eat in all price brackets, and offer an excellent selection of bars for coffee and snacks, including some of Rome's most historic cafés. Both areas also have small establishments from another age – the discreet Fiaschetteria Beltramme (➤ 143), for example – and more modern establishments such as Al Presidente (right), whose sleek minimalism wouldn't be out of place in London, Sydney or New York.

Agata e Romeo €€€
The environs of the station are an unlikely location for this excellent restaurant. The cooking is modern Roman mixed with pan-Italian and international dishes, and gives the lie to the notion that creative cuisine, especially in Italy, is invariably pretentious or unsuccessful. Thus you might eat a traditional dish such as *baccalà* (salt cod), but salt cod that has been smoked and cooked with an orange sauce; or be tempted by a flan of *pecorino* (sheep's cheese) with honey. The setting is simple but comfortable – brick arches and plain walls with the occasional painting. The wine list contains an interesting selection. Reservations are essential.
🚹 209 E4 ✉ Via Carlo Alberto, 45
☎ 06 4 46 61 15; www.agataeromeo.it
🕐 Mon–Fri 12:30–2:30, 7:30–10.
Closed 2 weeks in Aug and 1–2 weeks in Jan

Al Presidente €€€
You are guaranteed a memorable – albeit expensive – evening at Al Presidente. With its cool, elegant design, this restaurant near the Quirinale and the Fontana di Trevi (➤ 124) is a good bet for a leisurely meal, which you can eat outside in warm weather. The cooking is Italian but distinctly modern, so expect a twist on traditional favourites, which include soups, pasta and risottos, and some wonderful fish dishes – the *coda di rospe* (monkfish) served with lentils is recommended. The wine list has more than 500 varieties, including wines by the glass. In the evenings you can try one of the taster menus to sample the full range of the kitchen's capabilities.
🚹 202 C2 ✉ Via in Arcione, 94–95
☎ 06 6 79 73 42; www.alpresidente.it
🕐 Tue–Sun 1–3:30, 8–11:30. Closed 3 weeks in Jan and 3 weeks in Aug

Alla Rampa €/€€
It may be packed with tourists but this cheery restaurant, with its lovely outside terrace, is a great place for an excellent-value meal. Take advantage of the delicious spread of antipasti on the buffet before moving on to a simple pasta or grill. Credit cards are not accepted.
🚹 202 C2 ✉ Piazza Mignanelli, 18
☎ 06 6 78 26 21
🕐 Mon–Sat 12–3, 7:30–10:30

Antica Birreria Peroni €/€€
This wonderful old beer hall, wood-panelled and frescoed, has been serving Peroni on draught since 1906. They pride themselves on the

beer and the straightforward, hearty cooking, which specializes in well-sourced grilled meat and *Würstel* (frankfurters). It's ideal for both a quick lunch or a good-value dinner, served with true Roman spirit.

🟩 202 C1 ✉ Via San Marcello, 19
☎ 06 6 79 53 10 🕐 Mon–Sat 12–12.
Closed Aug

Cantina Cantarini €€

The tiny tables may be cramped, but the food makes up for it at this well-priced trattoria. Menus are meat-based for the first half of the week, then feature fish and shellfish from Thursday to Saturday; the locals ensure a great atmosphere. There are tables outside in summer.

🟩 203 E3 ✉ Piazza Sallustio, 12
☎ 06 48 55 28
🕐 Mon–Sat 12:30–2:15, 7:30–10:15.
Closed 3 weeks in Aug, 2 weeks in Dec–Jan

Fiaschetteria Beltramme €/€€

You could easily miss this historic but humble-looking trattoria, which is incongruously located on one of the smart streets near Via Condotti. That may be the idea, for this is a deliberately understated place frequented by locals, artists, shopkeepers, society ladies and – on one famous occasion – by the pop legend Madonna. The interior is little more than a long single room whose walls are topped with wicker-covered wine bottles and almost completely covered in paintings left, bought or donated by locals over the years. Food is simple, well cooked and thoroughly Roman. Everything is recommended. You can't reserve a table here, so just turn up and hope that you'll be lucky. Credit cards are not accepted.

🟩 202 B3 ✉ Via della Croce, 39 ☎ 06 69 79 72 00; www.fiaschetteriabeltramme.info
🕐 Mon–Sat 12:15–3, 7–10:45

GiNa €

The cool, clean lines as much as the food and ambience draw all-day grazers to this relaxed and good-value bar-cum-café-restaurant off the west end of Piazza di Spagna. People drop in for everything from a late breakfast through lunch to a light dinner, or just to enjoy a well-made aperitif. The menu is eclectic, with Italian staples on offer beside home-made soups, imaginative salads and delicious ice cream sundaes. They also prepare picnic hampers, complete with glasses and cutlery; order ahead for a romantic outing to the Borghese gardens.

Insider Tip

🟩 202 C3 ✉ Via San Sebastianello, 7A
☎ 06 6 78 02 51; www.ginaroma.com
🕐 Mon 11–5, Tue–Sat 11–11, Sun 11–8.
Closed 2 weeks in Aug

Il Margutta €/€€€

Il Margutta has been in business for many years, which is no small achievement given that it is a vegetarian restaurant, something that until recently was barely known in Italy. The famed film director Federico Fellini lived nearby and dined regularly here. The stylish dining area is airy and filled with modern art, a nod to the restaurant's position on Via Margutta, home to many of the city's leading commercial art galleries. At lunch there's a good set-price all-you-can-eat buffet menu. You can also drop by most of the day for a tea or snack in the bar area.

🟩 194 B3 ✉ Via Margutta, 118
☎ 06 32 65 05 77; www.ilmargutta.it
🕐 Daily 12:30– 3:30, 7:30–11

Pommidoro €/€€

This is where the *letterati* Alberto Moravia, Dacia Maraini and Pier Paolo Pasolini met and philosophized about the merits of *spaghetti carbonara* or *all'amatriciana*. The landlord has never cashed Pasolini's last cheque, issued on the eve of his death. To this day, the venue remains a favourite haunt of the artists and glitterati of San Lorenzo.

🟩 210 C5 ✉ Piazza dei Sanniti 44
☎ 06 4 45 26 92

🕐 Mon–Sat 1–3:30, 7:30–11

TramTram €/€€
One of the dignified, traditional old trattorias. The name comes from the tram that passes here on its way to the Porta Maggiore. The cuisine is Roman with Sicilian and Apulian influences. Try the *orecchiette alla Norma*, ear-shaped pasta with -vegetables, or the *gnocchi con Bacala*, potato *gnocchi* with cod.
➕ 210 C5 B Via dei Reti, 44 ☎ 06 49 04 16
🕐 12:30–10

BARS & CAFÉS

Antica Enoteca €
This wine bar opened in 1842 and has been restored in order to retain its pretty old-world appearance. You can order wine by the glass or bottle and choose nibbles from a cold buffet or eat in the restaurant to the rear.
➕ 202 B3 ✉ Via della Croce, 76b
☎ 06 6 79 08 96; www.anticaenoteca.com
🕐 Wine bar: daily 11:30am–midnight. Restaurant: daily 12:30–3, 7–10:30

Antico Caffè Greco €
The long-established Caffè Greco is Rome's most famous café. Though it has had its ups and downs in recent years (and may no longer be the city's best café), it is still worth the price of a cappuccino to enjoy the venerable interior and savour its historic atmosphere. Locals stand; tourists tend to crowd the sofas. Expect to pay slightly over the odds.
➕ 202 B2 ✉ Via Condotti, 86 ☎ 06 6 79 17 00
🕐 Tue–Sat 9–7:30, Sun, Mon 10:30–7:30

Insider Tip
Antica Fabbrica del Cioccolato SAID €€
Founded in 1923, the old chocolate factory in San Lorenzo will set your taste buds alight! The shop section in the front has a wonderful selection of chocolates, while the restaurant serves some fusion dishes with chocolate. The trendy café is full of young Romans sitting with a hot chocolate that is so creamy that the spoon stands up in it.
➕ 210 B5 ✉ Via Tiburtina, 135
☎ 06 4 46 92 04, www.said.it
🕐 Mon–Sat 10–10

Ciampini al Café du Jardin €
You will escape the crowds in Piazza di Spagna at this lovely café near the Villa Medici, but you won't escape the area's relatively high prices. However, it's worth paying a little extra for the setting – a calm outdoor area with pond and creeper-covered walls – and the superlative views. The café serves sandwiches, light pasta meals, snack lunches, breakfast, ice cream and cocktails.
➕ 194 C3 ✉ Piazza Trinità dei Monti
☎ 06 6 78 56 78 🕐 Thu–Tue 8am–1am (closes earlier in spring and autumn). Closed Nov–March

Dolci e Doni €
The perfect place to take a cake break. Alternatively, indulge in a late breakfast, brunch or light lunch in this chic pastry shop and tea room.
➕ 194 B2 ✉ Via delle Carrozze, 85b
☎ 06 69 92 50 01 🕐 Daily 11–9 or 10. Closed 2 weeks in Aug

Insider Tip
Il Gelato di San Crispino €
Walk just a few paces from the Fontana di Trevi and you arrive at this temple to the *gelato*. Most Romans consider it sells the city's best ice cream and sorbets; some say they are the best in Italy, which is close to saying the best in the world. There are no cones here, just cups: San Crispino's perfectionist owners, brothers Giuseppe and Pasquale Alongi, claim that cones, with their artificial additives, inter-fere with the purity and flavour of their fresh fruit and myriad other iced delights. Flavours change with what is seasonally available. This place is a must!
➕ 194 C2 ✉ Via della Panetteria, 42
☎ 06 6 79 39 24 🕐 Wed–Mon 12–12 or later. Closed mid-Jan to mid-Feb

Where to...
Shop

The streets at the foot of the Spanish Steps are the epicentre of Roman chic and the only area for shoppers in search of designer labels and luxury goods. Although **Via Condotti** is the best-known street, the parallel streets of Via Frattina and Via Borgognona are almost equally full of designer names. Smaller side streets in the vicinity increasingly have smart boutiques selling shoes, lingerie, leather goods and accessories. Some streets specialize in particular items: Via della Croce, for example, has a scattering of good food shops, while Via Margutta is home to galleries and antiques shops. Via del Corso and Via del Tritone are lined with mid-market clothes, shoes and accessory shops, providing a good alternative to the designer stores. The area around Piazza Vittorio Emanuele south of Termini is home to many of Rome's most recent immigrants, and as a result is full of specialist food and other stores selling Chinese, Korean, Somalian and other Asian and African goods. The local food market is now located in Via Baccina (Mon–Sat 7am–2pm).

DESIGNER STORES

The outlets of principal Italian and international designers are listed below by street. Note, however, that new outlets open regularly in these streets, and stores often change their locations. Opening hours for the designer stores are generally Tue–Sat 10–7:30 or 8; some may close Monday morning.

Via Condotti
Battistoni (Men's clothing)
✉ Via Condotti, 61 ☎ 06 69 94 19 34

Bulgari (Jewellery)
✉ Via Condotti, 10 (near Piazza di Spagna)
☎ 06 69 92 21 04
Giorgio Armani
✉ Via Condotti, 77 ☎ 06 6 99 14 60
Gucci
✉ Via Condotti, 8 ☎ 06 6 79 94 05
Furla (Handbags/leather goods)
✉ Via Condotti, 55 ☎ 06 6 79 19 73
La Perla
✉ Via Condotti, 79 ☎ 06 69 94 19 34
Max Mara
✉ Via Condotti, 61a ☎ 06 6 79 36 38
Prada
✉ Via Condotti, 90 ☎ 06 6 79 08 97
Trussardi
✉ Via Condotti, 49–50 ☎ 06 6 78 02 80
Valentino
✉ Via Condotti, 13 ☎ 06 6 78 58 62

Via Frattina
Marella
✉ Via Frattina, 129–131 ☎ 06 69 92 38 00

Via Borgognona
Brunello Cucinelli (Cashmere)
✉ Via Borgognona, 33 ☎ 06 6 78 76 80
Ermenegildo Zegna
✉ Via Borgognona, 7e ☎ 06 6 78 91 43
Fendi
✉ Via Borgognona, 36–40 ☎ 06 69 66 61
Frattelli Rossetti (Shoes)
✉ Via Borgognona, 5a ☎ 06 6 78 26 76
Laura Biagiotti
✉ Via Borgognona, 43–44 ☎ 06 6 79 12 05
Roberto Cavalli
✉ Via Borgognona, 7a ☎ 06 69 92 54 69

Also: **Missoni** (Piazza di Spagna, 78; tel: 06 6 79 25 55), Krizia (Piazza di Spagna, 87; tel: 06 6 79 37 72), **Valentino Donna** (Women, Via del Babuino, 61; tel: 06 36 00 19 06), **Emporio Armani** (Via del Babuino, 140; tel: 06 36 00 21 97) and **Armani Jeans** (Via del Babuino, 70a; tel: 06 36 00 18 48).

ANTIQUES

Antiques hunters will have a field day in Via del Babuino and Via Margutta. Antichità is one of several tempting shops on these streets, specializing in old fabrics and furnishings.

Antichità Di Castro
✉ Piazza di Spagna, 5 ☎ 06 6 79 22 69
🕐 Tue–Sat 9–1, 3:30–7:30

Bottega del Marmorato
Here you'll find all manner of grand ornaments in marble, including copies of ancient busts.
✉ Via Margutta, 53b ☎ 06 3 20 76 60
🕐 Mon–Sat 9–1, 3:30–7:30

BOOKS

Feltrinelli
Renowned Italian bookseller with four bookstores, good assortment of Italian and international literature, CDs and DVDs.
✉ Via del Babuino, 39/40; Via E. Orlando, 84; Largo di Torre Argentina, 5a ☎ 6 68 66 30 01, www.lafeltrinelli.it 🕐 Mon–Sun 10–9

CHILDREN'S CLOTHES

🏵 La Cicogna
This chain of shops sells chic – and expensive – children's clothing.
✉ Via Frattina, 138 ☎ 06 6 79 19 21
🕐 Mon–Sat 10:30–7:30, Sun 11–7

🏵 Mettemi giu
The name of this pretty children's clothing shop means "put me down!". Jackets, blazers, children's jeans – colourful and casual.
✉ Via dei due Macelli, 59e ☎ 06 6 78 97 61
🕐 Mon–Sat 10–8

COSMETICS

Materozzoli
If you want to purchase quality beauty products, then you will enjoy shopping in Materozzoli. This refined shop dates from 1870 and sells a variety of top-of-the-range toiletries, perfumes, cosmetics and bathroom items.
✉ Piazza San Lorenzo in Lucina, 5
☎ 06 68 89 26 86
🕐 Tue–Sat 10–1:30, 3–7:30, Mon 3:30–7:30

DEPARTMENT STORES

TAD
There are plenty of goodies under one roof. You can buy clothes, shoes, perfumes and cosmetics, browse the CDs and magazines, have your hair done or grab something to eat or drink. Expensive labels and expensive people make for a high-end shopping experience.
✉ Via del Babuino, 155A ☎ 06 32 69 51 31
🕐 Tue–Fri 10:30–7:30, Sat, Mon 12–7:30

FOOD & WINE

Buccone
One of the best places in Rome to buy good quality wine and other alcoholic drinks such as *grappa* and *amaro*. Wine is available by the glass, and a small but excellent selection of snacks and fine foods.
✉ Via di Ripetta, 19 ☎ 06 3 61 21 54
🕐 Mon–Thu 12:30–2:30, 9–10:30, Fri–Sat 8–midnight

Pasta all'Uova
This little place that sells a variety of fresh and dried pasta. The pastas in unusual colours and designs make inexpensive gifts.
✉ Via della Croce, 8 ☎ 06 6 79 31 02
🕐 Mon–Wed, Fri–Sat 7:30–7:30, Thu 8–3:30 (8–7:30 in summer)

Inside Tip

Salumeria Focacci
Like Pasta all'Uova, this is one of Rome's landmark food stores. You will find a truly excellent selection of cheeses, meats and other gastronomic treats.
✉ Via della Croce, 43 ☎ 06 6 79 12 28
🕐 Mon–Sat 8–8

HATS & GLOVES

Borsalino
Hats, hats and more hats: for the past 150 years, the wide-brimmed Borsalino has been *the hat for* gentlemen, gigolos and gangsters alike.
✉ Via di Campo Marzio, 72A ☎ 06 6 78 39 45
🕐 Mon–Sat 10–7:30, Sun 10:30–7:30

Sermoneta

Giorgio Sermoneta's intimate shop has been selling just about every size, colour and style of Italian glove for over 35 years.

✉ Piazza di Spagna, 61 ☎ 06 6 79 19 60
🕐 Mon–Sat 9:30–7:30, Sun 10:30–7

JEWELLERY & WATCHES

Bulgari

Whether or not you are going to buy anything – it is worth browsing in Bulgari, easily Rome's most exclusive jewellers.

✉ Via Condotti, 10 ☎ 06 69 62 61
🕐 Mon–Sat 10:30–7:30, Sun 11–7

Melis

Massimo Maria Melis crafts very special necklaces and rings using antique coins and 21-carat gold.

✉ Via dell'Orso 57 ☎ 06 6 86 91 88
🕐 Tue–Sat 9–8

LAMPS

Artemide

Lighting from the classic table lamps, the Tolomeo and the Tizio, to the silver pendant light Alfiere.

✉ Via Margutta 107 ☎ 06 36 00 18 02, www.artemide.com 🕐 Mon–Sat 10–8:30

LINENS

Frette

Hotels or Italian households who have any pretensions to style would not use anything but Frette bed or table linens. Goods are expensive, but you can expect outstanding quality and excellent service too.

✉ Piazza di Spagna, 11 ☎ 06 6 79 06 73
🕐 Mon–Sat 10–7:30

LINGERIE

Demoiselle

If you adore gorgeous lingerie, the truly exquisite and sensual whisps of silk and lace nightwear and lingerie will send you diving for the plastic in this pretty store, which also sells swimsuits and beachwear by Missoni and Pucci.

✉ Via Frattina, 93 ☎ 06 6 79 37 52
🕐 Mon–Sat 10–8

Rossati

The window displays may be a little dated, but step inside this traditional lingerie shop to find the best of Italian products. They stock everything from soft silk and wool vests, pyjamas and nightgowns, to fine silk peignoirs trimmed with lace.

✉ Piazza di Spagna, 52 ☎ 06 6 79 00 16
🕐 Mon 3–8, Tue–Sun 10–8

SHOES

Fausto Santini

Some of the designs may seem far-fetched, but none can be called boring, and the quality is excellent.

✉ Via Frattina, 120 ☎ 06 6 78 41 14
🕐 Mon–Sat 10–7:30, Sun 12–7:30

Tod's

Flexible yet elegant cult shoes for stylish women and smart young entrepreneurs. Tod's CEO Diego della Valle is considered the inventor of the *gommini*, his trademark rubber-studded shoes, and is known as a socially committed businessman – he recently donated 25 million euros towards the restoration of the Colosseum.

✉ Via Fontanella Borghese, 56a ☎ 06 68 21 00 66; www.tods.com 🕐 Daily 10–7:30

STATIONERY

Pineider

The pens and stationery here are the finest and most exclusive in the city.

✉ Via dei Due Macelli, 68 ☎ 06 6 78 90 13
🕐 Mon–Sat 10–7, Sun 10–2, 3–7

Vertecchi

This pretty shop crammed with pens, paints, stationery and all manner of items covered in marbled paper, is a good place for gifts to take home.

✉ Via della Croce, 70 ☎ 06 33 22 82
🕐 Mon–Sat 9:30–7:30

Where to...
Go Out

CLASSICAL MUSIC

The **opera season** in Rome runs
from October to May at the
19th-century auditorium, the
Teatro dell'Opera, which lies just
a few steps from Piazza dei
Cinquecento at Via Firenze 72/
Piazza Beniamo Gigli 8 (tel: 06 48
16 01, 06 4 81 70 03; www.opera
roma.it). The reputation of Rome's
opera house is not exceptional,
however, it is often easier to obtain
tickets here than in Milan or elsewhere. The box office is generally
open Tuesday to Saturday 9–5,
Sunday 9–1:30 on days when
there is no performance or
10:45am to half an hour before
the start of any performance. Free
phone in Italy for information (tel:
80 00 16 665) between 10am and
1:30pm. Making a booking by
phone is almost impossible, so
visit the box office in person or
book online. Contact the visitor
centre or the opera house for information on summer outdoor
performances.

North from here is Rome's
best performing arts centre, the
Auditorium Parco della Musica
(Viale Pietro de Coubertin 15; tel:
06 06 08, 89 29 82, 06 3 70 01 06;
www.auditorium.com). This is a
superb complex of concert and
exhibition spaces, designed by
Renzo Piano (2006) and now
offers a programme of extraordinary scope that includes everything from symphony to jazz. The
box office is open Monday
to Friday. Browse the website and
book ahead online; alternatively,
just go for a look at this exciting
venue – worth it for the architecture alone.

NIGHTLIFE

Even though many Romans still
head to Trastevere and Testaccio
when they are in the mood for a
party, the trendy nightlife district is
Monti. The area around Stazione
Termini, Via Cavour, Via Serpenti,
and Via Nazionale offers something
for everybody. Depending on the
mood, you can kick off the evening
with a pizza in the rustic **Est Est Est**.
It is one of the oldest pizzerias in
Rome and has being going since
1888 (Via Genova, 32; tel: 06 4 88
11 07; Tue–Sun 6–midnight), or in
Cavour 313 (Cavour, 313, tel: 06 6
78 54 96; Mon–Sat 12:30am–
12:30pm), a typical Roman *enoteca*
(wine bar) with excellent selection of
wine, small snacks and fresh salads.

In a similar vein is **Monti Doc** (Via
Giovanni Lanza, 93; tel: 06 48 93 04
27; Tue–Sun 7pm–1am) a relaxed
wine bar with good wines and eats.

For those who prefer beer and
whisky, then the pub **Druid's Den**
(San Martino ai Monnti, 28, tel: 06
48 90 47 81, daily 5pm–2am) is the
place for you.

The hip museum restaurant,
Open Colonna on the rooftop of the
Palazzo delle Esposizioni, is particularly popular on Saturdays
(Scalinata di Via Milano, 9a; tel: 06
47 82 26 41; www.opencolonna.it;
closed Sun, Mon nights and Aug).

For nightclubbers the **Micca Club**
on the Piazza Barberini (formerly
Termini) offers sets by international
DJs (Via Avignonesi, 73, Piazza
Barberini; tel: 39 39 33 23 62 44;
Thu–Mon 10pm–4am).

Piper (Via Tagliamento, 9; tel:
06 8 41 44 59; Thu–Sat 11pm–4am)
is one of the longest-running clubs
in Rome – frequent revamps have
allowed it to ride out changing
trends. If you want to dance or
listen to live music in the city
centre, the only club is the busy
Gregory's near Piazza di Spagna
(Via Gregoriana, 54a; tel: 06 6 79
63 86; Tue–Sun 7pm–2am).

Vatican City

 Little Treats

Coffee in the cupola

After taking in the view from the dome of
the **Basilica di San Pietro** (➤ 158), enjoy a cup
of coffee at the souvenir stand.

Divine peace

The small, tranquil cemetery, **Camposanto
Teutonico** (➤ 156, entrance left of the cathedral), is the burial site for pilgrims to Rome.

Heavenly messengers

The most beautiful pedestrian bridge in
Rome, the **Ponte Sant' Angelo** (➤ 173), is
adorned with ten statues designed by Bernini.

Getting Your Bearings

The Vatican is the world's smallest independent state – yet it contains two of the highlights of any visit to Rome: the immense Basilica di San Pietro (St Peter's), and the Musei Vaticani (Vatican Museums), home to the world's richest and largest collections of paintings, sculptures and other works of art accumulated by the papacy over the centuries

Inscribed in the apse of St Peter, the largest basilica of Christianity, are the words, "You are Peter, and upon this rock I will build my church". In the fourth century, part of the area became the site for a huge basilica – the first St Peter's – built over or close to the tomb of St Peter, who was crucified sometime between AD64 and 67. By the 10th century, attacks by Lombards and Saracens had led to the building of a defensive wall around the Vatican, and later to the use of the Castel Sant'Angelo as a papal fortress.

For more than 1,000 years the territories of the Papal States – the secular and political domain of the papacy – covered all of central Italy. The Papal States came into being in 756, when the Frankish king Pepin and his son Charlemagne donated territories to the papacy, and lasted until 1870, when, following a referendum, they were annexed to the Kingdom of Italy. The papacy rejected this and withdrew to the Vatican. The situation was only resolved by the Lateran Treaty in 1929, concluded under

Getting Your Bearings

TOP 10

At Your Leisure

Mussolini, which saw a return to normal relations between the Holy See and the Republic of Italy.

Today, the area has its own shops, banks, newspaper, and helicopter pad and radio station. Most is out of bounds to the general public, with the important exceptions of San Pietro, the Musei Vaticani and – if you reserve a visit in advance – parts of the Vatican Gardens.

It should take just a couple of hours to see St Peter's, though you may be tempted to linger in the dome, which offers the best views in Rome. Just before (or after) seeing Basilica di San Pietro you might spend an hour in the Castel Sant'Angelo – these days outside the Vatican – a fascinating Roman building overlaid with later fortifications and papal apartments.

From there, or from St Peter's, it is just a short walk to the highlights of the Musei Vaticani – especially the Sistine Chapel and the Raphael Rooms – and you should set aside a whole morning to explore them.

Vatican City

The Perfect Day

If you're not quite sure where to begin your travels, this itinerary recommends a practical and enjoyable day exploring both St Peter's Basilica and the Vatican Museums with the highlight of the Sistine Chapel. However, it is best to take more time and explore the area at your leisure over two days.

🕘 9:00am

The Musei Vaticani are always crowded, so get there early. Book tickets online in advance to avoid queues. Remember that the entrance to the Vatican Museums is located in Viale Vaticano, a ten minute walk from St Peter's Square. Start with the ⭐🟡 **Museo Pio-Clementino** (ill. right, ➤ 162), which contains the best of the Vatican's sculpture collection.

🕙 10:00am

Have a quick look at the Etruscan highlights in the 🟥 **Museo Gregoriano Etrusco** (➤ 170) before moving from its upper floors through the 🟥 **Sala della Biga** (➤ 170) to the Gallerie. These corridors link the main museum buildings to the Vatican palace: the Galleria dei Candelabri (candelabra), the Galleria degli Arazzi (tapestries), and the Galleria della Carte Geografiche (frescoed maps).

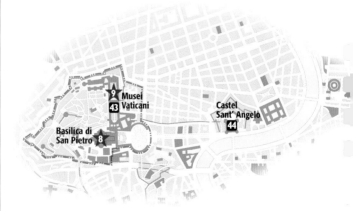

⏰ 11:00am

The Gallerie funnel visitors through to the ⭐**Stanze di Raffaello** (➤ 164), rooms covered in frescoes by Raphael, and the **Cappella di Niccolò V** (➤ 165), before steps take you down to the tiny **43 Appartamento Borgia** (➤ 171) and on to Michelangelo's ⭐**Cappella Sistina** (➤ 166).

⏰ 12:00pm

Follow the signs through the **43 Biblioteca Apostolica Vaticana** (➤ 171) to the Cortile and the **43 Pinacoteca Vaticana** (➤ 172), well worth a quick glance.

⏰ 1:00pm

Take a break in the Musei Vaticani cafeteria, or you could try **Taverna Angelica** (➤ 175).

⏰ 2:00pm

Walk down to **Piazza San Pietro** (ill. right). Stroll around the piazza to admire its columns and the façade of ⭐**Basilica di San Pietro** (➤ 154), then explore the interior. Security queues into Basilica di San Pietro may take as long as an hour to get through at the busiest times of day.

⏰ 4:00pm

The Via della Conciliazione leads to the **44 Castel Sant'Angelo** (➤ 172). After the tour of the castle take in the view of the nearby Ponte Sant'Angelo (ill. above).

⏰ 5:00pm

You can walk back to the city centre via the bridge, or take the 40 or 64 bus.

Vatican City

⭐8 Basilica di San Pietro

The Basilica di San Pietro (St Peter's) is the world's most famous church, an important place of Catholic pilgrimage, and the one sight in Rome that you simply must see, even though there are few important works of art inside.

History of the Basilica

The church is built over the shrine of St Peter, one of the Apostles and the first pope. The huge basilica you see today is not the original. St Peter himself was crucified during the persecutions of Emperor Nero somewhere between AD64 and 67, probably on the hilly slopes above the present church, and his followers then buried him in a cemetery nearby. The position of his tomb is reputedly marked by the present-day high altar, a notion supported by extensive archaeological work that has taken place around the site since 1939. Some sort of shrine to the saint probably existed by 200, but the first church for which records survive was raised in 326 by Pope Sylvester I during the reign of Constantine the Great, the first Christian emperor. This church survived for well over 1,000 years.

The majestic Piazza San Pietro was designed by Bernini

By 1452, however, its main fabric was in a precarious state, leading Nicholas V, pope at the time, to suggest the construction of a new basilica, funds for which would be collected from across the Christian world. Nicholas had 2,500 wagonloads of stone removed from the Colosseo and carried across the Tiber to prepare for construction. In the event, building only began in 1506, and would proceed – with many false starts and alterations to the original plans – for the best part of 300 years.

Basilica di San Pietro's Architects

The architect charged with designing the new church and pulling down the old one – a task that required 3,000 labourers – was Donato Bramante. He died in 1516, and it was 1539 before Giuliano da Sangallo won a commission to complete the building. His plans proved ill fated, however, and in 1546 Pope Paul III called in Michelangelo to salvage the increasingly troubled project. The artist, then aged 72, demolished Sangallo's additions and advanced an ambitious plan for a colossal dome. Much work on this dome was accomplished by the time of Michelangelo's death in 1564, only for it to be amended in 1590 by another architect, Giacomo della Porta.

In 1605, Carlo Maderno was asked to redesign the church yet again, a scheme that involved, among other things, the construction of the present facade in 1612. Finishing touches were added by the baroque architect,

Vatican City

Gian Lorenzo Bernini. The new church – a monument to
architectural compromise – was eventually consecrated
on 18 November, 1626, precisely 1,300 years after the
consecration of the original basilica.

The Piazza and Basilica
Bernini was responsible not only for last-minute refinements
to the church, but also for **Piazza San Pietro** (1656–67),
the enormous square (340m by 240m/370 by 260 yards)
that provides the Basilica di San Pietro's grand setting.
The piazza's vast colonnades reach out in two half-circles,
symbolizing arms stretching out to embrace visiting pilgrims. The colonnades are four columns deep and contain
284 columns – be sure to hunt out the famous pair of
stone discs, one near each of the square's fountains.
These mark the focus of each colonnade's ellipse, and
the point at which the four sets of columns appear to
line up as a single pillar. The statues surmounting the
colonnades represent 140 saints, while the colossal
350-tonne **obelisk** at the centre of the piazza was brought
to Rome from Egypt by Caligula in AD37. The orb at the
top contains a fragment of the Holy Cross (it was thought
at one time to contain the ashes of Julius Caesar).

The Facade
Note the central balcony, from which a new pope is
proclaimed and where the pope proclaims sainthoods
and delivers his "Urbi et Orbi" blessing on holy days.
Note, too, the statues, which depict Christ, John the
Baptist and 11 of the Apostles – the missing disciple is
St Peter. The most celebrated of the five portals is the

The sheer
scale of
Bernini's
ornate
baldacchino
impresses
many visitors

The dome floodlit at night

one on the extreme right, the **Porta Santa**, which is opened only during Holy Years, the most recent of which was the year 2000. Inside, the overwhelming impression is one of immense size: the church measures 185m (200 yards) long, 119m (390 feet) high at the dome, and can accommodate upward of 60,000 people. For many years it was the largest church in the world. Just inside the entrance, look out for the series of brass line inscriptions on the marble floor which set out the world's next 14 largest churches. Look out, too, for the red porphyry disc a few metres from the entrance which marks the spot where Charlemagne was crowned Holy Roman Emperor in 800.

Fine Arts

The items of genuine artistic merit found among the swathes of marble and decorative artifice are actually few in number, and take less time to see than you might imagine. The first of these is also the greatest: Michelangelo's statue of the *Pietà* (1498–99), which shows Mary cradling the dead Christ. Created when the sculptor was 23, it is Michelangelo's only signed work, the sculptor having reputedly added his name when he heard onlookers disputing the statue's authorship.

Vatican City

A Place of Worship

Farther down the church, the crossing is marked by the high altar – used only by the pope on special occasions – and a vast altar canopy, or *baldacchino* (1624–33), created by Bernini using bronze removed from the roof of the Pantheon. It was created for Urban VIII, a member of the Barberini family, hence the repeated appearance on the work of the Barberini symbol – the bee. Behind you on your right as you face the canopy is a 13th-century statue, *St Peter Enthroned*, unmissable by virtue of its right foot, which has been caressed to smoothness following a 50-day indul-

gence granted by Pius IX in 1857 to anyone kissing the statue after confession. The statue's authorship is disputed: it was long thought to be a fifth-century work, but was later attributed to the 13th-century Florentine sculptor Arnolfo di Cambio.

The right foot of *St Peter Enthroned* has been worn smooth by the kisses of pilgrims

In the apse beyond the high altar stands Bernini's **Cattedra di San Pietro** (1656–65), a bronze canopy built to encase a throne reputedly used by St Peter (although probably dating from the ninth century). To its left and right lie two important papal tombs: Bernini's **Monument to Urban VIII** (1627–47) on the right, and Guglielmo della Porta's **Monument to Paul III** (1551–75) on the left. The latter's female figures of Justice and Prudence are said to be modelled on the Pope's sister and mother. Look also for Antonio Benci detto il Pollaiolo's **Monument to Pope Innocent VIII** (1498) – by the second main pillar of the nave on the right as you walk back toward the entrance. One of the artefacts saved from the old basilica, it shows Innocent twice – once sitting and once recumbent.

All else in the basilica, however, pales into insignificance compared to the views from the **dome**. The entrance is at the end of the right-hand nave, from where you can take the lift or steps to the first stage. From here, more steps lead to the higher drum and gallery, then continue up a steeper and narrower one-way staircase to the topmost lantern.

TAKING A BREAK

Taverna Angelica (➤ 175) is a good choice for a simple meal within easy striking distance of San Pietro.

✚ 204 C4 ✉ Piazza San Pietro, Città del Vaticano
☎ 06 69 88 37 31; 06 69 88 34 62; www.vatican.va
🕐 Basilica: April–Sep daily 7–7; Oct–March 7–6.
Dome: April–Sep daily 8–6; Oct–May 8–5. Grotto: as for Basilica.
🚇 Ottaviano-San Pietro 🚌 40 or 62 to Via della Conciliazione, 64 to close to Piazza San Pietro or 19, 23, 32, 49, 492, 990 to Piazza del Risorgimento
💶 Basilica: free. Dome: €7, Grotto and Treasury: €2.50

Piazza San
Pietro from
the topmost
lantern of
the dome of
the basilica

INSIDER INFO

- A **rigid dress code** is enforced in San Pietro, which is, of course, primarily a place of worship. Women should not wear shorts, short skirts or skimpy tops; they should also avoid displaying bare shoulders. Men should also avoid shorts and muscle shirts and dress with decorum. Romans consider sandals and socks inappropriate, not only in churches but also in restaurants.
- The one thing you should definitely do when you visit the Basilica di San Pietro is **climb the dome**, as the view of the city and surrounding countryside from the top is one of the finest in the area. Try to arrive early, as long queues develop, and pick a day when visibility is good.
- There is plenty to see beneath St Peter's, where you'll find the **Sacre Grotte Vaticane**, a crypt which contains the tombs of numerous popes. The entrance to the stairs down to the crypt is off the right aisle.
- The **Treasury** contains some liturgical relics, chalices and other gifts made to Basilica di San Pietro over the centuries, but its best artefacts are now held in the Musei Vaticani.

Insider
Tip

Centre of the Catholic cosmos

A number of architects worked for around one and a half centuries on St Peter's Basilica, and quite often made alterations to the plans of their predecessors. Nevertheless, the house of worship appears amazingly harmonious and dignified.

St Peter's has the largest nave in Christendom, with room for 60,000 people

❶ **Portico:** Five entrances with bronze latticework lead into the 71m (233 feet) wide, 13.5m (44 feet) deep and 20m (66 feet) high portico. The Porta Santa (Holy Door), which is sealed and only opened every 25 years during a Holy Year, is on the extreme right.

❷ **Nave:** The pillars that separate the chapels are enormous, fluted double pilasters with Corinthian capitals.

❸ **Bronze statue of St Peter:** Pilgrims like to touch the statue's right foot as it is said to bring blessings.

❹ **Cupola:** Four pentagonal columns support the cupola that Michelangelo created to crown the tomb of St Peter. It has a diameter of 42.3m (139 feet) making it slightly smaller than that of the Pantheon with 43.2m (142 feet). From here there is a wonderful view over the Vatican and the city of Rome.

❺ **Apse:** In addition to the Cathedra Petri, the altar created by Bernini, that covers the entire wall, is particularly noteworthy. The angelic hosts hover over it on clouds.

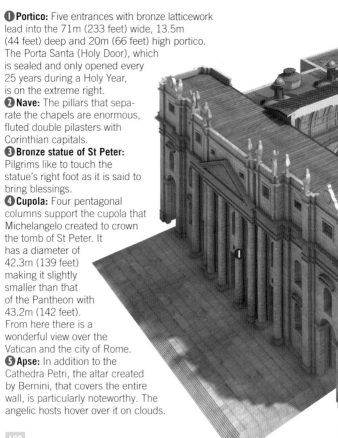

Basilica di San Pietro

6 Grottos and Necropolis: The remains of an earlier building, a Constantine basilica, and the graves of numerous popes can be found in the grottos under San Pietro. It is also said that the mortal remains of Peter the Apostle are preserved here. Peter first of all transferred the centre of the church from Jerusalem to Antioch and then to the capital of the Roman Empire.

The grace of Michelangelo's Pietà is still palpable despite the armoured glass that protects it

★9 Musei Vaticani

Start a visit to the Vatican Museums by concentrating on the main highlights – the Museo Pio-Clementino, which contains the best of the Vatican's many classical sculptures; the frescoes in the Stanze di Raffaello (Raphael Rooms); and the Sistine Chapel, celebrated for Michelangelo's famous ceiling paintings.

Since the inauguration of the new entrance complex in 2000, and extended opening hours, visiting the museums has become slightly less daunting. The scale is vast, and you'll have to be prepared for lengthy queues, random route changes and sudden gallery closures, but judicious planning will help. Check the screens near the ticket desk to see which galleries are open, and then take the escalators up to the gallery entrance to pick up an audio guide. You can get background information on the most popular sights – the Cappella Sistina (➤ 166) and the Stanze di Raffaello (➤ 164) – via the information boards in the Cortile della Pigna.

Museo Pio-Clementino and Galleries

Founded by Pope Clement XIV in 1771 and augmented by his successor, Pius VI, this museum made use of the papacy's immense collection of Greek and Roman antiquities.

These start with the Vestibolo Rotundo, which leads to the Gabinetto dell'Apoxyomenos, dominated by the **Apoxyomenos**, the only known Roman copy of a fourth-century BC Greek masterpiece. It shows an athlete scraping the sweat and dust from his body in the wake of victory. Returning to the Vestibolo, you move left to the **Cortile Ottagono**, which contains some of the greatest classical statues. The most famous is the **Laocoön**, an intricately carved sculptural group dating from around 50BC. Created by sculptors from Rhodes, a Roman copy of the bronze original was found near the Domus Aurea in 1506. It had a huge influence on Renaissance sculptors, especially Michelangelo, who was on site to inspect the new discovery.

Other works in the Cortile include the **Apollo del Belvedere**, a Roman copy of a fourth-century BC Greek bronze original, a masterpiece of classical sculpture which, like the *Laocoön*, greatly influenced Renaissance sculptors. The statue of the young god

Laocoön group, created by Greek sculptors, in the Museo Pio-Clementino

The coffered ceiling of the Galleria delle Carte Geografiche is adorned with frescoes

Apollo originally held a bow in one hand, and is thought to have held an arrow in the other. Also here is a statue of **Hermes**, another Roman copy of a Greek original, and the figure of **Perseus** by Antonio Canova, a 19th-century sculptor influenced by the sculpture of the classical world – his statue here, for example, shows the clear influence of the nearby *Apollo del Belvedere*.

Beyond the Cortile lies the **Sala degli Animali**, a truly charming collection of ancient and 18th-century sculpted animals. Moving on, you reach the Galleria delle Statue, where the highlights are the *Apollo Sauroktonos*, a magnificent Roman copy of a fourth-century BC original showing **Apollo** poised to kill a lizard, and the famed **Candelabri Barberini**, a pair of second-century lamps, which were discovered at the Villa Adriana in Tivoli (► 180). Close to the Sala degli Animali is the Sala delle Muse, which is dominated by the *Torso del Belvedere*, probably a first-century BC Greek work. The gigantic torso was much admired by Michelangelo, whose famous nudes, or *ignudi,* in the Cappella Sistina frescoes were influenced by the figure.

Insider Tip

Statues, Tapestries and Maps

Other statues worth hunting out include the *Venere di Cnido (Venus of Cnidus)* in the Gabinetto delle Maschere, a copy of a famous Greek nude rejected by the islanders of Kos because it was too erotic, and purchased by the Cnidians. Also visit the **Sala a Croce Greca** to see the Sarcofago di Sant'Elena and Sarcofago di Constantina, the sarcophagi – respectively – of the mother and daughter of Emperor Constantine.

Moving on, you should at some stage walk along the long galleries on the upper floors: one is the **Galleria dei Candelabri e degli Arazzi**, which is adorned with superb tapestries, candelabra and other works. This leads on into the **Galleria delle Carte Geografiche**, a long corridor decorated with beautiful painted maps (1580–83) of the Papal States, much of Italy, and the main cities of each region.

Stanze di Raffaello (Raphael Rooms)

Raphael was an artist who died aged just 37 and painted
relatively little. This makes the Stanze di Raffaello, or
Raphael Rooms, which are almost entirely covered in
frescoes by the painter, one of Italy's most treasured artistic
ensembles. The four rooms were commissioned from
Raphael by Pope Julius II in 1508 and completed after

The Stanze di Raffaello are decorated with frescoes by Raphael, here the Stanza dell'Incendio depicting the fire in the Borgo district

the painter's death in 1520 by his pupils: they include scenes inspired by Leo X, who became pope while work was in progress.

The order in which you're allowed to see the rooms varies from month to month, but if possible try to see them in the order in which they were painted. This means beginning with the **Stanza della Segnatura** (1508–11), which served as Julius' library and was the place where he applied his signature *(segnatura)* to papal bulls (edicts). The frescoes here are the rooms' finest – many critics call them an even greater achievement than the Cappella Sistina. The four main pictures provide a celebration of the triumph of Theology, Philosophy, Poetry and Justice, fusing classical, religious, artistic and philosophical themes in a complicated allegorical mixture; it is well worth buying a guide to help decipher the paintings.

Divine Inspiration

The next room to be painted was the **Stanza di Eliodoro** (1512–14), a private antechamber or waiting room. Here the paintings are a form of visual propaganda for Julius and Leo, although their professed theme is the timely intervention of Divine Providence in the defence of an endangered faith. Thus the battle scenes in *The Expulsion of Heliodorus from the Temple* – a reworking of a Biblical story – are an allusion to Julius' skill in defending the Papal States from foreign interference. Similarly, the panel ostensibly showing *Attila the Hun* turning back from Rome actually contains a portrait of the new pope, Leo X (the figure on a donkey). Note the three-part fresco showing *The Deliverance of St Peter from Prison*, the first time Raphael attempted to portray a scene set at night.

The third room chronologically is the **Stanza dell' Incendio** (1514–17), designed as a dining room for Leo X, who asked Raphael to paint a series of scenes that celebrated the achievements of two of his papal namesakes, Leo III and Leo IV. Thus the main frescoes portray the *Coronation of Charlemagne* (a ceremony conducted by Leo III in 800); the *Oath of Leo III* (when Leo denied accusations levelled at him by rivals); the *Battle of Ostia* (where Leo IV showed mercy to a defeated Saracen navy in 848, an allusion to Leo X's attempts to forge a crusade against the Turks); and the *Fire in the Borgo* (in which Leo IV – painted here as Leo X – extinguished a fire near Basilica di San Pietro by making the sign of the Cross).

Much of the Stanza dell'Incendio was painted by pupils working to designs by Raphael, as were the four principal frescoes on the life of the Emperor Constantine in the last room, the **Stanza di Costantino** (1517–24).

Before moving on from the Raphael Rooms, be sure to see the nearby **Cappella di Niccolò V**, a small chapel covered in beautiful frescoes by Fra Angelico showing scenes from the *Lives of St Stephen and St Lawrence* (1447–51).

Vatican City

Cappella Sistina (Sistine Chapel)

You will not want to miss the Cappella Sistina (Sistine Chapel), but expect crowds and considerable pressure to move on to make way for visitors behind you. This can make for a rather unsatisfactory visit, but detracts little from the majesty of Michelangelo's breathtaking frescoes.

The chapel was built for Sixtus IV between 1477 and 1481, and received its first pictorial decoration between 1480 and 1483, when the lower walls were frescoed by several of the leading artists of their day, notably Perugino, Domenico Ghirlandaio and Sandro Botticelli. A quarter of a century elapsed before Michelangelo was commissioned to fresco the chapel's ceiling, which up to that point had been adorned with a simple wash of blue covered in gold and silver stars.

Michelangelo Marvels

Michelangelo supposedly proved reluctant to accept the commission, partly because he viewed painting as a lesser art than sculpture, and partly because he was more concerned with creating a tomb for Julius (never completed). In the event the ceiling would occupy him for four years, work being completed in 1512. The frescoes – controversially restored between 1979 and 1994 – consist of nine main panels, beginning with the five principal events in the Book of Genesis: *The Separation of Light from Darkness; The Creation of the Heavenly Bodies; The Separation of Land and Sea; The Creation of Adam;* and *The Creation of Eve.* These are followed by *The Fall and Expulsion from Paradise; The Sacrifice of Noah, The Flood* and *The Drunkenness of Noah.* Scattered around the ceiling are various painted Prophets, Sibyls, Old Testament characters, and 20 *ignudi,* or nude youths. In all, the painting covers an area of 930sq m (1,110sq yards) and more than 300 individual figures.

Michelangelo's celebrated ceiling frescoes are the most famous paintings in the Cappella Sistina

The ceiling on its own is a masterpiece, but the chapel contains a second, and probably greater, fresco by Michelangelo, the huge ***Last Judgement*** (1536–41) that covers the entire wall behind the altar. Bear in mind while you admire the painting that it was painted a full 22 years after the ceiling frescoes, during which time Rome had been sacked by the forces of Emperor Charles V in 1527, an event which apparently deeply affected Michelangelo and effectively brought to an end the period of optimism of the Renaissance years.

Something of the darker forces affecting the city and the painter can be glimpsed in Michelangelo's uncompromising vision of a pitiless God venting his judgement on a cowering humanity. Those spared in this judgement are portrayed in the fresco rising to Paradise on the left, while those doomed by it are shown sinking to hell on the right. The dead rise from their graves along the lower part of the painting, while Christ stands at its centre, surrounded by the Virgin, Apostles and assorted saints. Of the 391 figures

Vatican City

in the picture, only one is painted gazing directly at the onlooker – the famous damned soul hugging himself as he awaits his doom.

TAKING A BREAK

If you need a respite from sightseeing, visit the Musei Vaticani café or try **Non Solo Pizza** (➤ 174), a few blocks north of Piazza del Risorgimento.

✚ 204 B4–5 ⊠ Viale Vaticano
☎ 06 69 88 46 76; 06 6 98 31 45; mv.vatican.va
🕑 Mon–Sat 9–6 (last entrance 4pm), last Sunday of the month 9–2
(last entrance 12:30pm). Closed on religious and public holidays
🚇 Ottaviano-San Pietro or Cipro-Musei Vaticani 🚌 19, 23, 32, 49, 492, 990
to Piazza del Risorgimento 🎫 €16. Free last Sun of the month (➤ 169).
Book tickets in advance to avoid queues online at biglietteriamusei.vatican.va

One of the Vatican Museums' elaborately decorated corridors

The beautiful ancient mosaics and statues of the Sala Rotonda in the Museo Pio-Clementino

INSIDER INFO

- It's a 10-minute walk from San Pietro to the entrance of the Vatican Museums; if you take a bus or taxi then get out at Piazza del Risorgimento.
- Entrance is **free on the last Sunday of the month**, but this means waiting time can be 2–3 hours. The Musei Vaticani are **open on Monday.**
- Labelling is very poor, so pick up a museum guidebook or an **audio guide**.
- **Binoculars** make sense for the Cappella Sistina.
- From May to October there are guided Friday **night tours** of the Vatican offered by companies such as www.viator.com from €35 (plus €16 museum ticket), but these are booked up very quickly.
- For a glimpse of the inner sanctum of the Vatican City take a **guided tour** of the Vatican Gardens (book at least one week ahead on 06 69 88 46 47 or email visite-guidatesingoli.musei@scv.va).
- It's worth buying **guides** to the Stanze di Raffaello and Cappella Sistina to help appreciate the allusion and meaning in the paintings.

Insider Tip

At Your Leisure

⓭ Musei Vaticani

The following museums and rooms are also part of the Musei Vaticani, to which most visitors will devote less time, or simply walk through en route to the main attractions. Entry details are the same as for the main museum complex (► 168). There are still more museums not discussed below: these include the **Museo Sacro**, the Museum of Christian Art, next to the Sistine Chapel (sacred art from catacombs and early Christian churches in Rome); **Museo Storico** (includes saddles, sedan chairs, carriages and coaches used by the popes, also weapons); **Museo Missionario Etnologico** (anthropological artefacts brought to Rome by missionary and other expeditions); **Museo Chiaramonti** (a huge quantity of Greek and Roman sculpture); and **Museo Gregoriano Profano** (a collection of secular or "profane" art – mostly more Greek and Roman sculpture).

Museo Gregoriano Egizio

The Vatican's Egyptian collection was founded by Pope Pius VII and collected in this nine-room museum by Pope Gregory XVI in 1839. Housed in its 22 rooms are a wide range of mummies, monumental statues, headstones, papyri and sarcophagi from the third millennium BC to the the third century AD. Many were found in and around Rome itself, having been brought to the city from Egypt, which formed part of the Roman Empire for several centuries. Highlights include the sixth-century BC statue of Udya-horres-ne in Room I, the head of a statue of Pharaoh Monthuhotep II (2100–2040BC) in Room V and the bronze censers in room VI.

Museo Gregoriano Etrusco

This 22-room museum is excellent if your interest in the Etruscans – who dominated central Italy before the rise of Rome – is not enough to take you all the way to the much larger Etruscan collection of the Villa Giulia (► 141). Like the Villa Giulia, this museum has its fair share of urns and vases, but it also contains some of the greatest of all Etruscan artefacts. The most celebrated of these is the *Mars of Todi* (Room III), a large bronze statue named after the Umbrian town in which it was found. Also worth special attention are the exhibits of Room II, most of which were taken from the **Regolini-Galassi Tomb** (*c.* 650BC), uncovered in 1836 at Cerveteri just north of Rome. The Etruscans, like the Egyptians, buried the deceased with all manner of everyday items they might need in the afterlife, thereby providing archaeologists with a graphic picture of their domestic and artistic habits.

Sala della Biga

This single marble-decked room, at the entrance to the three galleries (► 163), features a Roman *biga*, or two-horsed chariot, reconstructed in 1788 from first-century elements. Part of it may once have formed a votive offering, but for years was used as an episcopal throne in the church of San Marco. Niches around the walls contain accomplished Greek and Roman statues: some date back as far as the fifth century BC.

Appartamento Borgia

This suite of apartments was built for Pope Alexander VI, a member of the notorious Borgia family, during his papacy (1492–1503). Almost a palace within a palace,

Inside the sumptuous interior of the Biblioteca Apostolica Vaticana

it proved so sumptuous that subsequent popes chose to use it as their principal lodgings for the next hundred years. Room I, the Sala delle Sibille, is where the infamous Cesare Borgia is said to have had Alfonso of Aragon, the husband of his sister, Lucrezia Borgia, murdered. Today, the room is more remarkable for its frescoes, part of a fine series of paintings in the suite executed between 1492 and 1495 by the Umbrian artist Pinturicchio. The pictures cover a wide variety of themes, embracing religious, humanist and mythical subjects – the best are in Room V, the Sala dei Santi. Other rooms in this complex

are given over to the **Collezione d'Arte Religiosa** Moderna, a collection of modern religious art.

Biblioteca Apostolica Vaticana

The Vatican Library easily rates as the world's most valuable collection of books and manuscripts. Books were accumulated by the popes for centuries, but only found a permanent home in 1474 during the papacy of Sixtus IV. Material has been systematically added to the library ever since, amounting

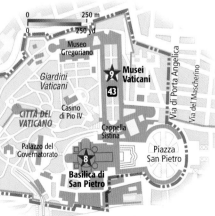

Vatican City

to some 100,000 manuscripts, 70,000 archive volumes, 800,000 printed works, 100,000 prints and maps, and around 75,000 hand-written and illustrated books.

The library has been closed to tourists since 2007, functioning as an academic research library only, and its treasures are no longer on display. You can, however, admire the decorated hall (Salone Sistino), which once housed the library.

Pinacoteca Vaticana
Even on its own, the Vatican's Pinacoteca, or art gallery, would be considered one of Rome's major collections of medieval, Renaissance and other paintings. Its 18 rooms offer a chronological insight into the development of religious art, and would be richer

An apostle in Angeli e Apostoli Musicati by Melozzo da Forlì, Pinacoteca Vaticana

still had Napoleon not pilfered many of their treasures at the beginning of the 19th century.

44 Castel Sant' Angelo
A few hundred yards east of the Vatican the bulwarks the mighty fortress of Castel Sant' Angelo rise on the banks of the Tiber. Today, the castle is a museum, but it started life in AD130 as a mausoleum for Emperor Hadrian. Its circular design – which formed the basis for all subsequent structures on the site – was copied from the Mausoleo di Augusto near the Capitoline Hill, which in turn was probably based on the design of Etruscan tombs. The mausoleum was used as a

---

HISTORY AND GEOGRAPHY WITH A DIFFERENCE
The views from the top of the dome of the **Basilica di San Pietro** (➤ 158) will delight children, although the climb up may be difficult (you have to be very fit to be able to carry a toddler up all the steps). The **Castel Sant'Angelo** (➤ above), not only looks like a "real" castle but is also fascinating to children with its eerie atmosphere, dark corridors and hidden corners.

In the Vatican Museums you can make a choice between the animal figures in the **Sala degli Animali** (➤ 163), the maps of the **Galleria delle carte Geografiche** (➤ 163) or the mummies in the **Museo Gregoriano Egizio** (➤ 170).

At Your Leisure

OFF THE BEATEN TRACK

For a glimpse of the inner sanctum of Vatican City (most of which is reserved for those people working or living in this tiny state), book on to one of the tours of the **Vatican Gardens** (► 169). Outside Vatican City, the small grid of streets known as the Borgo – between Borgo Sant'Angelo and Via Crescenzio – is the least-visited enclave near St Peter's.

Insider Tip

offer excellent views across the city. Immediately below, look out for the Ponte Sant'Angelo, a bridge adorned with statues of angels sculpted to a design by Bernini. The castle's various military and other exhibits are fairly dull, unlike the beautifully decorated papal apartments and libraries woven into the fortress's labyrinth of rooms.

➕ 205 D4
✉ Lungotevere Castello, 50 ☎ 06 6 81 91 11; www.castelsantangelo.beniculturali.it
🕐 Tue–Sun 9–7:30
🚌 30, 49, 70, 87, 130, 186 and other services to Piazza Cavour and Lungotevere
💶 €8.50

resting place for emperors until AD271, when it was incorporated into the city's defences. It then remained Rome's principal fortress for more than 1,000 years.

On entering the castle, you walk along subterranean passages, part of the original Roman-era mausoleum, then climb up to the ramparts, which

Statues of angels line the Ponte Sant'Angelo on the way up to Castel Sant'Angelo

Where to...
Eat and Drink

Prices
Prices are for a starter and a main course excluding drinks:
€ under €30   **€€** €30–€50   **€€€** over €50

The area around St Peter's and the Vatican suffers from a shortage of good restaurants compared to other parts of the city. Once, the grid of streets between Via della Conciliazione and Via Crescenzio, an area known as the Borgo, was filled with artisans' workshops and traditional little eating places. Most have gone now. But not to worry, there are enough options for a quick snack.

Dal Toscano €€
This lively restaurant is convenient for the Vatican Museums, being just east of the entrance on Via Germanico between Viale Ottaviano and Via Vespasiano. It's also popular with locals and families, so reservations are recommended, at least in the evenings. As the name suggests, this is not a place for Roman specialities, but rather the thick *bistecca alla fiorentina* (T-bone steaks), ribollita soups, and other staples of Tuscany.
➕ 204 C5 ✉ Via Germanico, 58–60
☎ 06 39 72 57 17
🕐 Tue–Sun 12:30–3, 7:30–11.
Closed 1 week in Dec and 2 weeks in Aug

Gran Caffè Esperia €
Right beside the river, and not far from Castel Sant'Angelo (➤ 172), this beautifully restored, *fin-de-siècle* café is open all day for everything from a true Roman coffee and *cornetti* (croissant) breakfast to lunchtime sandwiches and evening long drinks and cocktails. The setting is lovely, and there are tables outside.

➕ 205 F5 ✉ Lungotevere dei Millini, 1
☎ 06 32 11 00 16 🕐 May–Sep daily 7am–midnight, Oct–April 7am–9:30pm

Les Étoiles €€€
This is one of the great Roman restaurants for a treat or celebration. From the moment you enter the stylish dining room and see the view of San Pietro you know you're in for something special. The Italian food and courteous service are as good as the view, and the menu changes from day to day. The restaurant forms part of the Atlante Star hotel, and has a roof garden and a terrace for dining outside.
➕ 205 D4 ✉ Via dei Bastioni, 1
☎ 06 6 87 32 33 🕐 noon–2:30, 7:30–10:30

Isola della Pizza €
This long-established and much-loved local restaurant got a complete facelift in 2010, but the welcome remains as warm and the pizza just as good. There's a huge antipasto choice, pizza featuring well-sourced ingredients from all over Italy, and they also serve grills and pasta.
➕ 204 C5 ✉ Via della Scipione, 45
☎ 06 39 73 34 83
🕐 Thu–Tue 12:30–3, 7:30–midnight

Non Solo Pizza €
Non Solo Pizza (Not Only Pizza) serves pizza by the slice (and full pizzas after 7pm) and a selection of Roman-style deep-fried delicacies: stuffed olives, rice and cheese balls, courgette flowers and the like. It also serves a limited daily

selection of inexpensive hot dishes, a good option for lunch after a visit to the Vatican Museums. The restaurant is in a side street north of Piazza Risorgimento.

➕ 204 C5 ✉ Via degli Scipioni, 95–97
☎ 06 3 72 58 20 🕐 Tue–Sun 8:30am–9:30pm

Osteria dell'Angelo €€

You need to reserve a table at this popular restaurant on a side street just north of the busy Viale delle Milizie. The sophisticated cooking goes beyond the usual local and Italian staples, while the decoration is dominated by sporting photographs, a nod to the rugby-playing past of the owner, the eponymous Angelo. On balmy evenings you can eat outdoors.

➕ 204, north of B5 ✉ Via Giovanni Bettolo, 32
☎ 06 3 72 94 70 🕐 Tue–Fri 12:45–2:30, 8–11, Mon, Sat 8–11

Osteria Croce €

This is a reasonably convenient option for the Vatican Museums: just walk north up Via Leone IV and turn right after six blocks to find this very popular and traditional trattoria patronized mostly by Romans.

➕ 204, north of B5
✉ Via Giovanni Bettoio, 24
☎ 06 3 72 94 70 🕐 Tue, Fri 1–2:30, 8–11, Mon, Wed–Thu, Sat 8–11

Paninoteca da Guido €

If you want a quick snack after a morning in the Vatican, you'll find a counter full of tasty ingredients at this tiny place on a street just behind the Via della Conciliazione. Choose your *panino* and it will be filled with meat, salami, cheese and salad ingredients, which you can eat on the spot – there are a few tables outside – or take away. There are also delicious pasta dishes at lunchtime and a range of snacks is available all day.

➕ 205 D4 ✉ Borgo Pio, 3
☎ 06 6 87 54 91
🕐 Mon–Sat 8–6

Pizzarium €

A few minutes' walk from the Vatican Museums, this snack bar is a good bet for all-day pizzas and drinks. Unlike many tourist-aimed joints, this one offers the real thing, combining slow-rise dough with imaginative toppings, which make use of local, seasonal ingredients, including fresh rocket, aubergine, pesto or artichoke.

➕ 204 A5 ✉ Via della Meloria, 43
☎ 06 39 74 54 16
🕐 Mon–Sat 12:30–2:30, 7–11

Taberna de' Gracchi €/€€

The Taberna de' Gracchi is a reliable and convenient restaurant for lunch if you have visited the Castel Sant'Angelo, for it lies just north of the Castel, close to Piazza Cola di Rienzo.

➕ 205 E5 ✉ Via dei Gracchi, 266–8
☎ 06 3 21 31 26; www.tabernagracchi.com
🕐 Tue–Sat 12:30–2:30, 7:30–10:30, Mon 7:30–10:30

Taverna Angelica €€

This best mid-range restaurant within easy reach of St Peter's lies in the heart of the Borgo. Despite its location, it is not a typical Roman trattoria, for the modern interior is minimalist, and the cooking light, innovative and biased toward seafood. The wine list is excellent, and includes some by the glass. Tables are limited, so make a reservation.

➕ 204 C4 ✉ Piazza Amerigo Capponi, 6
☎ 06 6 87 45 14; www.tavernaangelica.it
🕐 Dinner only: daily 7pm–midnight, plus Sun lunch 12–2:30. Closed 3 weeks in Aug

Tre Pupazzi €/€€

If you can't get into Taverna Angelica, try this 400-year-old place just around the corner. It is far more traditional in appearance and cuisine, and serves good fish, pizzas and pasta dishes.

➕ 205 D4 ✉ Via dei Tre Pupazzi, 1
☎ 06 6 86 83 71
🕐 Mon–Sat 12:30–2:30, 7:30–11

Where to…
Shop

The shops surrounding the Vatican and St Peter's mainly sell **religious souvenirs** and postcards. Some of them are acceptable, but most are just expensive kitsch. Borgo's grid of streets contain the occasional **artisan's workshop**, but nothing to compare with the workshops on Via dei Cappellari and around Campo de' Fiori (►86). One exception is **Italia Garipoli** (Borgo Vittorio, 91a; tel: 06 68 80 21 96, closed Sun), which sells linens, curtains and fabrics.

Where you will find a variety of shops is in the mainly modern streets north of Via Crescenzio, and in particular Via Cola di Rienzo, one of the busiest shopping streets in northwest Rome. The street has a wide variety of shops selling mid-range clothes, shoes and other commodities, but is especially known for its *alimentari* – **food shops**. One of the best known is **Castroni** (Via Cola di Rienzo, 196; tel: 06 6 87 43 83; www.castroni.com; closed Sun), which combines Italian staples (cheese, hams, olive oils and so on) with food specialities from around the world.

Alternatively, visit **Franchi** (Via Cola di Rienzo, 200–204; tel: 06 6 87 46 51; closed Sun), one of Rome's most mouth-watering delicatessens, where you can buy picnic provisions or order delicious take-out sandwiches and snack lunches.

Prati has a very flash new gourmet store, **Romeo Chef and Baker (**Via Silla, 26a; tel: 06 32 11 01 20; 9am–midnight), an ultra-modern branch of the well-known Roscioli delicatessen in the city centre.

Where to…
Go Out

Since 1958 the **Auditorium Conciliazione** (formerly the Auditorio Pio; Via della Conciliazione, 4; tel: 06 68 43 91, 800 90 45 60; www.auditorium conciliazione.it), close to St Peter's, has staged a variety of classical music concerts.

Rome's foremost classical musical association, the **Accademia Nazionale di Santa Cecilia** (tel: 06 80 24 25 01, www.santacecilia.it) has its own orchestra, and also organizes concerts with visiting choirs, orchestras and other ensembles.

Superb choral and organ music can be heard in St Peter's. The Accademia is among many organizations that perform at Rome's spectacular **Auditorium Parco della Musica** (►148).

Music of a different sort can be heard two blocks north of the entrance to the Vatican Museums at **Alexanderplatz** (Via Ostia, 9, off Via Leone; tel: 06 39 74 21 71; www.alexanderplatz.it, Mon–Sat 9pm–2:30am). This is probably Rome's best venue for live jazz; international jazz greats such as Dave Brubeck and Chet Baker have left their autographs and graffiti on its walls.

Another good pub-club for hearing live jazz, blues and rock is the long-running **Fonclea** (Via Crescenzio, 82a; tel: 06 6 89 63 02; daily 7 or 8pm–2am; admission usually free except Sat).

Similar music can be heard farther north, in a side street off Via della Giuliana, at the **Four Green Fields** pub (Via C Morin, 38; off Via della Giuliana; tel: 06 3 72 50 91; daily 6pm–2am; admission generally free).

Excursions

Excursions

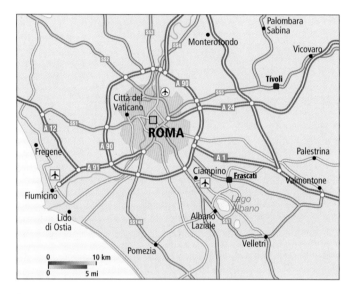

Rome is so filled with museums, ancient monuments and other sightseeing temptations that many people on a short visit prefer to stay in the city, rather than visiting the variety of towns and sights within the vicinity.

However, there are two interesting excursions, which are easily made and offer an excellent counterpoint to the city and – should you need it – an escape from its often busy streets. The most popular is **Tivoli**, a town to the east of Rome, known for its gardens and the **Villa Adriana**, the ruins of Emperor Hadrian's vast private villa. The second is **Frascati**, a town nestled on the slopes of the Alban Hills, the volcanic peaks that rise just south of the city. Easily reached by train from Termini, the town is best known for its white wine, cooling summer breezes and lofty views over Rome.

Those with more time to spend exploring the area might also want to investigate **Ostia Antica**, Rome's old sea port, and today an extensive archaeological park to the west of the city. Farther up the coast to the north are **Cerveteri** and **Tarquinia**, two major Etruscan towns with large ancient necropolises containing thousands of tombs, while inland to the south lies **Palestrina**, known for its great pre-Roman temple.

If you want a complete change, consider **Orvieto**, a fascinating Umbrian hill town with an outstanding cathedral, around 80 minutes from Rome by train.

Tivoli

The ancient town of Tivoli – Roman Tibur – is the most popular one-day excursion from Rome. Some 36km (22 miles) from the city, it's known for two principal sights: the Villa d'Este, a Renaissance villa celebrated for its gardens, and the Villa Adriana, a vast Roman-era villa and grounds created by Emperor Hadrian. Also worth seeing are the more recent and more rugged grounds of the Villa Gregoriana.

Villa d'Este

The Villa d'Este began life as a Benedictine convent, but was converted into a country villa in 1550 for Cardinal Ippolito d'Este. The cardinal was a wealthy collector, patron of the arts and a scion of Italy's noble families – he was the son of Lucrezia Borgia. Today, following years of restoration, the villa and its extraordinary gardens are a UNESCO World Heritage Site. Stroll through the frescoed, stuccoed rooms of the villa, with its panoramic terraces and balconies, before walking into the gardens, the main reason for visiting the villa.

First laid out as an escape from Rome's summer heat, it was **water** that inspired the gardens' design, and it cascades, spouts, falls, tumbles and trickles in small fountains – there are more than **500 jets**. Don't miss the **Viale delle Cento Fontane** (Avenue of One Hundred Fountains), a long walk lined with cascades and jets of water; Bernini's elegant **Fontana della Bicchierone** and the **Fontana dell'Organo Idraulico**, mechanical **Organ** and **Owl Fountains**, of which the former plays music, while the latter has singing birds which fall silent when an owl appears.

Detail of water spouts along the Viale delle Cento Fontane path

Villa Gregoriana

The Villa Gregoriana is generally less crowded than the Villa d'Este and – although not particularly well maintained – is perhaps more interesting and beautiful. Centred on a pair of waterfalls and a 60m (200-foot) gorge cut by the River Aniene, it lies in the town's northeast corner about 300m (330 yards) from the Villa d'Este. The park was created in 1831 when Pope Gregory XVI built tunnels to divert the waters

Excursions

of the Aniene to protect Tivoli from flooding. From the ticket office follow the path signposted to the Grande Cascata, or Large Waterfall, which brings you to steps and a terrace overlooking the waterfall. Other paths nearby meander around the lush and often overgrown park, passing through the ruins of a Roman villa, among other things, and dropping down to the valley floor past ancient shrines and grottos before a long climb up the other side of the gorge past the ruined Temple of Vesta.

Villa Adriana

Leave plenty of time for the Villa Adriana as its site covers an area equal to that of early Republican Rome on the Capitoline and Palatine Hills – making it probably the largest villa ever created in the Roman world. It was begun in AD125 and completed ten years later by Emperor Hadrian. Many of its treasures, statues and stone have long gone, but the site remains a wonderfully pretty and romantic place, and enough survives of the villa's many buildings to evoke their original grandeur.

Hadrian reproduced or adapted the designs of many of the great buildings he had visited during his travels around the Empire: the "Pecile" colonnade through which you enter, for example, reproduces the Stoa Poikile of Athens in Greece. A small museum displays finds made in the ongoing excavations, but you will get most pleasure by simply wandering the site at random. Be sure to walk along the sunken stone passageway (known as a *cryptoporticus*) while exploring the Villa Adriana. Past artists have burned their names on the ceiling with candle smoke. To reach the Villa Adriana from Tivoli, take a taxi or catch the local CAT bus, No 4 or 4X, from the bus station in Piazza Massimo, or from the stop outside the tourist office on Largo Garibaldi.

The columns and statues that line the Canopus at the Villa Adriana are copies from the Temple of Serapis near Alexandria

TAKING A BREAK

A good restaurant choice in Tivoli is **Il Grottino della Sibilla dal** (Piazza Rivaroli, 21; tel: 07 74 33 26 06; closed Mon). Out of town, on the road to the Villa Adriana, the best option is **Adriano** (Largo Marguerite Yourcenar, 2; tel: 07 74 38 22 35; daily, closed Sun pm in winter); you can eat outside in summer. Alternatively, buy food and drink from shops in Tivoli and take them to the Villa Adriana for a picnic.

The Viale delle Cento Fontane at the Villa d'Este

Villa d'Este

✉ Piazza Trento, Tivoli ☎ Toll free in Italy: 199 76 61 66; 07 74 3 35 58 50
(for disabled bookings); www.villadestetivoli.info
🕐 May–Aug daily 8:30–6:45; Sep 8:30–6:15; Oct 8:30–5:30;
Nov–Jan 8:30–4; Feb 8:30–4:30; March 8:30–5:15; April 8:30–6:30 💶 €8

Villa Gregoriana

✉ Piazza Tempio di Vesta, Tivoli ☎ 07 74 39 96 77 01; www.villagregoriana.it
🕐 Apr to mid-Oct Tue–Sun 10–6:30;
March, mid-Oct to Nov Tue–Sat 10–2:30, Sun 10–4 💶 €6

Villa Adriana

✉ Via di Villa Adriana, just outside Tivoli, ☎ 06 39 96 79 00
🕐 May–Aug daily 9–7:30; March, Oct 9–6:30; April, Sep 9–7;
Nov–Jan 9–5; Feb 9–6 💶 €8

INSIDER INFO

Getting there The blue Cotral buses to Tivoli depart approximately every 10 to
20 minutes from the Ponte Mammolo station on the Metro B line. Note that the
fastest Roma–Tivoli bus, via the *autostrada*, takes about 50 minutes to the centre
of Tivoli, and thus near the Villa d'Este, but the bus stops some 2.5km (1.5 miles)
from the somewhat remote Villa Adriana. If you first want to visit Hadrian's villa,
rather take the Roma–Tivoli bus via Prenestina, the Villa Adriana stop is about
300m (330 yards) away. In summer there is a shuttle bus between the Villa Adriana
and the centre of Tivoli.

- Tivoli's **visitor centre** lies close to the entrance to the Villa d'Este on the north
  side of Largo Garibaldi (tel: 07 74 31 12 49).
- The Villa d'Este is extremely popular, so be prepared for lots of visitors.
  Try to get there as early as possible there.
- In the Villa Adriana look out for the **Teatro Marittimo**, or Maritime Theatre, a small
  colonnaded palace built by Hadrian on an island in an artificial lagoon. It is thought
  that this was the emperor's private retreat.

Insider Tip

Frascati

Frascati offers a cool, calm retreat from Rome's heat and hustle on hot summer days, providing a pleasant combination of good food, local wine and sweeping views of the city.

If you have time to spare, Frascati is the place to go. Trains depart from Termini approximately hourly and the journey takes about 30 minutes. You are treated to an ever-more attractive rural outlook as the train wends its way into the Colli Albani (Alban Hills), to the south of Rome. Steps from Frascati's small station lead through gardens to Piazzale (or Piazza) Marconi, the town's principal square, home to the visitor centre at No 1 (tel: 06 9420 33 1; www.aptprov roma.it). Above the square stands the **Villa Aldobrandini**, one of the few old buildings to survive the bombing during 1943 and 1944 that destroyed 80 per cent of old Frascati.

The villa was built for Cardinal Pietro Aldobrandini between 1598 and 1603 and is still owned by the Aldobrandini family. Though the villa itself is closed to the public, some of the grounds, which are noted for the excellent views over Rome in the hazy distance, can be visited. Look out for the gardens' Teatro dell'Acqua, a semi-circular array of fountains and statues in which the central figure of Atlas is said to be a representation of Pope Clement VIII.

Frascati's other major public park is the less appealing **Villa Torlonia**, entered from close to the town hall building (the Municipio) near Piazzale Marconi. In the rest of the town, leave a short time for the rebuilt Duomo in Piazza San Pietro and the church of the Gesù (Piazza del Gesù), known for its late 17th-century paintings by Andrea dal Pozzo.

Sculpture of Polyphemus in the gardens of Villa Aldobrandini

TAKING A BREAK

Cacciani (Via Armando Diaz, 13; tel: 06 9 40 19 91; closed Mon, also Sun pm in winter), which has an outdoor terrace for dining in summer, is the best restaurant in Frascati. For something simpler and less expensive, try **Zarazà** (Viale Regina Margherita, 45; tel: 06 9 42 20 53; closed Mon, also Sun pm Sep–May).

Villa Aldobrandini gardens

🕐 Apr–Sep Mon–Fri 9–1, 3–6; Oct–March 9–1, 3–5

💶 Free, though passes must be obtained from Visitor Centre (see above; closed Sat pm and all day Sun)

Walks & Tours

1 GHETTO TO TRASTEVERE
Walk

DISTANCE 4.25km (2.6 miles) **TIME** Allow 3–4 hours
START POINT Piazza del Campidoglio ✚ 207 E4
END POINT Campo de' Fiori ✚ 205 E3

This walk takes you to three of the city's smaller and prettier enclaves: the old Jewish Ghetto area, a lovely labyrinth of quiet streets; the Isola Tiberina, an island on the River Tiber; and the Trastevere district, an equally appealing but better-known collection of cobbled lanes, tiny squares, shops, cafés and restaurants.

🔲–🔲

Start in **Piazza del Campidoglio** (►50) just off Piazza Venezia. With the church of Santa Maria in Aracoeli on your left, walk to the rear of the piazza and take the lane on the right of Palazzo Senatorio, the palace ahead of you. Follow the lane as it winds downhill, admiring the views of the **Foro Romano** (►52) on your left. Turn right at the bottom on Via della Consolazione and cross Piazza della Consolazione. Bear left off the piazza down Via San Giovanni Decollato. At the end of this street on the left stands **San Giorgio in Velabro**. The church takes its name from the marshy area (the Velabro) by the Tiber where – according to legend – the shepherd Faustulus found Romulus and Remus, Rome's founding twins (►11). The church's simple Romanesque interior – almost bare save for an apse fresco – is one of the city's finest. There are two ancient arches nearby: the one adjoining the church is **Arco degli Argentari** (Arch of the Moneychangers) erected in AD204

in honour of Emperor Septimius Severus; the other, in the short Via del Velabro in front of the church, is the **Arco di Giano**, and dates from the time of Constantine (fourth century).

🔲–🔲

Continue down Via del Velabro and Passaggio di San Giovanni Decollato, which open into the large **Piazza Bocca della Verità**. On the right, in an area of grass

Isola Tiberina (Tiber Island) with the Ponte Rotto

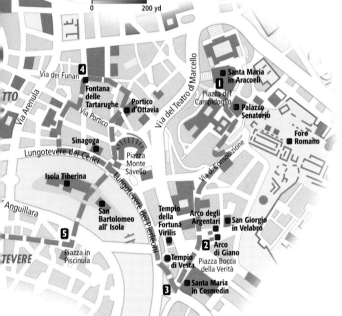

and trees, stand two almost perfectly preserved Roman temples: the circular Tempio di Vesta and rectangular Tempio della Fortuna Virilis (both second century BC). On the piazza's left (south) flank stands the 12th-century church of **Santa Maria in Cosmedin**. In the portico, on the left side as you face the church, look for the round stone relief (an old Roman drain cover) known as the Bocca della Verità (Mouth of Truth). Legend claims that the mouth will clamp shut on the hands of dissemblers. The church, one of the few in the city to have escaped a baroque makeover, vies with San Clemente for the title of Rome's loveliest medieval interior.

Walks & Tours

La Fontana delle Tartarughe in
Piazza Mattei

3–4

From the area in front of the
church walk northwest following
the line of the Tiber on Lungotevere
dei Pierleoni. Continue past Piazza
Monte Savello on your right until
Lungotevere dei Pierleoni becomes
Lungotevere dei Cenci and you
see Rome's distinctive **Sinagoga**
(synagogue) ahead of you on the
right. Turn right, before you pass
the synagogue, on Via del Portico
d'Ottavia. This takes you to the
Portico d'Ottavia, a tiny fragment
of a great Roman building begun
in 146 BC, now partly enmeshed
in the eighth-century church of
Sant'Angelo in Pescheria. Turn right
(north) here on Via del Sant'Angelo
in Pescheria and then left at the
top of the street on Via dei Funari.

This takes you to **Piazza Mattei**
and the heart of Rome's old Jewish
Ghetto, where Jews were segregated
after 1556 and the walls torn down
in 1848. But the worst day of the
ghetto was yet to come: 16 October
1943, at Portico d'Ottavia, the
Gestapo loaded 2091 Jews on to
trucks destined for concentration
camps – for many a journey of
no return. Despite this many
Jewish families are still based in
the area. Piazza Mattei is known
for having one of the city's most
charming fountains, the **Fontana
delle Tartarughe**, (Fountain of
the Tortoises). The fountain was
created by Taddeo Landini, but
the delightful bronze tortoises were
added by the great Gian Lorenzo
Bernini in the restoration of 1658.

4–5

From Piazza Mattei you should
explore some of the surrounding
side streets and piazzas for a
flavour of the area. Then take
Via della Reginella left (south) off
the piazza, and at Via del Portico
d'Ottavia turn right then left
through Piazza delle Cinque Scuole
to rejoin Lungotevere dei Cenci.
Turn left and then first right on
the Ponte Fabricio which crosses
the Tiber to the **Isola Tiberina**
(Tiber Island). Much of the island
is given over to a hospital, continuing a tradition begun in 291 BC
when a temple here was dedicated
to Aesculapius, the god of healing.
You can take the steps down to
the river before looking into the
10th-century church of San
Bartolomeo in the square in front
of the piazza, before crossing the
Ponte Cestio on the island's south
side. This brings you to the
Trastevere district (➤ 101).

5–6

Beyond the Ponte Cestio cross
the main, busy Lungotevere
dell'Anguillara and continue
straight into Piazza in Piscinula.

Go down the steps and turn right out of the piazza on Via della Lungaretta. Cross Piazza Sonnino-Viale di Trastevere and pick up the continuation of Via della Lungaretta and follow it to Piazza di Santa Maria in Trastevere and the church of **Santa Maria in Trastevere** (➤ 102). Walk out of the piazza to the right of the church as you face it, then bear right at the rear of the church into Piazza Sant'Egidio. From the piazza follow Via della Scala until you reach Via Garibaldi. Turn right here on Via di San Dorotea, which leads to Piazza Trilussa, a small square almost on the Tiber. From here cross the Tiber on the pedestrians-only Ponte Sisto, turn left and then take the right fork into **Via Giulia**, which is framed by a pretty vine-draped archway.

Santa Maria in Trastevere

6–7

Walk down Via Giulia, one of Rome's most elegant streets, noting the stone skulls decorating the facade of **Santa Maria dell'Orazione e Morte** (➤ 106) on the left at the junction with Via dei Farnesi. Via Giulia was laid out in 1508 for Pope Julius II (hence Giulia), providing what, at the time, was the city's main approach to St Peter's. In 1655 a major city prison was established at the present-day No 52.

Where Via Giulia opens out into a piazza, turn right onto Vicolo della Moretta, a short street that takes you to a junction of several more streets. If you have time, turn left here and walk a little way down Via dei Banchi Vecchi, which, like Via Giulia, is dotted with interesting

shops. Otherwise, turn right on Via del Pellegrino and then turn first right on Via dei Cappellari.

7–8

Via dei Cappellari is one of the most distinctive streets in this part of Rome, chiefly because it retains some traditional workshops, most of which are given over to furniture-making and restoration. It has a long history of artisanship, taking its name from the *cappellari*, or hatters, who were once based here. Other streets in the vicinity are named after similar trades (Via dei Baullari – the street of the trunk-makers; Via dei Chiavari – the street of the locksmiths; and Via dei Giubonnari – the street of the tailors). Continue down Via dei Cappellari, passing under the dark arch midway down and you emerge into **Campo de' Fiori**, the ideal place to enjoy a lunch or a relaxing break (➤ 86).

PLACES TO VISIT

Santa Maria in Cosmedin

✚ 207 E3

✉ Piazza della Bocca della Verità, 18

☎ 06 6 78 77 59 🕑 Apr–Sep daily 9:30–6; Oct–March 9:30–5

2 PIAZZA VENEZIA TO PIAZZA NAVONA
Walk

DISTANCE 3km (1.9 miles) TIME Allow 2–3 hours
START POINT Piazza Venezia ✚ 207 E5
END POINT Piazza Navona ✚ 205 F3

This walk meanders through the heart of the medieval and Renaissance city, taking you to several key sights – notably the Fontana di Trevi (Trevi Fountain) – but also to a succession of lesser churches, streets and monuments that you might not otherwise discover on a tour of the area's major attractions.

Right: The magnificent Fontana di Trevi floodlit at night

❶–❷

Start on the northern flank of **Piazza Venezia** (►72) facing the Monumento a Vittorio Emanuele II. Walk out of the piazza to your left (east) along Via Cesare Battisti and turn left into Piazza dei SS Apostoli. On your right in the piazza stands the 15th-century Palazzo Colonna, home to the **Galleria Colonna**, an art gallery filled with first-rank paintings by mostly Italian masters. Alongside to the left lies the church of SS Apostoli. Behind a palace-like facade, the baroque interior is known for its huge altarpiece by Domenico Muratori, and Antonio Canova's 1789 Tomb of Clement XIV, in the north (left) aisle by the sacristy door. Continue to the end of Piazza dei SS Apostoli.

❷–❸

Turn right at the junction with Via del Vaccaro and first left on Via dell'Archetto. Cross Via dell' Umiltà and carry on down Via delle Vergini. Turn right on Via delle Muratte to emerge in the square containing the **Fontana di Trevi** (►124). Take Via dei Crociferi from the piazza's

northwest corner (to the rear left as you face the fountain) and continue straight on along Via dei Sabini to emerge on Via del Corso. Across the Corso to the right lies the open area of Piazza Colonna, named after the **Colonna di Marco Aurelio** at its heart. The column was raised between AD180 and 196 to celebrate the military victories of Marcus Aurelius in northern Europe. The sculpted reliefs portray episodes from the Emperor's campaigns.

❸–❹

Walk across Piazza Colonna and through either of the small streets off its western flank – Via della Colonna Antonina is the one on the left. Either one brings you to Piazza di Montecitorio, another large piazza, dominated by Bernini's 1650 **Palazzo di Montecitorio**, seat

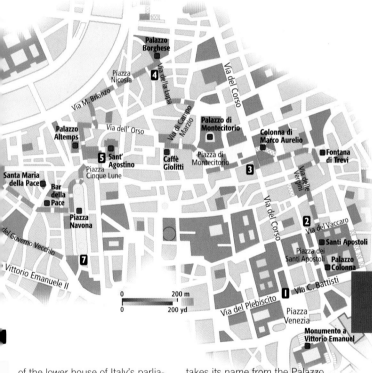

of the lower house of Italy's parliament, the Camera dei Deputati. Take Via Uffici di Vicario west off the piazza, passing the historic Caffè Giolitti on the left, then turn right up Via di Campo Marzio. Take the third left, Via dei Prefetti, and then turn right on Via della Lupa to emerge in **Piazza Borghese**, which

takes its name from the Palazzo Borghese, the large palace across the street.

4–5

Bear left from the piazza along Via del Clementino and continue on through Piazza Nicosia and west along Via di Monte Brianzo (the river is on your right). Turn left off Via dl Monte Brlanzo on Via del Cancello, right on Via dell'Orso, and then almost immediately left on Via Gigli d'Oro. You then emerge in Piazza di Sant'Apollinare with the **Palazzo Altemps** on your right (➤ 97). To your left down an alley stands the church of **Sant'Agostino** (➤ 106), known for Caravaggio's painting, *Madonna di Loreto* in the first chapel in the left aisle (➤ 27), Raphael's fresco, *The Prophet Isaiah* (third pillar on the left), and Jacopo Sansovino's statue, the *Madonna del Parto* (1521), venerated by expectant mothers.

5–6

Return to Piazza di Sant'Apollinare and walk south to the adjoining Piazza Cinque Lune and into **Piazza Navona** (➤ 88). Take Via di Sant'Agnese in Agone (which

TAKING A BREAK
Try the trendy, ever-popular Bar della Pace (➤ 114) or the equally hip, but quieter Bar del Fico (➤ 117). Alternatively, there are plenty of cafés from which to choose in Piazza Navona.

PLACES TO VISIT
Galleria Colonna
🔲 208 A5 ✉ Via della Pilotta, 17
☎ 06 6 78 43 50 🕐 Sat 9–1, or by request
🎫 €12

Sant'Agostino
🔲 205 F4 ✉ Piazza di Sant'Agostino
☎ 06 68 80 19 62
🕐 Daily 7:30–12:30, 4–6:30

Santa Maria della Pace
🔲 205 E4 ✉ Vicolo dell'Arco della Pace, 5
☎ 06 6 86 11 56
🕐 Mon, Wed, Sat 9–12

Chiesa Nuova
🔲 205 E3 ✉ Piazza della Chiesa Nuova
☎ 06 6 87 52 89
🕐 Daily 7:30–12, 4 or 4:30–7

becomes Via di Tor Millina) midway down the piazza on its west side. You might pause for a drink at Bar della Pace (➤ 114) on the corner of Via della Pace. As you face the bar, a short distance away to its right stands **Santa Maria della Pace**, a charming (if rarely open) church begun in 1482. It contains frescoes of the Sibyls by Raphael and a cloister added in 1504 by Bramante, one of the architects of St Peter's. Return to the bar and turn right down Via della Pace and then straight on down Vicolo delle Vacche and Via della Vetrina. Turn left on **Via dei Coronari**, renowned for its antiques shops. At the end of the street continue straight down the short Vicolo del Curato to emerge on Via del Banco di Santo Spirito. You may wish to turn right here to look at the **Ponte Sant'Angelo** and **Castel Sant'Angelo** (➤ 172).

6–7

If not, turn left and then first left on Via dei Banchi Nuovi. This leads eventually to **Piazza dell'Orologio**, named after the delightful clock tower or Torre dell'Orologio on the building on the piazza's far right. This forms part of the **Palazzo** and **Oratorio dei Filippini**, a complex built by the baroque master, Francesco Borromini, in the 17th century for the Oratory of Saint Philip Neri. For a closer look at the Oratorio's facade, turn right (south) off the piazza down Via dei Filippini. You emerge on the busy Corso Vittorio Emanuele II in front of the richly decorated interior of the16th-century **Chiesa Nuova** ("New Church"). Of particular interest are Pietro da Cortona's ceiling frescoes (1647–65) and three paintings by Peter Paul Rubens in the presbytery around the high altar. Return to Piazza dell'Orologio and turn right to follow Via del Governo Vecchio to Piazza di Pasquino and the short Via di Pasquino back to Piazza Navona.

3 ALONG THE VIA APPIA ANTICA, THE "QUEEN OF ROADS"

Walk or Cycling tour

DISTANCE 4.5–9km (2¾–5½ miles) **TIME** Allow 1–3 hours
START POINT Porta S. Sebastiano ✚ 209, south of D1
END POINT Mausoleo di Cecilia Metella ✚ 209, south of D1

If at all possible, you should plan to make this wonderful walk along the Via Appia Antica on a Sunday or public holiday when sections of the "Queen of Roads" are turned into a pedestrian precinct and a – rather bumpy – paradise for bicyclists. Walk past ancient tombs on the original Roman era pavement in the shade of umbrella pines. Visit the most famous Christian catacombs and enjoy the panoramic view far into the Roman Campagna.

1–2

Begin your stroll at the **Porta San Sebastiano**, a gate in the Aurelian Wall. This is the start of the Via Appia Antica, with which the Roman censor Appius Claudius Caecus set an immortal memorial to himself in 312BC. It runs almost dead straight from Rome to Capua and then on to Brindisi, the Roman Empire's most important port. This is the route Roman rulers, armies and merchants followed to the south. At the time, it was possible for two horse-drawn carriages to pass each other comfortably on the 4.10m (13.5 feet) wide consular road. After just a few steps, you will see on the right a copy of a milestone with which the Romans marked the 365 miles to Brindisi. A Roman mile measured 1,000 paces or 1.5km (just under 1 mile). Continue past the Campus Martius (Field of Mars) until you reach the small **Domine Quo Vadis** church where it is said that Peter, fleeing persecution in Rome, had a vision of Christ. When Peter asked: "Lord, where are you going *(Domine, quo vadis)*?", Jesus answered: "To Rome, to be crucified anew!". This persuaded Peter to return to Rome where he suffered death as a martyr. There is an information centre and you can hire bicycles opposite the church (tel: 06 51 35 51; 9:30–5).

2–4

The **catacombs** are not a Christian invention. During the Etruscan era entire cities

Walks & Tours

for the dead (necropolis) were cut into the tuff and the Romans were also not allowed to bury their dead within the city walls. For this reason, countless tombs, which reflected the status and wealth of their builders – such as the tomb of the **noblewoman Priscilla** diagonally opposite the Quo Vadis church – were built along the Appian Way starting in the 2nd century. A small detour to the Via Ardeatina will not only take you to one of the early Christian burial sites, the **Catacombs of St Domitilla**, but also to a modern place of burial and prayer, the **Mausoleo Fosse Ardeatine**. This is where the German Wehrmacht shot 355 innocent Romans on 24 March 1944 as a reprisal for an attack on the SS a day before in Rome. The Catacombs of Callixtus are just a few steps away. Until well into the 5th century, this was the most important Christian necropolis in Rome with many graves of popes and martyrs.

🜂–🜃

Back on the Via Appia Antica you soon reach the magnificent baroque church, **San Sebastiano**, one of the seven Pilgrim Churches of Rome, where the bones of Saints Peter and Paul were preserved in early Christian days. There you will have access to the **Catacombe di San Sebastiano**, the best-preserved Christian necropolis, which is also well-worth a visit. On the left side, you will see an ancient arena, the Circo di Massenzio, a racetrack for ten thousand spectators, and the tomb of Romulo – not the founder of Rome but the son of Emperor Massenzio – who died at an early age in the year AD309. The most striking building on the Via Appia Antica is the crenellated **Tomba di Cecilia Metella**, the tomb of a rich Roman woman who was a general's daughter. The battlements were not added until the 14th century. This is the start of the most beautiful

TAKING A BREAK
Hostaria Antica Roma (Via Appia Antica, 87; tel: 06 513 28 88; closed Mon) is a traditional inn that many Roman families like to visit on Sunday where the host, Paolo, provides his guests with great atmosphere and good food. You can sit in idyllic surroundings and enjoy good Roman cuisine in the garden of the **Antica Hostaria l'Archeologia** (Via **Insider Tip** Appia Antica, 139; tel: 06 7 88 04 94; closed Mon, Tue) with water babbling in its little fountain and blossoming roses.

CATACOMBS
Catacombs of St Domitilla, Via Sette Chiese, 283; Sun–Mon 9–noon and 2:30–5; admission €8
Catacombs of Callixtus, Via Appia Antica, 110; Thu–Tue 9–noon and 2:30–5; admission fee €8
Catacombs of St Sebastian, Via Appia Antica, 136; Mon–Sat 9–noon and 2:30–5pm; admission fee €8
Mausoleo Fosse Ardeatine, Via Ardeatina, 174; Mon–Fri 8:15–3, Sat–Sun 8:15–4.45; free admission
Tomb of Cecilia Metella, daily 9–5; €7, also as combined ticket with the Baths of Caracalla
Transport: bus 218 (from S. Giovanni in Laterano), bus 118 (from Metro B: Circo Massimo). Archeobus from Piazza Cinquecento (Termini) to the Tomb of Cecilia Metella, Fri–Sun 8:30–4:30 (every hour), ticket €12.

section of the Appian Way. You stroll under pines and cypresses, past countless ancient graves surrounded by ivy, dazzling red field poppies and daisies. This is also where the ancient Roman paving has been exposed and you will be able to see ruts and wheel tracks that are 2,000 years old. Caesar's travelling coach was so well sprung that the Imperator was supposedly able to write down his orders while he was underway. However, modern bicyclists should be prepared for a romantic, but bumpy, ride.

Practicalities

Practicalities

WHAT YOU NEED

		USA	Canada	Australia	Ireland	Germany	Ireland	Netherlands	Spain
● Required	Some countries require a passport to remain valid for a minimum period (usually at least six months) beyond the date of entry – check before you travel.								
○ Suggested									
▲ Not required									
Passport/National Identity Card		●	●	●	●	●	●	●	●
Visa (regulations can change – check before you travel)		▲	▲	▲	▲	▲	▲	▲	▲
Onward or Return Ticket		●	●	●	○	○	○	○	○
Health Inoculations		▲	▲	▲	▲	▲	▲	▲	▲
Health Documentation (▶ 192, Health)		●	●	●	●	●	●	●	●
Travel Insurance		○	○	○	○	○	○	○	○
Driving Licence (national)		●	●	●	●	●	●	●	●
Car Insurance Certificate		●	●	●	●	●	●	●	●
Car Registration Document		●	●	●	●	●	●	●	●

WHEN TO GO

High season

Low season

JAN	FEB	MAR	APR	MAY	JUN	JUL	AUG	SEPT	OCT	NOV	DEC
7°C	8°C	12°C	14°C	18°C	25°C	28°C	32°C	23°C	18°C	13°C	9°C
43°F	43°F	46°F	50°F	55°F	61°F	66°F	66°F	61°F	55°F	48°F	45°F

☀ Sun   ⛅ Sunshine & showers   🌧 Wet   ☁ Cloudy

Temperatures are the **average daily maximum** for each month. Average daily minimum temperatures are approximately 6 to 10°C (10–18°F) lower. Temperatures of over 35°C (95°F) are likely in July and August, making the city extremely hot and uncomfortable.

The best times of the year for good weather are May, June, July, August and September. Thunderstorms are possible in summer and through September and October. Winters (January and February) are short and cold, but snow is extremely rare. Spring starts in March, but March and April can be humid and sometimes very rainy. Autumn weather is mixed, but often produces crisp or warm days with clear skies.

GETTING ADVANCE INFORMATION

Websites
Official tourism board
of the City of Rome:
www.romaturismo.it
www.060608.it

Museum online reservations:
www.ticketeria.it
Official Vatican site for all
aspects of the Holy See:
www.vatican.va

In Italy
The website (www.060608.it)
has replaced the main tourist
office in Italy

Practicalities

GETTING THERE

By Air Rome has two main airports: Leonardo da Vinci (better known as Fiumicino) and Ciampino. Most UK and other European and international carriers fly to Fiumicino. Low-cost and charter airlines usually fly to Ciampino. There are many non-stop flights to Rome from London (Heathrow, Gatwick and Stansted) as well as regional airports in the UK, most major European cities and many US and Canadian cities. Flights from Melbourne and Sydney make one stop, usually in Bangkok; from other cities in Australia and New Zealand, the best connections are in Hong Kong or Singapore.

Ticket prices tend to be highest at Easter, Christmas and in summer. Best prices are obtained the further you reserve in advance but check airlines, travel agents, newspapers and the internet for special offers. Non-direct flights via hub airports such as Heathrow or Frankfurt may offer substantial savings. Short stays are generally expensive unless a Saturday night stay is included. City-break packages include flights and accommodation.

Airport taxes are included in ticket prices and no fee is payable at either Rome airport.

Approximate flying times to Rome: New Zealand (24 hours), east coast of Australia (21 hours), western US (11 hours), eastern US and Canada (8–10 hours); London (2 hours), Frankfurt (1 hour).

By Rail Ticket prices are usually the same or more than equivalent air fares. Numerous fast and overnight services operate to Rome from most European capitals, with connections from major towns. Rome has several stations, but most international services stop at Stazione Termini or Roma Tiburtina.

TIME

Rome is one hour ahead of GMT in winter, one hour ahead of BST in summer, six hours ahead of New York and nine hours ahead of Los Angeles. Clocks are advanced one hour in March and turned back one hour in October.

CURRENCY & FOREIGN EXCHANGE

Currency Italy is one of the majority of European Union countries to use a single currency, the euro (€). Coins are issued in denominations of 1, 2, 5, 10, 20 and 50 cents and €1 and €2. Notes are issued in denominations of €5, €10, €20, €50, €100, €200 and €500.

Exchange Most major **travellers' cheques** – the best way to carry money – can be changed at exchange kiosks *(cambio)* at the airports, at Termini railway station and in exchange offices near major tourist sights. Many banks also have exchange desks.

Credit cards Most credit cards *(carta di credito)* are accepted in larger hotels, restaurants and shops, but cash is often preferred in smaller establishments. Credit cards can also be used to obtain cash from ATM cash dispensers, although this can be expensive – most credit cards charge a fee for this. Contact your card issuer before you leave home to find out which machines in Rome accept your card and confirm the dates you will be in Italy. Failure to do this may mean your credit card is refused.

In the UK
ENIT
1 Princes Street
London W1R 8AY
☎ 020 74 08 12 54

In the US
ENIT
630 Fifth Avenue
Suite 1565
New York NY 10111
☎ 21 22 45 56 18

In Australia
Italian Consulate
Level 24,
44 Market Square
Sydney NSW 2000
☎ 02 92 62 16 77

Practicalities

WHEN YOU ARE THERE

NATIONAL HOLIDAYS

1 Jan	New Year's Day
6 Jan	Epiphany
March/April	Easter Monday
25 April	Liberation Day
1 May	Labour Day
29 June	St Peter and St Paul Day
15 Aug	Assumption of the Virgin
1 Nov	All Saints' Day
8 Dec	Feast of the Immaculate Conception
25 Dec	Christmas Day
26 Dec	St Stephen's Day

ELECTRICITY

 Current is 220 volts AC, 50 cycles. Plugs are two-round-pin continental types; UK and North American visitors will require an adaptor. North American visitors should check whether 110/120-volt AC appliances require a voltage transformer.

OPENING HOURS

○ Shops ● Post Offices
● Offices ● Museums/Monuments
● Banks ● Pharmacies

8am 9am 10am noon 1pm 2pm 4pm 5pm 7pm

☐ Day ☐ Midday ☐ Evening

Shops Usually Tue–Sat 8–1, 4–8, Mon 4–8.
Restaurants 12:30–3, 7:30–10:30; many close Sun evening and Mon lunchtime.
Museums Hours vary: usually Tue–Sat 9–7, Sun 9–1.
Churches Daily 7–12, 4:30–7pm; closed during services.
Post offices Mon–Fri 8:15–2, Sat 8:15–12 or 2pm.

TIPS/GRATUITIES

Tipping is not expected for all services and rates are lower than those elsewhere. As a general guide:

Pizzerias/Trattorias	€0.50–€2.50
Smart restaurant	5–10 per cent or discretion
Bar service	€0.10–€0.25
Tour guides	Discretion
Taxis	Round up to nearest €0.50
Porters	€0.50–€1 per bag
Chambermaids	€0.50–€1 a day

ROMAN QUEUES

Queue-jumpers will not be tolerated by the locals, so when standing in line in bars and restaurants, shops and when using public transport, it's a case of drawing a fine line between surging forward and giving as good as you get, or hanging back and getting nowhere.

TIME DIFFERENCES

Rome (CET)
12 noon

←
London (GMT)
11am

→
New York (EST)
6am

→
Los Angeles (PST)
3am

→
Sydney (AEST)
9pm

Practicalities

STAYING IN TOUCH

Post Rome's central post office
(ufficio postale) is at Piazza
San Silvestro 18–20. Stamps
(francobolli) are bought from
post offices and tobacconist
(tabacchi) kiosks usually marked
with a 'T'. Mail boxes are red
(per la città – slots for city mail
and *tutte le altre destinazioni)*
other destinations), or blue for
the more efficient *posta prioritaria* (priority post).

Public telephones Phone cards *(carta telecom no
distance*; €5.10 or €10) can be bought from post
offices or *tabacchi*. To dial numbers in Rome while
there, dial the 06 code then
the number. Dial 170 to
make reverse charge calls.
Dial 12 for operator or directory
enquiries.

International Dialling Codes
UK:	0044
USA/Canada:	001
Irish Republic:	00353
Australia:	0061

Mobile providers and services in the UK, Australia
and NZ mobiles work in Italy, but not the US.
The main providers are Tim (www.tim.it), Vodafone
(www.vodafone.it) and Wind (www.wind.it); all have
outlets throughout Rome, but check call rates with
your provider before travelling.

WiFi and internet Much of Rome is covered by wireless
hot spots sponsored by the city council. Once you
open your browser you'll need to register, using your
mobile phone number, then log on; access is free
(www.romawireless.com). In addition, many hotels
have built-in dataports, and even budget places will
allow you to plug into their phone systems. Download
speeds are excellent. There are numerous **internet
cafés**; try EasyEverything (Via Barberini, 2; 8am–2am
daily; €2 per hour; 250 terminals).

PERSONAL SAFETY

Rome is generally safe.
However, pickpocketing
is rife in the main tourist
areas, so take precautions:

- Men should never put
  wallets in back pockets,
  and women should wear
  bags across their bodies,
  and keep a hand on top
  in crowded buses.
- Keep cameras looped
  around your wrist or on a
  strap across your body.
- Take particular care of
  children working as
  thieves, who will often
  try to distract your attention; they work in pairs.
- At night avoid parks and
  the streets around
  Termini, Trastevere and
  the Campo de' Fiori.
- If you are a victim of
  crime, you must make
  a *denuncia* (statement),
  and obtain a copy, at
  a police station in or-
  der to claim on your
  insurance.

Police assistance:
☎ 112 from any phone

EMERGENCY 113
POLICE 112 OR 113
FIRE 113 OR 115
AMBULANCE 113 OR 118

Practicalities

HEALTH

 Insurance Citizens of EU countries receive free or reduced-cost emergency medical treatment with relevant documentation (European Health Insurance Card).

 Doctors Ask at your hotel for details of English-speaking doctors.
Dental Services Travel insurance should cover dental treatment, which is expensive.

 Weather Minor health worries include too much sun, dehydration or mosquito bites: drink plenty of fluids, and wear sunscreen and a hat in summer. Insect repellent may be useful in summer.

 Drugs Prescription and other medicines are available from a pharmacy *(una farmacia)*, indicated by a green cross.
Opening hours are usually Mon–Sat 8:30–1 and 4–8, but a rota system ensures that some are always open. Two 24-hour pharmacies are: Piram (Via Nazionale 228; tel: 06 4 88 07 54); Farmacia della Stazione (Piazza dei Cinquecento-corner Via Cavour; tel: 06 4 88 00 19).

 Safe Water Tap water is safe. So, too, is water from public drinking fountains unless marked "*Acqua Non Potabile*".

CONCESSIONS

Young People/Senior Citizens Young visitors (18–25) from EU countries and senior citizens over 65 are entitled to reduced rates to most galleries. A passport will be required as proof of age.
Roma Pass This 3-day pass gives entrance to two museums, reductions on museum entries, travel on public transport and a city map. It costs €30; available from Tourist Information Points (▶ 33) and at www.romapass.it.
Archeologia Card: €27.50, valid for 7 days with admission to several sights and museums (▶ 32).

TRAVELLING WITH DISABILITIES

Rome is a difficult city for those with disabilities, especially if you use a wheelchair. Streets are narrow, busy and usually filled with badly parked cars. Transport, museums, hotels and other public spaces are improving, but much remains to be done. For information, contact the Consorzio Cooperative Integrate (CO.IN), Via Enrico Giglioli, 54a; tel: 06 7 12 90 11; www.coinsociale.it.

🧒 CHILDREN

Most hotels, restaurants and bars welcome children, but few have baby-changing facilities.
  In this guide special attractions for children are indicated by the icon above.

TOILETS

Rome has few public toilets. Bars usually have toilets. Ask for *il bagno* or *il gabinetto*.

LOST PROPERTY

Airport 06 65 95 33 43
Buses 06 5 81 60 40
Metro 06 4 87 43 09 (Line A); 06 57 53 22 64/5 (Line B)

EMBASSIES & HIGH COMMISSIONS

UK
☎ 06 42 20 00 01

USA
☎ 06 4 67 41

Ireland
☎ 06 6 97 91 21

Australia
☎ 06 85 27 21

New Zealand
☎ 06 4 41 71 71

Useful Words and Phrases

SURVIVAL PHRASES

yes/no **sì/non**
please **per favore**
thank you **grazie**
You're welcome **Di niente/prego**
I'm sorry **Mi dispiace**
Goodbye **Arrivederci**
Good morning **Buongiorno**
Goodnight **Buona sera**
How are you? **Come sta?**
How much? **Quanto costa?**
I would like... **Vorrei...**
open **aperto**
closed **chiuso**
today **oggi**
tomorrow **domani**
Monday **lunedì**
Tuesday **martedì**
Wednesday **mercoledì**
Thursday **giovedì**
Friday **venerdì**
Saturday **sabato**
Sunday **domenica**

DIRECTIONS

I'm lost **Mi sono perso/a**
Where is...? **Dove si trova...?**
    the station **la stazione**
    the telephone **il telefono**
    the bank **la banca**
    the toilet **il bagno**
Turn left **Volti a sinistra**
Turn right **Volti a destra**
Go straight on **Vada dritto**
At the corner **All'angolo**
the street **la strada**
the building **il edificio**
the traffic light **il semaforo**
the crossroads **l'incrocio**
the signs for... **le indicazione per...**

IF YOU NEED HELP

Help! **Aiuto!**
Could you help me, please?
    Mi potrebbe aiutare?
Do you speak English? **Parla inglese?**
I don't understand **Non capisco**
Please could you call a doctor quickly?
    Mi chiami presto un medico, per favore

RESTAURANT

I'd like to book a table
    Vorrei prenotare un tavolo
A table for two please
    Un tavolo per due, per favore
Could we see the menu, please?
    Ci porta la lista, per favore?
What's this? **Cosa è questo?**
A bottle of/a glass of...
    Un bottiglia di/un bicchiere di...
Could I have the bill?
    Ci porta il conto

ACCOMMODATION

Do you have a single/double room?
    Ha una camera singola/doppia?
with/without bath/toilet/shower
    con/senza vasca/gabinetto/doccia
Does that include breakfast?
    E'inclusa la prima colazione?
Does that include dinner?
    E'inclusa la cena?
Do you have room service?
    C'è il servizio in camera?
Could I see the room?
    E' possibile vedere la camera?
I'll take this room
    Prendo questa
Thanks for your hospitality
    Grazie per l'ospitalità

NUMBERS

0	zero	12	dodici	40	quaranta	400	quattrocento
1	uno	13	tredici	50	cinquanta	500	cinquecento
2	due	14	quattordici	60	sessanta	600	seicento
3	tre	15	quindici	70	settanta	700	settecento
4	quattro	16	sedici	80	ottanta	800	ottocento
5	cinque	17	diciassette	90	novanta	900	novecento
6	sei	18	diciotto	100	cento	1,000	mille
7	sette	19	diciannove	101	cento uno	2,000	duemila
8	otto	20	venti	110	centodieci	10,000	diecimila
9	nove	21	ventuno	120	centoventi		
10	dieci	22	ventidue	200	duecento		
11	undici	30	trenta	300	trecento		

Useful Words and Phrases

acciuga anchovy
acqua water
affettati sliced cured meats
affumicato smoked
aglio garlic
agnello lamb
anatra duck
antipasti hors d'oeuvres
arista roast pork
arrosto roast
asparagi asparagus
birra beer
bistecca steak
bollito boiled meat
braciola minute steak
brasato braised
brodo broth
bruschetta toasted bread with garlic or tomato topping
budino pudding
burro butter
cacciagione game
cacciatore, alla rich tomato sauce with mushrooms
caffè corretto/ macchiato coffee with liqueur/ spirit, or with a drop of milk
caffè freddo iced coffee
caffè lungo weak coffee
caffè latte milky coffee
caffè ristretto strong coffee
calamaro squid
cappero caper
carciofo artichoke
carota carrot
carne meat
carpa carp

casalingho home-made
cassata Sicilian fruit ice cream
cavolfiore cauliflower
cavolo cabbage
ceci chickpeas
cervello brains
cervo venison
cetriolino gherkin
cetriolo cucumber
cicoria chicory
cinghiale boar
cioccolata chocolate
cipolla onion
coda di bue oxtail
coniglio rabbit
contorni vegetables
coperto cover charge
cornetto croissant
coscia leg of meat
cotolette cutlets
cozze mussels
crema custard
crostini canapé with savoury toppings or croutons
crudo raw
digestivo after-dinner liqueur
dolci cakes/desserts
erbe aromatiche herbs
fagioli beans
fagiolini green beans
faraona guinea fowl
farcito stuffed
fegato liver
finocchio fennel
formaggio cheese
forno, al baked
frittata omelette
fritto fried
frizzante fizzy
frulato whisked
frutti di mare seafood

frutta fruit
funghi mushrooms
gamberetto shrimp
gelato ice cream
ghiaccio ice
gnocchi potato dumplings
granchio crab
gran(o)turco corn
griglia, alla grilled
imbottito stuffed
insalata salad
IVA VAT
latte milk
lepre hare
lumache snails
manzo beef
merluzzo cod
miele honey
minestra soup
molluschi shellfish
olio oil
oliva olive
ostrica oyster
pancetta bacon
pane bread
panna cream
parmigiano Parmesan
passata sieved or creamed
pastasciutta dried pasta
pasta sfoglia puff pastry
patate fritte chips
pecora mutton
pecorino sheep's milk cheese
peperoncino chilli
peperone red/green pepper
pesce fish
petto breast
piccione pigeon
piselli peas
pollame fowl
pollo chicken

polpetta meatball
porto port wine
prezzemolo parsley
primo piatto first course
prosciutto cured ham
ragù meat sauce
ripieno stuffed
riso rice
salsa sauce
salsiccia sausage
saltimbocca veal with prosciutto and sage
secco dry
secondo piatto main course
senape mustard
servizio compreso service charge included
sogliola sole
spuntini snacks
succo di frutta fruit juice
sugo sauce
tonno tuna
uova strapazzate scambled egg
uovo affogato/in carnica poached egg
uovo al tegamo/fritto fried egg
uovo alla coque soft-boiled egg
uovo alla sodo hard-boiled egg
vino bianco white wine
vino rosso red wine
vino rosato rosé wine
verdure vegetables
vitello veal
zucchero sugar
zucchino courgette
zuppa soup

Street Atlas

For chapters: see inside front cover

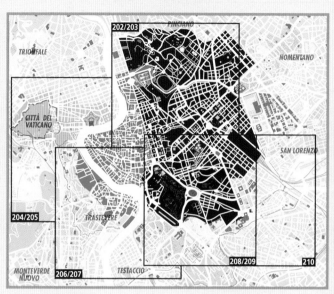

Key to Street Atlas

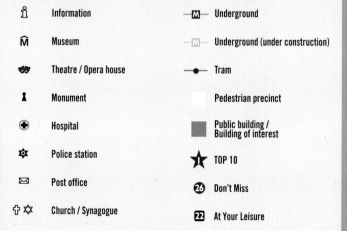

ℹ	Information	—Ⓜ—	Underground
⋒̂	Museum	—Ⓜ—	Underground (under construction)
🎭	Theatre / Opera house	—●—	Tram
♟	Monument		Pedestrian precinct
⊕	Hospital		Public building / Building of interest
✿	Police station	★	TOP 10
✉	Post office	26	Don't Miss
✝ ✡	Church / Synagogue	22	At Your Leisure

1 : 13.200

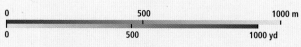

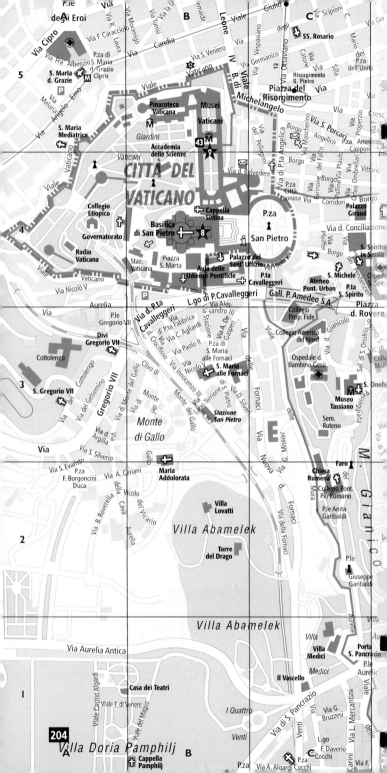

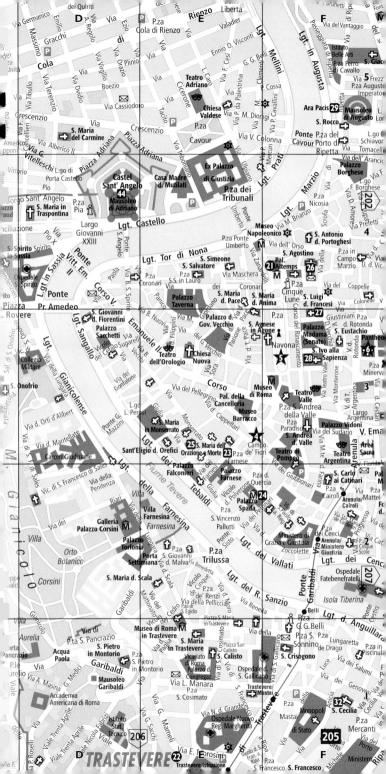

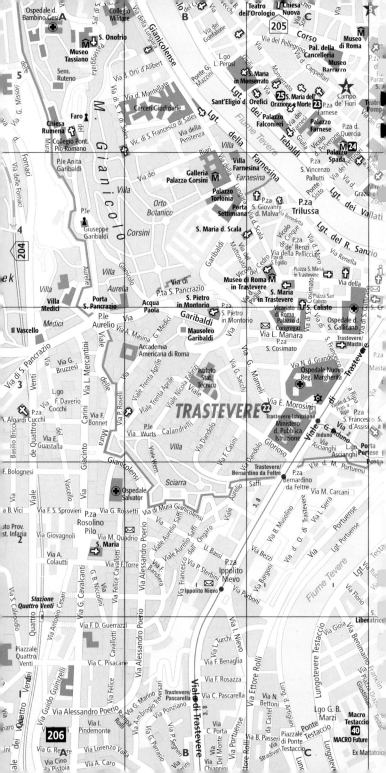

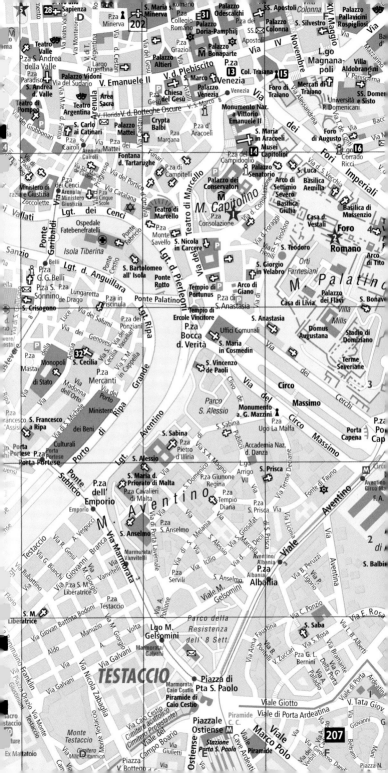

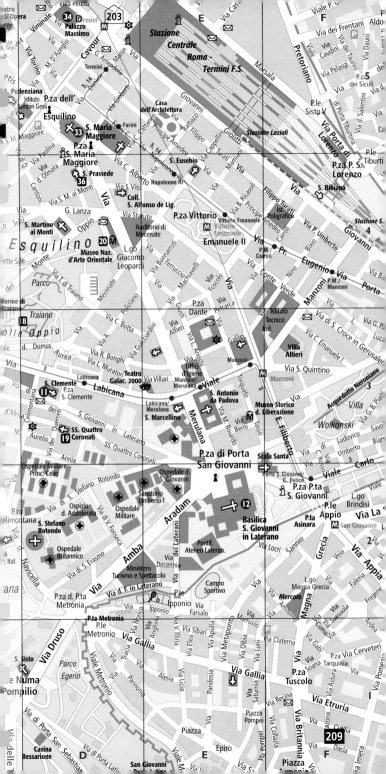

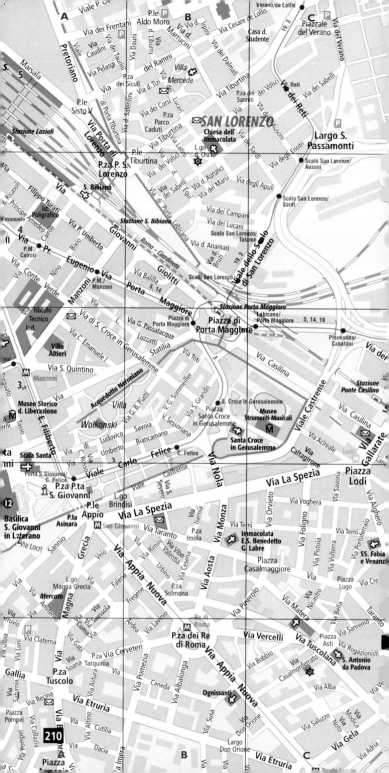

Street Index

Street Index

Street Index

Street Index

Street Index

Index

Index

Index

Index

Picture Credits

Credits

1st Edition 2015

Worldwide Distribution: Marco Polo Travel Publishing Ltd
Pinewood, Chineham Business Park
Crockford Lane, Chineham
Basingstoke, Hampshire RG24 8AL, United Kingdom.
© MAIRDUMONT GmbH & Co. KG, Ostfildern

Authors: Tim Jepson, Swantje Strieder
Editor: Jessika Zollickhofer
(Bintang Buchservice GmbH, www.bintang-berlin.de)
Revised editing and translation: Margaret Howie, fullproof.co.za
Program supervisor: Birgit Borowski
Chief editor: Rainer Eisenschmid

Cartography: © MAIRDUMONT GmbH & Co. KG, Ostfildern
3D-illustrations: jangled nerves, Stuttgart

Printed in China

Despite all of our authors' thorough research, errors can creep in.
The publishers do not accept any liability for this. Whether you
want to praise, alert us to errors or give us a personal tip –
please don't hesitate to email or post:

MARCO POLO Travel Publishing Ltd
Pinewood, Chineham Business Park
Crockford Lane, Chineham
Basingstoke, Hampshire RG24 8AL
United Kingdom
Email: sales@marcopolouk.com

FSC
www.fsc.org
MIX
Paper from
responsible sources
FSC® C020056

10 REASONS
TO COME BACK AGAIN

1. Celebrated in song, the **gelato a limone** is pure poetry here.

2. Nowhere else are the **carabinieri** so charming to female tourists.

3. The vibrant nightlife usually takes place on the **piazza**.

4. In ancient times it was said that as long as the **Colosseum** remains standing, so too will Rome.

5. Nowhere else do taxi drivers talk as much about **football** as here.

6. You have only seen half of the city's **monuments**, **churches** and **palaces** – at the most.

7. **Sunset from the Pincio** garden terrace is truly breathtaking.

8. The best **cappuccinos** are to be found at simple bar counters.

9. No other city has so many **fountains** burbling day and night.

10. A **coin** thrown into the **Fontana di Trevi** means you have already secured your return ticket.